# Wait Until I'm Dead!

Sarah & Leslie

Enjoy the book!

*E Lde M Danb*

# Wait Until I'm Dead!

*A Novel of Family Secrets*

ELDA M. DAWBER

Cover design: Jeannette Jacobs
Cover photo: Mariellen Langworthy
Book design by: Helene Berinsky

ISBN-13 978-1499766349
ISBN-10 1499766343

*For all survivors of childhood sexual abuse and the caring adults who have borne witness to their pain. May you find comfort, and perhaps gain courage from this book.*

*My hope is that we arrive, together, at a day when there truly are no more of these stories to tell.*

# 1 · PEELING THE ONION

*I have a memory of myself as a young adult in the first house I owned, standing beside my pre-clicker, pre-color, pre-cable TV, channel-surfing all three stations. Settling on The Phil Donahue Show, I adjusted the volume and sank into my grandmother's ancient couch—sank being the operative word here for this solitary piece of living room furniture whose three worn cushions, now concave, had sheltered the behinds of many a relative.*

*Phil was doing his usual routine of flitting through the audience, microphone in hand, looking for all the world like an albino hummingbird seeking delicious nectar from the numerous fertile plants offering themselves to him. The topic of the day was child sexual abuse, the numbers of victims astonishing, the need for intervention urgent—the guest authority of the day quoted statistics that were, in fact, quite frightening.*

*Hands shot up throughout the audience. Phil darted down one aisle and half-way up another, microphone at the ready. Stretching across three people, he hovered in front of a woman who asked, "So, how do we keep these children safe? What do we tell them to do?"*

*All eyes shifted to the expert. He paused for a moment, turned his palms up as if pleading with the universe for wisdom, and said in an almost-whisper, "Tell them not to go home."*

*Oxygen sucked out of the room with one great gasp. Then silence. No one dared breathe. Even Phil was stricken. He perched heavily on the arm rest of the nearest seat, raised the microphone to his lips, and then lowered it again—a suddenly flightless albino hummingbird.*

*"Tell them not to go home," I repeated to no one in my living room.*

*If only it were that simple.*

# Friday

"When we honestly ask ourselves which person in our lives means the most to us, we often find that it is those who, instead of giving advice, solutions, or cures, have chosen rather to share our pain and touch our wounds with a warm and tender hand. The friend who can be silent with us in a moment of despair or confusion, who can stay with us in an hour of grief and bereavement, who can tolerate not knowing, not curing, not healing and face us with the reality of our powerlessness, that is a friend who cares."

Excerpted from *Out of Solitude* by Henri J.M. Nouwen. Copyright 2004 by Ave Maria Press, P.O. Box 428, Notre Dame, IN 46556. Used with permission of the publisher.

# ONE

THE MANUSCRIPT LIES DEAD CENTER between them, arranged like an *objet d'art* on the massively imposing rich ebony desk, curled edges of the first thirty pages testament to the fact that someone has at least read to Chapter Three—perhaps more than once from the looks of things.

DJ Brava, famed author of the romance genre, sits on the wrong side of the desk, shoulders slightly hunched, left leg over the right—the movement of that leg gaining momentum by the second. Words from somewhere back in time push to the forefront of her consciousness. *Hot potato, hot potato, hot potato…*

"What on earth is this supposed to be?"

DJ looks up to see the long and elegantly manicured pointer finger poking furiously at the title page.

"You," and now the finger is directed at her, "are a romance writer. The entire reading world awaits the sixth book in your latest series. And you send me *this*?" The question is accompanied by the zipper-like sound of the pages being quickly flipped in anger.

He levels what he hopes passes for an authoritarian glare at her. "I got it. I read it. It's not romance, that's for damn sure. What am I supposed to do with this?"

"Publish it. It's good. It'll sell. With my name on it, it will sell big."

Donna Jean Brava, Queen of Lust-and-Thrust, allows her shoulders to relax and leans forward, both hands on the highly polished desk surface, purposefully leaving her mark.

"Cole," she says, throaty voice competing with the sound of his deep leather chair scooting back from her closeness, "this is the one. This is the book I have needed to write from the beginning. It is what I have needed to say for my entire life but have never had the words or wisdom. Until now. Right now."

"But, the series is progressing nicely and the readers-"

"The series has to wait. No sixth or seventh book about Serpentine's misadventures in the land of the lovelorn can claw its way into my head and out of me just now. But this one..." She indicates the manuscript Cole has pulled closer to his side of the desk. "This one is next. After that, I'll give you as many sequels or new series as you want. You're my editor. You can make it happen." She sits back once again, taking satisfied note of the ten pronounced smudges she has left upon his almighty desk, and waits.

Regaining his imperiousness, Cole Alexander thinks of reaching into his pocket for a monogrammed handkerchief to wipe the prints from his desk. Containing himself for the moment, he says, "This is not what we pay you for, DJ. We're a big company, and you're a big part of that, yes, but you don't control what gets published here."

"Here or somewhere else, Cole. It's your call. Here or somewhere else." DJ reaches onto the seat of the next chair for her canvas case. "I'll need to know by next week. You can reach me on my cell. I have some traveling to do and a few people to see before news of this book gets out." She rises and leaves the room, with an ever-so-slight last second tug at the door meant to convey her determination.

Cole sits quietly for a few minutes, fingers tented and resting against his chin. He reaches for the manuscript and twice flips a stack of pages between his thumb and forefinger, listening to the sound of money. He knows good when he sees it, and this is very good; knows it will sell, and sell big. But at what price, and to whom?

Picking up the phone, he deliberately touches the same number three times. Cole hears the phone being answered. "We have trouble," he says, and hangs up.

# TWO

D J STANDS ALONE in the hall outside Cole's office, allowing herself a momentary satisfied gloat at how she handled herself with him before her anxiety takes a monumental leap. She turns left down the corridor, passing framed copies of million-selling book covers, and ducks into the first restroom she finds. Locking it behind her, she presses the small of her back into the door, trying to ease her tightening muscles. "Shit," she says, tossing her bag on the sink top and rushing into the stall just in time to lose the small breakfast she had allowed herself to eat.

She finds her cell phone in her pants pocket and dials.

"I've gone and done it," she whispers. "I really did it, Kate."

"OK, then," comes the reply. "Pick your butt up off the bathroom floor and get on over here. Tuck and I have been talking about this."

"How did you know-" DJ starts, but is immediately interrupted.

"Your voice always takes on that tinny quality when you toss your cupcakes, Deej. Are you okay enough to get here on your own? We can come and get you."

"No, I can manage. Thanks. I just need to get myself out of this place." DJ lifts herself off the floor, bones creaking as she stands. "I'll take the T and be there in an hour." She moves toward the sink to rinse her mouth and splash water on her face.

Kate is still on the line and not quite finished with her yet. For a fourth-generation Irishwoman who has barely touched a toe to the old sod, Kate is quite capable of reaching deep into the recesses of her genes and pulling out a respectable brogue when needed. This, apparently, is just such a time.

"And for the love of Mike, DJ, stop at the pharmacy and get yourself a toothbrush and some paste." Kate is nothing if not direct, often irritating, but always practical. "Puking can rot the enamel off what's left of your teeth."

"Katie," DJ says, "must you always be so graphic?"

"Well *that* can't be the worst thing I've said to you in the last thirty-five years, can it? So get over it and get moving."

DJ manages a small smile. "Tell me again why I need a social worker as a best friend?" she asks, sarcasm oozing from each clipped word.

"To help you find your way through the crap you just placed yourself in, for starters," is the retort, followed by the click of the call ending.

When she makes herself presentable enough and spritzes the restroom with the deodorizer she finds on the vanity, DJ does one last check in the mirror. Judging herself safe to meet the world, she opens the door and stares directly into a picture of herself on the opposite wall. It was her very first book jacket and, in spite of the fifteen years that have passed since then, DJ can't help but be startled by the difference between that picture and the image she viewed in the mirror just seconds ago. "Christ," she thinks, "I really do need to get my shit together."

She puts her head down, purposely not looking at any of the other thirteen book jackets of hers lined along the wall. Sucking in a deep breath, DJ tucks the empty briefcase well up under her armpit and makes her way down the elevator and out of the largest publishing house in New England. Within minutes she is at the Park Square subway station, boarding the Red Line for Porter Square.

THE TRAIN IS CROWDED in mid-morning, mostly with students on their way to class. An avid people-watcher always on the lookout for material for her novels and desperately needing to distract herself from her morning encounter with the imperious Cole, DJ engages in her favorite pastime when traveling. Her love of public transportation fuels her tendency to project fantasy lives onto the young people around her, giving them relationships and torments, ambitions and vices.

She spots two young men four seats up to her right, heads bent towards each other in intimate conversation. Lovers, she decides, planning their wedding in Provincetown this Christmas, pouring over the guest list, saddened by the anticipated absence of close family members. The taller male in the Red Sox cap puts his arm around his partner and kisses his head.

Kate loves to say that DJ can turn a ten minute bus ride into a soap opera with a four year run. She just might be right about that.

Smiling at the memory, DJ thinks fondly of her long history with Kate. It was a college room-mate match that worked from day one. She was the shy and fairly inarticulate scholarship girl from Providence, Rhode Island, rooming with the bronze-haired, brazen, Boston Irish beauty, Katherine Eleanor Brennan.

They clicked immediately, DJ slowly uncoiling herself in the presence of Kate's relentless sense of humor and tendency to skirt the edges of propriety. Before long, and almost universally led by Kate, they were both testing and breaking the limits of boundaries only Catholic colleges felt an imperious right to impose. By senior year, they were president and vice-president of student government, loved by their classmates and just barely tolerated by the powers that were.

They had remained close friends, although their paths had gone in such different directions. Kate and her life partner, Audre Tucker—"Tuck" to her friends—were social workers with a thriving private practice in Somerville, seeing abused children and adolescents, and providing expert testimony in court cases.

DJ's attention is pulled back to the present when a group of students cheers a young man walking down the aisle. He has apparently just been named captain of the rugby team and is being congratulated. The youngsters are vibrant and eager, reminding DJ what she loves so much about these mid-October days when students approach a new phase of their lives with such intense expectation. She did, too, in those days.

The irony of the situation is not lost on her.

*Now look at me,* she thinks. *I'm weathered and worn and weary. And starting something brand new… Can I really pull this off?*

Anticipating where this new venture will take her is also, at the moment, giving her heartburn. She digs for an antacid in the corners of her briefcase, relieved to find one last foil-wrapped piece.

DJ catches sight of her profile in shadow as the train, lit from the right side, passes along a wall to the left. "Well, I'm no spring chicken," she muses, "but I still have a lot of kick, and I'm about to use it. I have certainly paid my dues".

And pay her dues, she has. Right after college, DJ worked at a small newspaper in rural Vermont for four years while plugging away at a master's degree in journalism at UVM in Burlington. She moved to a larger paper in New Hampshire, living and working there for almost seven years, until a piece she did on the political ramifications of running an educational system in an income-tax-free state garnered a national prize and caught the attention of the *Boston Globe*.

Boston has been all she had hoped for. When she first arrived, Kate was in town with her partner, both social workers struggling within an inadequate child welfare system. The *Globe* gave DJ the chance to write solid newsworthy pieces as well as the lighter "lifestyle" shorts she found her readership loved. She was close to her best friends, to culture, and once again, to the heart of action and renewal. Her enthusiasm spilled over into an urge to write. Then the urge became a need, and when she had enough to present to an agent, and the agent found an editor who was interested, DJ made the break with the *Globe*—and the rest, as the saying goes, was history.

DJ smiles at the memory of that September morning. She had called Kate and Tuck, shared the thrill of her news and invited them to dinner courtesy of the advance from her new publisher. Just about seventeen years had passed since then, and the three friends still shared a formidable bond.

DJ exits the subway at Porter Square, ducks into the local pharmacy for the required items, and walks the short distance to their professional office building on Massachusetts Avenue.

*I'm going to need Katie and Tuck now, more than ever,* she thinks, *so much more than ever.*

# THREE

COLE ALEXANDER, EDITOR EXTRODINARE, sits quietly at his desk, eyes and thoughts still focused on the manuscript before him. He had asked his secretary to hold his calls, told her he did not want to be disturbed by anyone other than his boss, Stan Whitman, and had—against all of his impulses—chosen not to wipe DJ's fingerprints off his desk.

DJ had been with Whitman, Westminster and Yarrow for her entire writing career. They had made her a rich woman.

"OK," he mutters, "her writing has made her rich—and the company as well, if we are to be honest about it." No author at any publishing house was as prolific in the romance writing department. Of course he didn't want to lose her. She was their moneymaker. But it was more than that. Cole had been with her from the beginning. Sixteen, almost seventeen, extraordinary years of working together, fourteen best-selling books, lectures, book signings and travel, and still she remained an enigma.

Still shy and self-effacing, she hated touring, TV interviews and anything that even vaguely hinted of publicity. But when she wrote, she packed a wallop with her words. DJ's descriptive sense was the best in the business, and readers and critics alike often commented that they "saw" what she had written, that the pages moved, characters took shape and became real to them. They literally couldn't get enough of her novels. She had taken romance and turned it into literature. She had made an honest woman out of a genre that used to be a joke.

"My god, if they only knew," he says to the manuscript. "They think they know her. They think she is the heroine of her own novels." None of this distresses him, of course. He's been in the business close to thirty years and knows this is what makes the books sell, and when his books sell, he is a happy, contented man. Put quite simply, he likes money and he likes what he can get with it.

But he also likes DJ. And he worries about the step she now wants to take, and the role he will play in it. No closer to an answer about what course of action to take, Cole reaches for the neatly typed pages, and thumbs them one more time. His pulse quickens and tiny beads of sweat form along his upper lip.

"So this is, finally, what you want all of us to know about who you are," he says. He opens *Peeling the Onion: The Autobiography of Donna Jean Brava*, turns to Chapter Three, and begins to read it for the third time since it arrived in the mail four days ago, along with the ominous Post-it note from DJ about when she would drop in to discuss it.

*Truth be told*, he admits to himself, *it was more like an order than a discussion.*

He drums his fingernails across the top of the manuscript.

*What's the price of obeying, I wonder? And why do I feel like I'm damned if we do and damned if we don't?*

## 3 • Peeling the Onion

*I had a brother when I was growing up, just a year older than myself. My strongest memory of the quicksilver of his life was my father chasing him into the street outside our home, our old bamboo clothes pole in his hands, beating JJ across the back until the top of the pole split into thin, weakened strips the way bamboo does. The sound, when the broken strips bounced off his back and hit the street, was similar to what a musician creates when the brushes caress the drums—except, of course, sharper, more painful, more crushing to the spirit.*

*That was the day that something important left my brother's eleven-year-old soul—and something close to evil entered it. I watched him crawl to the curb and wrap himself into a ball, thin streams of blood appearing across the back of his T-shirt. Too frightened for myself if I went to him, I crouched behind the hedge across the street and watched as my father, breathing heavily, heaved the pole toward JJ. Missing him, it bounced once, twanged against* the asbestos siding of the house and rolled into the gutter. Our father swore, tucked his shirt back under his belt, got into his car and drove away.

I felt rather than saw the shards of bamboo enter my brother's soul, felt them pierce his heart, felt them burn into his being with a heat so intense it melted the most important part of him into a protective, impenetrable shield. He turned to glass before my eyes. The thick, transformer glass I used to see on the top of telephone poles, insulators against charges the intensity of which a mere human could not withstand. Then he slowly came back to himself, unwound his body, sat, and pulled himself up. He lifted his head toward me, silently mouthing "No more".

The darkness in his eyes was deeper than any night my childhood fears could have conjured. He limped into the passageway between our tenement and the next, right hand grabbing the fence for support. We had been in this together since I was seven and I knew that being essentially defenseless on my own was a dangerous thing. Together, we had found some small sense of safety that we could retreat to when necessary. Now, I knew, I would have to fight the demon on my own.

That is not what killed his body, of course. But from that day his spirit and his mind were altered, twisted into a caricature of malevolence. He goose stepped around the yard when angered, obeying my father's orders with a heel-clicking, "Heil, Hitler", accompanied by a Nazi salute. He played with fire in the alley behind the house, put fire crackers into ant hills to watch them blow up, and trip-wired the basement at ankle level so that the unsuspecting would become entangled and enraged. He adopted a British accent and a rather pompous way of looking down his nose at anyone who asked a question of him.

Despite the closeness of our bond, JJ was hard to like—even at the best of times. The only male child, he was favored by my father's family as if only he had value. He lived with my grandmother on the third floor of our tenement, and he was cooked for and cleaned up after in ways we four younger kids, all girls, both envied and hated.

As is frequently the case in homes like ours, there was a pecking order to the type of abuse we endured, and when our parents left the house, JJ became the major tyrant, striking out with a force and frequency not at all tempered by his own experience.

Empathy seemed to have fled his being, racing away from his movement through the world. He had no soft curves—only hard edges that resisted any emotion that dared drift his way. He could stare down the strictest teacher, bore holes through younger kids with his eyes, scoffing at acts of tenderness and mercy.

There were moments, of course, when we managed to enjoy small pieces of our lives, stolen and cherished. One torrid summer day, so hot the road tar formed little bubbles we loved to poke with sticks, our mother sent us to our grandmother's dry goods store two blocks away for something called Modess. We were given a box wrapped in brown paper that was then placed in a brown paper bag. Too hot to carry anything at all, my brother tried getting me to take it.

"What's in it, anyway?" I asked.

He didn't know.

We were curious, and just naughty enough that we sat on the wall of the neighborhood church, peeled through the brown paper, and opened the blue box.

The white puffy pads bewildered us and we could not imagine what they were, but in our hands they became weapons. We batted each other. They became bandages, tied to our foreheads and arms, and we rolled with laughter onto the grass and under the trees.

One loud "Uh, oh", from JJ was warning enough. I turned in time to see our mother, shoulders hunched, fists clenched and pumping, running out of the alley  screaming for us to stop. Someone must have seen us and called her. JJ and I shed our weapons and bandages, and took off laughing up the hill. We hid until dark, thinking we really would be in trouble this time. But we were met with absolute silence about the incident. It was one of a number of luxuriously conspiratorial moments we managed to share.

JJ often retreated into the study of history, especially in researching old boats, steamships and ferry lines. After high school, he found work in the engine room of the local ferry boat, and that led him to similar employment on an oceanographic research vessel, the Robert J. Conrad, where he had his chance to see the world—or at least a good part of it. JJ went to South Africa, Australia, New Zealand, South America, and all points in between, crossing and re-crossing the equator. He documented on film and in diaries the celebratory practice of Crossing the Line, during which new sailors are initiated by way of rituals and ceremonies that run the gamut from silly to painful: being pelted with raw eggs, made to dress as women, or being tied up and flogged.

His ship was at the scene of the discovery of the remains of the USS Thresher, the submarine that went down with all hands off the coast of New

*Jersey in 1963. This he loved. It gave him a sense of pride he never seemed to allow himself from any other arena. For all the ways our relationship as siblings was a mess, I loved that he had this one great adventure.*

*From ninth grade on, JJ's body was staging its own rebellion against the years of beatings and terror and anger. There are still those within my family who will tell you that his cancerous spinal tumors must have been caused by being checked against the boards in youth hockey—which he hated beyond all reason, but was forced by our father, the jock, to play—or by the time his fellow altar boys beat him up and kicked him when he was down.*

*Not me.*

*I know, beyond any fleeting murmur of doubt, that it was the bamboo pole—along with every other beating, whack, hit and body blow driving the shards so deep within his being that they wrapped themselves around his spine, clung to it, and grew and grew until they burst forth in fury and revenge so encompassing that it eventually took away his capacity to walk, to move.*

*The last interaction I had with JJ was when I was away at college and he was hospitalized for the final time. I borrowed a car and drove to him, staying in the parking lot until our mother's car was gone, then went in to sit with him in his third day of coma. He stirred, opened his eyes and startled me with how present and clear he was. We talked, we said goodbye, and he slipped away—just like into the crack between the houses so long ago. I went back to college.*

*He died the next morning. He had just turned twenty-five.*

*I think of JJ often. I do not miss him, or wish that he were here. I think the whole world was far too painful for him. I fear he would be labeled psychotic today, and perhaps be institutionalized. He moved with the kind of anger and pain that tends to make others afraid. He carried the memory of his terror in his body, and I believe that others—especially children—could sense that and were wary of him.*

*No, I am most often reminded of him when someone gives me change and places one quarter in my palm. Twenty-five. I close my hand over that coin and bring it to my heart.*

*Chemicals have a half-life. Food has a shelf-life. Human beings, we believe, have a right to a whole life, a full life. JJ had twenty-five years. One quarter of a whole life.*

*But he was already turned to glass and shattered by age eleven.*

*Quicksilver.*

*No more.*

# FOUR

COLE LETS OUT A WHOOSH OF SOUND, and rolls his head to relax the muscles of his neck and back, wrung to knots with each successive chapter. He stands and stretches, pushes back his chair, and bends to the floor, counting to ten. Ten deep breaths and a long stretch toward the ceiling follow before he again drops into the soft leather seat. He pulls open the top drawer, withdraws an index card and uses it to hold his place in the manuscript.

His secretary knocks quietly and enters. "Stan is here to see you," she says and steps aside. "I'll bring coffee."

"Thanks, that would be great, Maya," replies Cole as he stands to welcome his boss. Shaking hands, Cole leads him to the chairs in the alcove across from his desk. "Glad you had the time, Stanley. I really need to run this situation by you."

"Something happening with our star writer?" he asks, lowering himself into a chair and loosening his tie. "It's not a health thing, is it?"

"No, nothing like that, Stan. It's just that she's written a novel she wants us to publish, and it's so off track from what she's been putting out that it might be a problem for us, and perhaps for her as well." Cole begins to perspire, his hands feel sticky and he rubs his palms nervously back and forth on the upholstered chair arm. Maya's return with the coffee tray is a welcome relief for the brief time it takes for them to settle with their drinks, and it gives Cole a chance to gather himself for what he has to say.

He begins. "Stan, I think the trouble I referred to may have to do with the fact that I haven't been completely forthcoming with you about DJ from the beginning."

Stan Whitman, of Whitman, Westminster and Yarrow, is not the least bit pleased with how this conversation has started and where it might be headed. He levels a look at Cole that is meant to wither him like poison ivy's response to weed killer. It almost does.

Cole raises both hands, palms up to Stan. "Hang on just a sec before you go off on me, Stan, if you can. Let me explain and then you can decide, but I think what I did will make sense to you. I hope so, anyway." He slides back, sits up straight, takes a long gulp of black coffee and begins.

"You may recall that we worked pretty diligently with DJ when she first came to us. We recognized her talent and we agreed that our efforts would be rewarded—and they have been, many times over. The first two years were mainly rewrites and editorial sessions and more rewrites. When we finally had a publishable manuscript, something happened that you're going to think is right out of a Hollywood B movie, but I swear to you every word is true."

"Get to the point, will you, Cole?" Stan pushes.

"I was still married then. It was my birthday and my wife and I had dinner plans at Club Café. As I was leaving the building here, I was told my limo was waiting. Thinking it was a surprise from my wife, I jumped in. There was someone in the car. Not just any someone, however. This guy I recognized immediately. It was Zip Martone."

That name gets Stan's attention.

"The Zip Martone who controls the entire East Coast entertainment industry?" he asks, forming air quotes around the last two words. "The *porn* king?" he continues, now clearly interested in what Cole has to say. He is intrigued, and perhaps a bit in awe of Cole having commanded the interest of such a nefarious person.

"The Zipper himself," Cole responds heavily, "actually, the Zipper, one of his bodyguards, and his gun."

Stan responds by lowering his voice, as if the room could suddenly hear their conversation. "Oh," was all he could say.

They both sit in the quiet for a long moment. Stan's inner processing of this information is visible on his face, concern turning to puzzlement.

"Wait just a second here, Cole. What in all hell has this got to do with DJ? What's the connection? She's not writing trash for him is she, because if she is and you knew it, it'll end your career this minute. I mean it-"

"Whoa, Stan, hold on here, will you? Let me explain." Cole is on his feet and comes around the table to sit closer to his boss.

"No, she doesn't write for him or anyone besides us. And we've always known she's related to him. She legally took her mother's maiden name when she became a reporter up there in New Hampshire for just this reason. She needed to avoid any connection with him. Now I really understand why. Wait 'til you read this manuscript."

Stan is still skeptical, giving Cole a long, hard stare.

"All right," he finally says, unbuttoning his shirt at the neck and nodding his head for Cole to continue. "Tell me about this threat. And this time, tell me everything, you hear me?"

Cole returns his boss's nod. "Christ, Stan, I thought I was going to die in that limousine and I had no effing clue what the hell I ever did to *this* guy, of all people. I mean, I'm probably one of the few people on the entire coast who's never even been in one of his shops, for crying out loud."

Stan makes a rolling motion with his hand, urging Cole to move along quickly.

"So he said 'Happy Birthday'. Then he told his driver to head over to Club Café and I was freaking out. He knew it was my birthday, for Christ's sake, and he knew where my wife and I were going to eat. I didn't have a clue what the hell was going on."

Cole is now in full-sweat mode, moving anxiously in the chair and making little eye contact with his boss. He fills a water glass from the carafe Maya has left, drinks the entire measure and fills it again.

*This guy's a wreck*, thinks Stan, who wants nothing more than to tell Cole to get to the god-damned point and stop being such a drama queen, but the strong scent of fear coming off his editor holds him back. Of all the things Cole might be, Stan can't think of any instance of him being an alarmist. He holds his impatience in check and lets Cole set the pace.

"The next thing the guy said to me was that he'd heard we're going to publish his niece's book, and he wanted to know what it was about. Me, I couldn't even think of who he was referring to and I must have given him some kind of look he didn't care for. He picked up the gun, pointed it in my face and told me to think about it real quick. I was almost soiling my pants and I wanted to ask him who the hell he was talking about, but he must have guessed.

"He said, 'Donna Brava. What's the book about?'"

"I told him it's a romance novel and he starts to laugh. Me, I'm thinking I'm a dead man and he's laughing like a maniac. Then he says—get this Stan—'Why, she's just a chip off the old block, isn't she? That's the damndest thing I ever heard'. I manage to ask him what the heck that means, but he keeps laughing and says, 'Never thought she'd follow in my footsteps. I provide sexual entertainment for men, and she's cornering the market for women. Good for her.'"

"Jesus, Cole. I hope you set the guy straight on that, man. He's a seriously twisted guy if he thinks pornography and romance can even be found in the same dictionary of civilized human behavior," Stan says. "You did say something, didn't you?"

"Give me a break here, Stan. The guy had my balls in a vise, for god's sake. It's a wonder I could say anything. Listen to me, will you? I'm trying to tell you. I'm in this limo. I don't know what the hell is going on, but all I can really see is his gun. I still see it in my nightmares sometimes. Damn! But he's laughing, then suddenly stops, gets real serious and tells me we'd better publish her book. That he'd hold me personally responsible if anything ever happened to her.

"I was thinking, OK, what's the big deal? We were going to publish her and make her rich and famous, so I was in the clear, right? That's what I thought anyway, but I was wrong. Evidentially he works out of a whole other playbook. He picked up his gun again, pushed it against my left kneecap and told me he'll pop both my caps if we ever print anything she writes about her family, especially about him. Then he asked if I understood his meaning. I could only nod in agreement.

"The car pulled over, someone opened the door, grabbed me by the collar, and I was literally dumped on the sidewalk, right in front of the restaurant and my wife. I could hear him laughing as the limo pulled away. I can still hear him laughing. And damn it all to hell, Stan, that laughing gets louder the more of her manuscript I read."

Cole is exhausted now, and sags limply in the chair.

Stan's face is red and he is trying to control his temper, pulling his tie completely out of his collar and wrapping it around his hand.

"So, you get threatened with violence by one of the most powerful guys in town and you don't think this worthy of a mention to me or the other heads of this company? What the hell is wrong with you?"

Cole knows this is coming and is prepared. "In hindsight, I absolutely should have. But, Stan, this was, what, almost seventeen years ago? I was low in the ranks here—still a junior editor—and so eager to prove myself with this new find of ours that I rationalized the entire thing. You know, she's writing romance, not underworld exposés. Remember how we all felt about romance novels in those days? That stuff was thought of as just this side of trash in most places. I didn't think we'd ever have to deal with this, Stan. Tell you the truth, I just didn't think, period. I just wanted it to go away."

Stan's impatience boils over and he paces the length of the office and back.

Cole is aware of his own blood pulsing against his temples. *I am absolutely going to get canned,* he thinks. *And I probably deserve it.*

When Stan stops his pacing, his back is to Cole and he takes a moment to observe a cargo tanker maneuver itself into the docking area way over in Boston Harbor. Cole watches him put the tie around his shirt collar again and perform the rote task of manipulating a perfect Windsor knot. It seems to Cole that Stan has reached a decision.

"Okay, Cole," Stan says as he turns to confront his editor, "we'll deal with what you've done—and what you didn't do—later, after I speak to the others. Just tell me what brought all this up now. You say she's written a new novel. More romance, right?"

"Wrong, Stan," is Cole's weary reply. "It's not even a novel. It's a memoir, an autobiography, and it is about her family. I'm on my third reading right now, and I am overwhelmed with the intensity and the amount of raw emotion it holds. Her early life wasn't a picnic. Not by any stretch of the imagination. It's not pretty, but trust me, it's dynamite—literally— and it's destined to be a best-seller."

"And it's going to bring the Zipper out of the woodwork." Stan's voice has a tone of resignation to it that Cole has not heard before.

"Yes, it is." Cole exhales so strongly the cover page of DJ's manuscript flutters.

"I need to read it. And you're going to need protection. I'm calling Tony." Stan picks up the phone.

DJ's 'hot potato' of a manuscript still holds center stage on Cole's desk.

It's been less than two hours since DJ left, yet the manuscript and its contents have been the catalyst for Cole's call for help to Stan, and Stan's call for protection for Cole.

Cole's sweat glands are working overtime.

# FIVE

JUST AS DJ SUSPECTS, Kate and Tuck have, indeed, closed their practice for the day and are seated at their conference table, mugs of tea and coffee respectively cooling close at hand, waiting for her to arrive. In this office also, a copy of the manuscript holds center stage. The turned-down corners and tea stains give evidence that this copy has clearly been read more frequently than Cole's. Exhausted, Kate holds her head in her hands, elbows on the table, glaring at the thickness of the more than five hundred pages in front of her.

"You know, Tuck, I've known all of this for years, decades in fact, but seeing it in print... Christ, it makes it all the more real—more intense, I guess is what I'm trying to get at."

Tuck takes a sip of coffee, grimacing at the bitterness. "More power to her, I say. My guess is that she'll still have to deal with a shitload of fallout from both her family and her readers. She's got the right, though. She's done her work. She wants to say her piece about what her father and uncles did; I say we back her one hundred percent no matter what."

Kate looks up, leans heavily on her hands and rises, walks to the double window, pulls back the curtain, and looks right toward the T stop, searching the crowds for DJ.

"It's the 'no matter what' that I'm most worried about, lovey. She's bitten off a large chunk of downright painful past. And as you well know from what we do here every day, there's always the risk of the past biting you right back and taking a huge chunk out of your butt."

Tuck spins a yo-yo out into 'walk-the-dog' mode, and looks up expectantly as Kate turns from the window.

"No, can't see her yet," Kate says, collapsing into a bright red bean bag chair. She realizes her mistake immediately and stretches her hand out to Tuck.

"Oh, damn, help me out of this thing, will you? I keep forgetting I can't do this anymore. Last week, I had to wait until Taya's session was over before I could scooch over to the desk and pull myself out of this."

Tuck laughs and takes advantage of the moment to pull Kate into a firm hug, both women bracing for what they will face once DJ arrives.

"You're wound tight as a tick, Kate. I'll get fresh tea going for both of us. That nice Irish breakfast blend you brought back from our last trip. How about some of that?"

Kate nods her thanks, grateful for the concern on her partner's face, and the years of bringing out the best in each other. Something about those strong shoulders and long legs had moved Kate to love her years ago, and she was lucky enough to have had Tuck well received by her large Catholic family.

"There's something special about the cut of that gal's jib," her sailor father used to say. "Can't help but like her. Must have some Irish blood in her somewhere. And for sure she can handle you." Kate smiles at the memory. Tuck is as dark as a Godiva hazelnut truffle, and just as meltingly delicious.

The Tucker family was less amused at their daughter's choice of life partner. Oh, they were pretty much okay with Audre being a lesbian, difficult as that was to entertain. They had become resigned to it long before she had come out to them. They could also handle the fact that Kate was white. There had been intermarriage in this family, way back on Tuck's mother's side anyway.

The Irish part was more troublesome, and required more accommodation. According to family consensus—with Tuck concurring—Kate was a flaming, red-headed, brassy, bossy, opinionated, in-your-face, fun-loving, pain-in-the-ass kind of Irish. And apparently—but only to Tuck's point of view—quite charming as well.

For the past twenty years, Kate and Tuck have run *Reaching Out,* one of Boston's foremost child and adolescent therapeutic practices, dedicated to the assessment and treatment of psychological trauma, with sexual abuse being their specialty. Between themselves, they call the practice 'PTO', shorthand for Peel the Onion, a rather apt reference to how long-term therapy has a tendency to go after issue under issue under issue, until the often raw sources of pain and behavior can be exposed and dealt with. And then the healing can begin.

"Tea would be just perfect, with honey. Put some extra water on so we can have some ready for DJ when she comes in, would you? My guess is she'll be needing a wee bit of hydration."

"Good idea," Tuck responds, and adds more water to the kettle.

"You know, Tuck, I admire DJ's persistence in all this. First her therapy, then writing the manuscript, and now doing the hard work of telling her family. I actually feel honored she's asked us to walk through it with her."

"In for a penny, in for a pound, as the saying goes, right?" Tuck turns the electric kettle to high.

Back at the conference table, Kate reaches for the manuscript. She glances at Tuck who has taken her place by the window. "Anything?"

When the answer comes in the form of a head shake, Kate opens the tome to Chapter Four.

## 4 · Peeling the Onion

*There is something more that needs to be said about my brother. Because he was not only good, or only bad, or only weird. He tormented me. He ridiculed me. He hit me with the pecking order precision that left all of us taking the torment we experienced and doing it to the next in line—and if we had had a dog and a cat and a bird and a fish, they would each have done wrong to the smaller and weaker of them as well. That was just the way it was.*

*But he also saved me. He saved me from rape. He saved me from rape and it made all the other things he did seem so unimportant. It is why the day he was beaten with the pole and mouthed to me "no more", I knew I was truly on my own. I knew what he meant, and I knew he had his survival to deal with. And I knew I would have my own.*

*My brother saved me from rape on a day when the daffodils had just opened and I could smell the earth where the sun had lain upon the empty gardens between our house and the next house down the hill. Patches of snow still hid in corners and I was wearing my corduroys, red flannel shirt and beloved Buster Browns. It was a lazy Saturday afternoon, and I was seven and a half.*

*Our mother had sent my brother and me to pick up a coffee cake that the elderly woman next door had baked for us. It would be on the kitchen table and we were to go in even if they weren't there, and bring it home. Uneaten, we were reminded.*

*We knocked, but there had been no car parked in front of the garage so we went in to retrieve the bread. The smell in the kitchen was delightfully yeasty, full of cinnamon and caraway and butter. The oven was still warm and on the table was the plated coffee ring covered with a clean kitchen towel. Our family name was written on a tented piece of paper, and sat perched upon the towel.*

*As we argued about who would get to carry the coffee cake, someone called from the living room, inviting us in to say hello. It was Donny, the adult son of the couple, a Navy man, recently home from action in Korea. He had on tan pants, a white T-shirt, black shoes, and a tan web belt with a navy anchor on the bronze buckle. He was sitting in a tapestried easy chair, newspaper open on his lap, feet extended onto a green leather hassock.*

*Donny talked to both of us, telling us about his ship and the big guns on the bow that he said shot huge bullets into Korea. He told us he had earned medals in the war and asked if we wanted to see them. Excitedly, we agreed. He said they were upstairs and that he would show them to us one at a time. JJ insisted he go first, him being the oldest, but Donny said "ladies first", and I remember making a ha-ha face at my brother, and sticking out my tongue.*

*And so, taking me by the hand, Donny brought me up the stairs and into his room and told me to sit on the bed. He turned to get the medals from his dresser drawer and I marveled at the mystery of a room I'd never seen before. Framed pictures of navy warships sailed above an old oak desk, trophies of various heights lined a matching bookcase and I recognized the Hardy Boys series my brother had just started. A crucifix graced the wall behind my head.*

*When he turned back to me, his pants were open, his zipper down, and something reddish-purple and growing bigger poked out of his hairy belly, pointing its way toward my face. He pushed me back on the bed, grabbed my waist and began pulling at my corduroys, tugging them roughly downward. I wriggled and turned away, telling him to stop, suddenly, vividly, clearly certain he meant me harm—although I was far too young to understand the nature of the harm he intended. He slapped my face. I screamed and squirmed and twisted down the bed, trying to get away. He gave up trying to deal with my pants and grabbed his penis and my hair, whisper-shouting at me to be quiet and open my mouth.*

*I did open my mouth. I yelled louder, screaming for my brother. JJ hol-*

lered up the stairs, wanting to know what was going on. Donny yelled for him to stay there. I screamed for him to come get me. JJ ran up the stairs, scream-ing at the man to leave me alone. Caught, trapped, afraid of being seen by JJ, Donny let loose of my hair and put his penis inside his pants just as JJ found the room we were in.

The man's face was red with sweat beads as he zipped himself up. The white T-shirt was wet under the arms and he smelled nasty. He drove his fist into the dresser, knocking pictures and coins to the floor. My brother grabbed me by the arm and pulled me from the bed. We ran down the stairs. He snatched the coffee cake from the table as we rushed past, out the door and home.

That's what my brother did for me. What he meant to me. And when I lost him, I lost one of the few things that made me feel I could find safety anywhere in the world.

We ran up the grassy slope to our house and in the back door to the kitchen. My mother took the bread, asked why we brought the towel when it wasn't ours, and turned away. We were jumping and yelling. "Mom. Mom. Mommy. Listen. Listen. Listen…"

---

THE SHRILL OF THE TEA KETTLE snaps Kate from her reading. "Every time I read this, I want it to be different. So many things could have stopped right there. Crazy, huh?" she asks, getting up to pour hot water over the ball of loose tea in her cup.

"I don't know how she'll handle all this—bringing it back up, I mean. Hell, I'm getting too old for drama. And DJ's family isn't known for deal-ing with anything well, especially that weird uncle of hers." Kate brings her cup back to the table and sits to read some more.

"You mean her Uncle Zip? The notorious Zipper?" Tuck turns from her post at the window. She looks over Kate's shoulder at where she is in the manuscript.

Kate swirls the tea ball in the steaming brew, lifting it and catching the last few drips in a napkin—but not before a few dark drops have landed on the manuscript. "He really is an odd one, but I have to tell you, on some level I actually like him. He is totally 'what you see is what you get'. Not subtle by any means. If he didn't do what he does for a living, he might be okay."

Tuck slides another napkin across to Kate. "Stop christening the book. It already looks like we dragged it around a barnyard. I'm glad you said might, because the jury's still out with me. I don't trust him in the least."

She takes the tea ball from Kate, opens it, and empties the wet leaves into the trash.

"We've been over this a hundred times, Katie, but I can't see how you can even say you like the guy. Not only don't I trust him, but he's a despicable creature who makes his money on the backs of women, literally, I might add. And for the life of me I just can't grasp why DJ thinks he's even human," Tuck says. "And the fact that she still has anything to do with him…honestly, it weirds me out."

Kate frowns as she looks at Tuck.

"I know. I know. But he's important to her on a really deep level—you can see that from her book. And we've always know that. It's not news."

"No, it's not, but the way she talks about him, and the way she writes about him in the book, it's like he's a fairy godfather or something. I don't want to rain on her parade when she has so little, but, clinically speaking, he scares the crap out of me."

"Well, we're in this with her, Tuck. We gave her our word," Kate says.

"Hey, don't take that to mean I want out. I'm just saying…" She lets the sentence drop into the ether.

Making her way back to the window, Tuck searches briefly for signs of DJ, then trades her yo-yo for a Rubik's Cube. "You know, it's been more than ten years since I last solved this thing. Perhaps I have finally lost my touch." She tosses the cube into a plastic basket filled with puzzles.

"Not with me you haven't, kiddo. You're still as much of a puzzle as ever," teases Kate.

Tuck smiles and wags a finger at her partner. "Ha! Good one," she says and continues her earlier train of thought. "Clearly, he loves Deej and she loves him. I guess that counts for something in his otherwise contemptible life. But it doesn't give him a free pass on the damage he's done to people just like these kids we see every day, not in my book anyway."

"No argument from me on that score, Tuck."

"And he's kept close to her all these years. Except for us, DJ's not close to too many people. Never has been. Trusting isn't her long suit," Tuck says, abandoning the toy shelf, and bringing her tea and some paperwork to the end of the table nearest the window so she can keep one eye on the street below.

"No, it's not, and I can damn well see why. For the love of God, that mother of hers is a royal piece of work." Kate slips easily into Irish mode when angry, and she has worn this topic down to a fine edge over the years of knowing DJ. "Just listen to this next part." She runs her finger down the page, searching for the last few words she has read, and continues aloud.

———————

*I wish I could tell you that my mother put down the dish she was drying, bent to our child level, and listened to us. I wish I could tell you she picked me up, sat me on the kitchen counter and tenderly placed her two warm palms against my cheeks, kissing my forehead. That she hugged me, and called my father, and that the police came and took the man away. And when evening came she rocked me until I slept and then carried me into the bed I shared with my sister, tucking me in, safe and sound.*

*I have wished these things a million times over, but they did not happen.*

*Nothing happened. Life just went on as if it never occurred at all. Perhaps because doing nothing when trouble took place made no sense to my child mind, I convinced myself that I had never spoken words about it out loud. Perhaps what happened was my own fault. Perhaps that was why my mother did nothing.*

*What did change, however, was that subtly, slowly, over time, I became aware that my mother responded to everything I said as if it were a lie.*

*I always remembered the incident itself. I never went into that house again, always fearful the man would be there. Even two years later, when we were told to keep our church clothes on and our parents piled all five of us kids into the car one Sunday because we were "going visiting", I refused to get out of the car once I learned whose house we were at—he had since married and moved away. I was ordered out of the car, but refused to move. I was terrified of seeing that man. I was left in the car in the freezing cold to teach me a lesson about being rude, but I still refused to move. I wouldn't say why, and at the time I believed it was because I hadn't told my mother what happened.*

*It was years later, decades actually, before I found out that my brother and I really did tell my mother that day. I was having quite a different conversation with my mother when that incident came into consciousness, and I revealed it to her. She told me she already knew this and asked why I was upsetting her by bringing "that old thing" back up again. Turns out we had told her that Saturday afternoon. I asked her what she did about it and she said she did nothing. She didn't believe me, us, didn't believe that we had been "gone long enough for anything like that to have happened", and she didn't want to start trouble when I was so clearly lying.*

*The day of the attempted rape changed my life.*

*I did not stop loving the world in the springtime. I did not stop loving daffodils or the earthy smell of warming soil after the long New England winters. I did not stop loving oven-warmed kitchens with the yeasty smells of bread and cinnamon and caraway. I did not stop loving my brother.*

*I stopped loving myself.*

*I stopped feeling free. I stopped throwing my arms wide open under the sun and twirling round and round, watching the clouds tumble into swirls of white over my head. I stopped ducking under sheets hung on the line, smelling the sun baked drying freshness of the wind upon the sails of my fantasy ships.*

*Flinging my arms open along the beach to catch the wind would leave me without protection. I began pulling my arms in and wrapping them around me, cocooning my soul inside itself.*

*Neither the attempted rape nor the inaction by my mother made me angry. What grew within me was a profound and visceral conviction that adults would not believe me or stand up for me. I stopped trusting in men as protectors of children, in mothers as sources of belief and safety from harm, and in home as a sanctuary from the perils of the world at large.*

*And I stopped believing in myself. Everything I said was suspect. I had become the child who lies. I was seven and a half, and I did not understand any of this for many years. I did not understand that I was turning myself into a caterpillar waiting for the chance to become a butterfly.*

*I believed myself, instead, to be a lying worm.*

---

THE END OF THE CHAPTER comes none too soon. The cadence of Kate's reading has escalated to a pounding, angry tempo and she fairly shouts, "seven and a half".

She spits each small word into a fiercely enunciated sentence, "Seven. And. A. Half. Jesus!" Kate slams the pages closed and slaps the manuscript with an open palm. "And a liar! DJ? Christ, how far off the mark of knowing your own kid can you get?"

It is with some relief that Tuck spots DJ coming out of the pharma-cy across from the trolley station. She moves behind Kate and massages some of the tenseness out of her shoulders. "She's coming, honey."

Kate lets out a breath she is unaware she has been holding. "OK," she says, gripping Tuck's hand against her neck, "Forever onward."

# SIX

AS DJ HURRIES TOWARD the towering blue-fronted building that houses the offices of her dearest friends, she catches sight of her compact frame in a passing storefront window. She moves instinctively to brush hair from her graying temples, only to smile as she remembers yesterday's appointment to have her hair styled and her last minute decision to have it shortened as well. *Creature of habit that I am*, she thinks, and wonders how long it will take her to adjust to the new look.

DJ had allowed herself to go gray years ago, but held on to her shoulder-length waves much longer, loving the comfort it gave her to twirl her fingers through the locks as she sat at her computer and contemplated the fate of the various villains and heroes who formed the meat of her many novels. It had been years, perhaps even a full decade, since anyone else had run their fingers through her hair in the throes of passion, however. *Queen of Lust and Thrust, indeed!*

She didn't think of this often. But when such notions did rise to the surface, she managed to ream them back down with the force of a jack hammer on a city street. What she hadn't planned on were the resulting cracks in the foundation of her psyche that had begun to take their toll.

Writing her memoir was meant to help her heal the cracks and release her from the grip the past held on her. "If only it could magically *poof* all of it into another hemisphere," she says to herself as she enters the elevator with its gleaming bronze interior and presses the button for the fifth floor.

When the elevator opens on five, Kate and Tuck meet DJ with hugs and tea, ushering her into their conference room and a plush maroon chair. "Absolutely love the haircut. Love it!" Tuck checks out the back of DJ's head. "Short, stylish, and oh so you. It looks great."

"Are you feeling OK after your bout with the bowl?" DJ can feel Kate taking her measure, scanning her from top to bottom and back again, looking for signs of damage the way a Geiger counter checks for radiation.

"Physically, I'm fine, or will be if you give me a chance to freshen up a bit." DJ digs into her purse and waves the strongly suggested toothbrush and paste at Kate. "Emotionally, however, I am a train wreck waiting to happen. I gave Cole the manuscript. Scared the living shit out of me to do it, but I did it. Now, I don't know what the hell else I'm supposed to do. I really don't. And I'm not sure I have any energy left to do much more than crawl into bed, pull the covers over my head and let whatever happens next just happen."

Exhausted from even that brief rant DJ sips at her tea. "That's good," she says, "but to really enjoy it, I need the facilities first." She again points the toothbrush at Kate, pistol-like, and walks down the hall and into the restroom, leaving Kate and Tuck to share a long look of concern.

"Onward." whispers Kate again, as if sending a prayer to the heavens for help. Only this time she adds, "Into the breach."

When DJ comes out of the restroom, she heads directly to the table and stands in front of her manuscript. She sits, placing one hand on the book. The other lifts her tea. After a long sip, she looks at her friends. "Okay, what next?"

"Here's what I like and what I don't." Kate pulls a chair up next to DJ. "First off, crawling under the covers, no matter the strength of that desire, means you relinquish control to other people about what happens next and whether or not this book gets published. And that would be so not you. Because, whatever else might have helped hold you together all these years, the fact that you are a total control freak—and I mean that in the nicest possible way, darlin'—is one of your major strengths. Period. Give it up to someone else now, and you are setting yourself up for one hell of a nose dive."

Kate leans toward DJ from across the table and looks directly into her eyes.

"Second," she says, "and this has always been true about you. What you might lack in confidence, you more than make up for in courage. What you lived through and what you have been able to do with your life in spite of it is truly remarkable. And that's what I think your book celebrates. So, what we have to do next is figure out, step by step, person by person, where the bumps are, the…" Kate pauses in thought. "OK, it's like moguls, there'll be moguls ahead-"

"Oh, please," Tuck jumps in. "Not the ski analogies. She gets what you mean. We both get what you mean. Please don't start that nonsense today." Tuck glances at DJ and then gives Kate a look of exasperation. "She's been doing this all fall. It's her new metaphor for everything difficult. Half the kids we work with have never even been to the beach, never mind a ski slope, but does that stop her? Not a chance." Tuck puts the brakes on before she, too, goes off on a tangent from which she may never return.

DJ rolls her eyes, more in amusement than exasperation. "Look, you two know me better than I probably know myself, so you should know I'm not about to fold. I've worked too hard to pack it all in now. But I didn't just fall off a turnip truck, either, to quote your famous saying, Kate. I spent years as a journalist, following up on these kinds of stories. People's feelings get hurt. Family ties suffer. People take sides. My readers will take sides, for God's sake. This could be the end of the 'Queen'. What happens when they find out there's never been a King, or a Prince, or even a Jester? Hell, there hasn't even been a Maid-in-Waiting. And yet I write like I've got a new one every day of the week. Do the words *fraud* or *fake* have any meaning here?"

"Sweet love of Jesus, DJ, there is nothing fake about you. You're a writer, an author. It's fiction. Its poetic license-"

DJ interrupts with, "What happened to the edict to write about what you know?"

The fact is, DJ loves to get Kate going on this topic and is enjoying herself immensely, giving herself a short break from the serious, and Kate a chance to flaunt her style. Kate's Irish is up, and there is no end to how long it will stay up.

Circling the table, Kate has a good wind and a long tail and her kite string is full out. "And just look at you," she rants, "You're writing the truth now, aren't you, toots? And since you've been at it, you've gone to hell in a hand basket, haven't you? Just what do you plan on doing next? Crawl on your hands and knees until you're bloody raw? Oh, wait, you already-"

Tuck intervenes with a shrill whistle, two fingers against her lips, and a seriously grim expression on her face. "I'm going to start charging you two for referee services if you don't quit this baloney right now. Kate, sit.

Let's get going on this. We cancelled a full day of clients, and I for one don't want to waste another minute. We have too much to do. DJ, where do you want to start first?"

DJ takes a deep breath and sits back in her seat. "Right, that's enough of that. Okay, then. Today's Friday. I think things with Cole will be fine over the weekend at least. After that, someone there is likely to leak the news to someone who will eventually tell the press. Shouldn't happen, but it will."

"So, this weekend, we cover your mother and your sisters. Is that right?" asks Tuck.

"And my uncle. Family beyond that… doesn't matter to me what they think right now," responds DJ. She looks from Kate to Tuck. "Are you both still willing to do this with me?"

Kate gives DJ one of her renowned 'what-the-hell-do-you-think-you-dummy' looks, while Tuck simply nods her head in one quick motion. DJ moves her hand over her heart, smiling at these two wonderful women. "Then let's start with my sisters. They're probably the easiest and most important. Then my mother."

"And she will not be a day at the beach, by any means," Kate chimes in. "It's been a while since I've had the pleasure." Sarcasm wraps around each word like bacon 'round a scallop before it's put into the pan to be fried to a crisp.

DJ toasts Kate's comment with her cup and drinks the last of the now tepid brew. "We'll save Raymond for last. He ought to be okay."

Tuck interrupts. "Raymond? The Zipper? Must we?"

"If we must, then we must," Kate says abruptly to Tuck, and then turns to DJ. "And why do you think he'll be fine with this?"

DJ's response is quick and sure. "He pretty much knows all this already. He'll support me. He's the one person who's never hurt me. Except for my brother, he's the only male in the family who ever really cared about me at all."

She turns to Kate and Tuck. "And please, you two don't keep calling him that offensive nickname. I hate it. It was fine when he was a kid playing football."

"What's that got to do with it?" asks Tuck.

"They called him Zip because he could cut through the defensive line faster than anyone else. He scored so many points his record still stands at Evans High."

"Oh," says Kate, "I thought you said it came from something having to do with the war in Vietnam."

"That, too," DJ says. "His army buddies thought the name fit him because his job was to zip up the body bags as the dead were being sent home. But that was then and this is now. I'm no fool. I know what he does for a living. And that nickname just reminds me of it. I hate it."

"It's so difficult when you mention him," Kate says, "because his name conjures up this image that I can't get out of my head, of some idiot's pants being unzipped as he reads porn. I'm way too visual and right-brained when it comes to this stuff. And you do know, don't you, that they sometimes refer to him as 'The Great *Un*-zipper'?"

"Once again, Kate, that's entirely too graphic. Thank you very much," says Tuck.

"Bottom line is this, girls. He means a lot to me. So call him Raymond, okay? I'm going to have enough to deal with once the whole world finds out I'm related to him anyway. I'm sure I'll be hearing enough of that kind of stuff then, thank you very much."

Tuck and Kate share an eyebrows raised look. "Okay," Kate replies, drawing out the word like she's pulling taffy, "Raymond it is. So we're off to see your sisters first. Do they know we're coming?" She points to herself and Tuck. "Because, as you are well aware, that spitfire sister of yours, Christine, and I have never been on the best of terms."

"Probably not," DJ says. "I didn't think to mention it when I set all this up. It will just have to be a delightful surprise, now, won't it?"

Kate groans, but DJ moves right along.

"We're all booked into the Peachtree in Atlanta for the night, and—"
Kate cuts her off.

"Atlanta? Not New York? I thought you said New York. Why in hell are we going all the way to Atlanta? Damn, DJ, you know how much I hate to fly," Kate says.

"Sarah's choice, since she has the furthest to fly. She's staying on to spend the week with an old friend. She and Chrissie should have flown in late yesterday to do some shopping." DJ looks around and finds the briefcase she had tossed onto a desk when she arrived.

"We should get going if we want to pick up our bags at your place, grab a quick lunch and get to the airport. Ah, maybe lunch first. I'm feeling a bit lightheaded," DJ says.

Kate stands, raising the manuscript with both hands. "Take this or leave it? What's your choice, madam author?"

"Oh god, I am not about to haul that brick on a plane, so let's leave it. Besides, I have no intention of giving anyone else a copy."

"All right, then, let's move," says Tuck, removing tea cups from the table and unplugging the kettle.

Kate runs through a checklist.

"Everything here is all set until Tuesday: answering service is on call; your dog's at the kennel; your car and overnight bag are at our place; we're both packed and ready." She looks around one more time. "Let's go."

"I really am hungry, girls," says DJ. "How about we just go downstairs and get something at *Au Bon Pain* before we head out?"

"Best idea I've heard all morning, my friend. Let's do it." Kate says, "Eat. Drive. Fly. Meet. Sounds like a great movie."

"It would if the 'meet' part didn't fill me with trepidation," DJ says, suddenly looking as weary as she sounds. She hesitates on her way to the office door, hand reaching for the knob.

"You know, I woke up this morning with an image in my head that I just can't seem to shake," she says. "I have four days to accomplish my goal of telling four people about this book. In my dream there were three huge rocks with names on them: one for my two sisters, one for my mother, and then my uncle."

Both Kate and Tuck stop moving and wait.

"I just can't help feeling like there's stuff under each of those rocks that I really don't want to know." She shakes her head and turns the door knob. "Guess we'll just have to roll each of them over to find out, though, won't we?"

# SEVEN

COLE HAD ASKED HIS SECRETARY to make a copy of the manuscript and deliver it to his boss hours ago. They had both agreed to do what they could to accommodate DJ's wishes and print the book—providing it lived up to the professional standards they would require of any author, new or an old veteran like Donna Jean. Cole himself had no doubt it rose to and exceeded that standard, but waiting for word from above was just about killing him. He was over-caffeinated to the point of leaking latte out his pores and, totally out of character for him, breaking into a cold sweat each time the phone rang. He fully expected that Stan went directly to the other two partners and that his future with Whitman, Westminster, and Yarrow was now on the line.

Two hours ago, Cole had tried to take control by dialing his boss again himself, only to be told that Stan wasn't to be disturbed. After that, he attempted to read more of the manuscript. One chapter later he abandoned any endeavor to sit still as his worry level rose with his blood pressure. He was a sweater caught on a nail, slowly unraveling, and he knew it. He paced. He arranged and then re-arranged his Red Sox baseball collection, setting each of his treasured relics at the proper angle to be able to view the player's autograph from his desk. He felt no better.

Now, in the waning hours of the afternoon, he detects and then adjusts a slight tilt to the framed and signed picture of Patriots' quarterback, Tom Brady, throwing for the conference-winning touchdown in a raging snowstorm.

"Desperate situations call for creative plays, don't they Tom, my man?"

Cole asks, tapping his finger on the glass. But the one-sided conversation leaves him feeling no more confident in himself at all.

Cole picks up a set of five-pound weights, positions his lanky frame dead center on his Persian carpet, lying on his back. He begins arm curls, humming the old theme from *Rocky*, trying valiantly to distract himself from his current situation and the reality that when he leaves the office tonight he will be protected by what he humorlessly envisions as *muscle*. He lowers the weights and begins to laugh.

"Given the industry that fucker Martone is hooked into," he says out loud to the ceiling, "I'm sure his muscle dude could beat the crap out of my muscle dude any day. Bet the asshole even has a bumper sticker on his limo."

The phone rings, snapping him out of his reverie and onto his feet. To his relief it is Stan calling, but only to say he is leaving for the weekend with the manuscript and will be in touch over the next couple of days. Cole wants more. He needs much more if he is going to survive the weekend—emotionally, at any rate.

"Give me a few seconds here, Stan. I think I have an idea. Can you stop down on your way out? Or I can run up? Your call."

"I'm already in the garage, Cole. What is it?"

"I think we need to do a pre-emptive strike, here. Let's call Martone, give him a heads up on this, give him a chance to read the manuscript."

"For Christ's sake, Cole, where's your head at anyway? We can't do that. Your slip is showing, man. Stop panicking for just one minute, will you? Calm the hell down and think straight so we can get a handle on this. There are rules against us taking an author's manuscript and giving it to someone else and you know it. I don't have time for this craziness."

"No, seriously, listen to me, Stan. He doesn't know about this yet. DJ was headed out of town. She told me she had family to see and tell before they found out some other way. She also said she was determined to get this published, here or somewhere else, and we both know exactly who would be more than thrilled to take it right out from under us."

Cole knows he has finally garnered Stan's attention when he hears him mutter the f-word into the phone. Levy Press has been nipping at their heels in the dwindling book publishing world and Stan is not about to let them bite this author in particular. She's too much their golden egg at the moment, and they are both quite certain that even if the earth went viral tomorrow, DJ's fans would still be clamoring for her words in print. They are that sure of her power and equally sure they will not let someone else horn in on their territory.

Levy tried in the past to best them in the romance book sales wars, and had almost succeeded. Not by wooing DJ away, but by coming up with someone almost as good. Almost, but not quite. It ended with a bang, when three of the genre's early—now elderly—romance writers filed a lawsuit citing Levy's new author for plagiarism of their works. It never got as far as court, but scuttlebutt in the industry placed the settlement amount well into the seven figures. DJ's popularity soared along with sales of her books during this media-mocked *Crisis in Romanceville.*

Taking advantage of Stan's silence, Cole rushes on. "Think about it, boss. We wait for him to find out from DJ, and he has all the reason in the world to come after us, well, me. I was warned, wasn't I? But if I contact him and let him know the situation up front, including how set DJ is on this, maybe we can get him to back off."

He pinwheels a pen across the top of DJ's manuscript, then lunges for it, grabbing air, as the pen spins wildly across his desk and flies off the edge.

"She's going to get this published somewhere, boss, and you and I both know it needs to be here. This guy is worried about something that only he seems aware of, as if the shit will hit the proverbial fan if she writes about her family. It doesn't matter that we don't understand what the problem is. Right now it only matters that he does, and we need to respond to that."

Cole pauses, giving his boss a moment to reflect, and sends a silent prayer to the heavens. He is begging for some help with this and he knows it. He is pretty sure Stan knows he's desperate as well. Resting his hand on the additional copy of the manuscript he had his secretary run off to give to the Zipper, he tries one more time.

"I really think it's our only shot," he continues, cringing at the aptness of his gun metaphor. "I really don't see working this out any other way."

"Do you know how to get in touch with him?"

Cole almost faints in relief. Finally something positive in the way of action, a way to take control of this mess. Oh, how he hates not being in control and to have been pushed to the point of humiliation by anyone, especially someone the likes of this Zipper person!

Cole's skinny-boned child's body had been the focus of harassment and bullying all of his early life. And, try as he has in adulthood to compensate, he knows himself to still be easily intimidated by power—even in the best of circumstances. This fear of Martone, however, is way beyond his capacity to cope, and has been giving him visions of plunging head-first into a pool of his own anxiety. And drowning.

Stan's response provides some relief. Cole is no less frightened of the Zipper. But at least they are doing something.

He tries to keep his excitement in check for the moment. "Not directly of course, no, I don't. But I can't imagine he won't respond to a call from us. Me. He certainly knows who I am."

"All right, then. Call him, set up an appointment. Check with my secretary first, because, Cole, I insist on being there as well. Got that?" Cole hears Stan start his car, signaling the call is over.

"I'll try my best with that, Stan, but you know who we're dealing with. He might be willing to come here; he might want us to go there—wherever that might be. But he certainly never gave me any warning the last time, and I don't think he'll have changed all that much since then. We might have to take what we can get."

"I want to be there, period. Keep me posted. And don't go anywhere without the guy we have on you, not even that gym of yours. You hear me?"

Cole responds with a strong "Yes, sir. And thank you," but Stan has already stabbed the Off button. Cole sinks back into the cushioned comfort of his soft leather chair. Maya, his secretary, has gone for the day so he reaches for the phone book and sets himself to the task of tracking down the notorious east coast porn king and calling him in for a chat. He chuckles at the absurdity of what he is about to do.

"If this works, it will be a flaming miracle. And if it doesn't, it'll just prove what a flaming asshole *I* am to think it will. Here goes nothing," he mutters, and flips the Boston yellow pages open to Adult Bookstores.

# EIGHT

THE THREE INTREPID TRAVELERS settle into their seats on the plane. Initially it was on time, but it's been sitting at the harbor end of the runway for almost half an hour. They are restless.

"You know, toots," Kate is clearly addressing DJ, "for all your wealth and prominence as the world's greatest author of the trashy novel, you could at least have set us up in first class. This is killing my old boney knees. I know you love to sit with your public, but as your closest and, dare I say, dearest friends, you really could have done much better than this, don't you think?"

"Give me some credit, will you. Those seats were already booked. Besides, I wanted to sit together so we could talk. Three across works better anyway, doesn't it?"

"Says she who commandeered the aisle seat closest to the restroom. Yes, it does, but I am about to take a nap, which would have been much more of a real nap in first class. I have to prep myself for this evening. Your sisters never stop talking, and I'm not going into that fray unprepared. Wake me when we get there, Tuck, providing we ever get off the ground in the first place."

"Wait, then." Tuck grabs her book and pillow from the pouch in front of her. "Katie, slide over to this seat. You can have the window and I'll take the middle. I'm not tired and I can chat better with DJ."

"I cannot just *slide* my butt over there. I'm trapped in here like a baby in a car seat. Besides, we're not supposed to take our seat belts off."

"Oh, just do it. Quick." Tuck is already up and stepping across Kate, raising the armrest in the middle so Kate can shift toward the window.

"See. Done," she says, just as the flight attendant announces, "Ladies and gentlemen, please remain seated with your seatbelts fastened. We will be taking off momentarily. We are sorry for the delay, but you must remain seated. Thank you for your cooperation."

"Hear that?" Kate glares at Tuck. "That's you she's talking about. And you're always blaming *me* for getting us into trouble."

Tuck changes Kate's book from one pouch to the other and straps herself into her new seat. "Oh, go take your nap," she quips. "It might improve your mood."

DJ smiles, "I am always amazed at how you two manage to have stayed together for, what, more than twenty-five years, isn't it?"

"Yeah, well, she's basically a sweet old thing and I love her. And a sense of humor does go a long way."

Tuck adjusts the air flow above her seat. "You know she didn't mean it about the tickets and first class. That's just Kate blowing hot air. You've been damned good to us—never could have opened our practice without your help. You know that, right?"

"Well, if I even thought for a second that that's why you were willing to help me with this, I'd have booked both of you into the baggage compartment," DJ says. "And, don't worry. I've had that girl's number since the second week of college. All bark and just as much bite, wrapped around a solid gold core. I'm so glad you found each other."

"So, how are you holding up? Really?" Tuck asks. "That turning over the rock image you mentioned as we were leaving the office sounds like you're worried this is all going to backfire on you."

DJ starts to answer but is interrupted by the rev of the engines and the announcement that takeoff is imminent. They settle back into their seats as the plane gains momentum and lifts, banking sharply over the bay and heading southward.

"You know," DJ says in response to Tuck's pre-take-off question, "mostly I'm just exhausted from the writing itself, and maybe the dream about the rocks simply comes with being this tired. I get really sapped when I'm wrapped up in my novels, anyway, but that's always been about the intensity of writing. This experience has been another thing altogether."

"Had to have been one hell of a trip down memory lane, DJ. I can't imagine-"

Tuck is cut off by Kate, who is wide-eyed and more than willing to contribute her opinion.

"I don't have to imagine. I know! You might as well have been a hermit the past eight months. Only came out of your cave twice that I can recall. And even then we had to bribe you with tickets to the Newport Folk Festival. Jeesh!" She tugs at her neck pillow and turns to face the window, sliding the shade down to screen out the brilliant sunlight.

Both Tuck and DJ laugh.

"We have to speak softly so as not to wake the gnarling giant," Tuck whispers.

"I heard that."

In a few minutes, Kate finally seems to have quieted for the flight.

Tuck turns to DJ. "You were saying…"

"The novels are pure fantasy. They basically have nothing to do with me or my life at all, and that makes them easy to write."

"Oh, yeah, I get it," Tuck says, "and the autobiography, of course, has *everything* to do with you."

"Yes… but it's more than that, I think." DJ bites the side of her lip, struggling for just the right words.

"It's been one thing to remember that I was abused. I think of that often. But it's been quite another to spend time dwelling on the particular *details* of those events—you know, exactly what my neighbor, then my father and uncles did to me. Especially, what my family did. But it's even more than that, actually. The hardest part is remembering what I *felt like* when those things were happening."

DJ takes a moment to reflect on what she has just said. She holds a finger up to let Tuck know she's trying to work out another thought.

"No, that's not totally accurate," she says. "It's more than just remembering what it felt like. What occurs is that my whole body reacts as if the abuse is really happening again in that very moment I'm thinking about it. With all the fear and the shame I felt years ago. That's the hardest."

"Ouch," was all Tuck could say.

"It was the not knowing when or if it would happen again. I spent years going to bed at night not knowing if it would happen this night, or the next, or the next. Would this be the weekend? Praying it wouldn't, or, sometimes even praying it *would,* just to get it over with."

"Kids tell me every day that they can't bear that feeling," says Tuck.

"Yeah. That's the part that had me walking the floor at two in the morning and clutching my gut most of the time I was in front of the computer writing about it. Probably had something to do with why I tossed my cookies this morning after I met with Cole, too."

"That's a dumpster load of stress to be carrying around, DJ. Frankly, I'm surprised you weren't prowling the cemetery playing *Whac-a-Mole* on your father's grave."

"Hah!" DJ says. "Oh, how I wish I'd thought of that. It really might have helped."

"I work with kids, remember? They come up with the best ideas in the world to handle grief and pain. They teach me new things every day," Tuck says. "Even had one little dudette who beat the crap out of her father's vintage motorcycle when she found out he died in a crash while riding one of his other bikes. Whatever works, I say."

"I'll remember that next time... Hell, it seems like I was a kid two or three centuries ago..." her voice trails off as the seat in front of her jerks back and crowds her space.

"Spending this past year facing all that again was just the pits, really. I feel so depleted that I must admit I was hoping this phase of bringing my family up to speed on what I've done would be easier. Then when I woke up with that image this morning..." DJ lets the sentence hang in the air for just a few tense beats. "So, I don't know, I might just be asking for too much."

"Small wonder, then, that this trip has you a bit spooked, girl," Tuck says.

"There's a feeling I just can't shake and it started to happen about the middle of the book. Something just doesn't add up and I can't figure it out. For the longest time I thought I had all the pieces, and now... now I'm not so sure. Some things don't quite fit right."

"Sounds to me like you're worried there might be some unburied skeletons somewhere," Tuck says.

"Unburied? Hah! Tuck, this is *my* family, remember? There are secrets and bones everywhere."

TUCK PICKS UP HER BOOK and flips the pages looking for her bookmark, thinking to give DJ some space to relax or sleep. When she sees that DJ is just sitting quietly, she lowers her tray table, sets her paperback down and removes her neck pillow.

"Let me ask you something, DJ." Tuck lowers her voice just a bit as the plane reaches cruising speed and the engine noises fall off a decibel or two. "What's your mother's story? I mean, I try like hell to have empathy but, honestly, Deej, she's quite a piece of work, as we say in the business. And I've worked with a lot of 'loosie-goosies', to quote Kate's name for far-too-inadequate parents. But some days I think that mother of yours could give lessons to the worst of them."

DJ smiles. "If I told you she's still a mystery to me after all these years, my friend, I wouldn't be lying."

"Seriously, Deej, I don't get her at all," Tuck says.

"I'm not sure I ever told you this, but very shortly after my mother was born, and I'm talking only a few days, my grandmother placed her into the home of a wet nurse for many months."

Tuck is interested. "You know," she says, "I remember hearing this before, but I never quite understood why."

"Well, it would have been near the end of that influenza-tuberculosis epidemic when she was born. My grandfather, her father, had contracted TB and ended up in an asylum in Rhode Island. He was one of the few Italians there and evidently miserable enough to beg my grandmother to let him come home to die. The health department wouldn't allow him to return with an infant in the household. My poor grandmother; she was young and primarily Italian-speaking, and faced with a terrible choice. And so, to help her husband die, she placed the baby out and only brought her home a few months afterwards, when the health department declared it safe."

"Wow, makes perfect sense then that your mother would have some trouble feeling connected."

"Honestly, it's the only thing I can think of that makes sense. There might be more, of course, because none of my relatives ever spoke about those times very much."

"Those years were pretty tough, DJ. War, depression, rationing—many people just closed into themselves and their families in order to survive, I suppose. And your mother's loss was a double whammy—separation from her mother after having her for a short time, then being returned to her while she was still grieving…" Tuck's voice just trails off.

DJ startles a bit when the tone sounds to indicate that seat belts can be unfastened. It is pronounced safe to roam around the cabin.

Awakened by the announcement, Kate drops her head onto Tuck's shoulder.

"Ack…she woke me up! And did she actually say 'roam' around the cabin? Seriously? The woman needs a reality check. She's been working at high altitudes and deprived of fresh air far too long." This produces a loud chuckle from the guy across the aisle as well as from Tuck and DJ.

Kate stretches. She lifts the shade.

"Anyone know where we are?" she asks.

She turns back to her seatmates.

"Can't sleep with you two jabbering away like magpies. What's going on? What'd I miss, anything good?"

"That's way too glary. It hurts my eyes." Tuck reaches across to pull the shade down again. "We're just talking about DJ's book, Katie. Nothing's happening. Sleep if you want and we'll try to be a bit quieter."

"Well, I *was* sleeping before the invitation to roam was issued," Kate says. "I hate flying. It always seems safer just to make myself comatose until it's over."

"Oh, that reminds me…" DJ reaches for her purse under the seat in front of her and grabs her iPod. "Here," she says to Kate, "I brought this so we'd have some tunes. Might help you relax."

Kate fits the ear pods in, turns it on, and closes her eyes. "Ah, nice," she says. "Thank you."

DJ's elbow is bumped by a passenger out 'roaming' the aisle on the way to the restroom.

"I'm so sorry," he says to her, "I'm sort of off kilter here."

The comment puzzles DJ, until she sees he is guiding a grinning two-year-old up the aisle with one hand and grasping the child's teddy bear with the other. "Slow down a bit there, buddy," he cautions, as the boy's unsteady legs pin-ball him forward from seat to seat.

Both Tuck and DJ laugh as they watch the boy pull harder and hear the father repeat the same apology right up to the first class curtain and beyond.

"Hey, Tuck," DJ asks, "did I ever tell you about the time I brought my aunt Lena a stuffed teddy bear, a really cute one, to keep her company when she was in the nursing home?"

"Seriously? No!" Tuck laughs. "Why a teddy bear? She was pretty old, wasn't she?"

"Yeah," DJ says, remembering. "I don't know. I visited when I could, and the place was always just so stark, so devoid of anything pertinent to her life. She had a roommate and all, but nothing was really hers—her very own. You know?"

"Yeah," Tuck says, "those places really creep me out. I'm great with kids, even with the most damaged of kids, but I don't think I have it in me to work with the elderly, especially in a nursing home."

"She was just so depressed in that place. Her mind was still alert. It's just that her body was giving out on her."

Tuck is reflective in the brief silence.

"I never know what's worse," she says, "having a body that's strong and a mind that fails, or a mind that's clear and a body that just gives up on you. Neither scenario is very appealing, I'd guess."

"I tell you, Tuck. My childhood was hell. But a person needs super powers to handle old age."

"I hear you there, DJ. I don't know if I'm ever going to be ready to deal with it gracefully when that day comes. And, for sure, I can't imagine Katie going softly into anybody's 'good night' as the saying goes." They share a laugh.

"So, did Lena like the bear?" Tuck prompts.

"Oh, yes. She cried and hugged it and told me she had always wanted one, had never had one. She loved it. She slept with it at night and it sat next to her in bed all day. It was the best gift I ever gave anyone."

DJ sits quietly with the memory, then just shakes her head and sighs.

"My mother happened to be there visiting as well and, as we were leaving, I kissed my aunt and said, 'I love you'. When we were walking to our cars, my mother asked why I had to keep telling Lena I loved her every time I saw her."

DJ rubs the back of her own neck, trying to release some tension. The self-massage is of little help, but the sight of the two-year-old who has escaped his father's grasp and is now running pell-mell down the aisle clutching his bear, relaxes her into a smile.

"My mother insisted that Lena knew I loved her—I was, after all, her niece," she continues. "I said that none of us knew how long Lena would live and that I wanted to be sure my words stayed in her heart, to comfort her, just like the teddy bear. My mother said, 'Oh, yes, and about that bear. Don't ever get me one when I get old. That's just silly.'"

"Whoa. Okay. Nothing touchy-feely for her, huh?"

"Nope. Not then. Not now. The shorthand version of my mother is this: nobody home emotionally. Lots of reasons why, of course, but none of them make up for the absence."

"Yeah," Tuck says. "And the other truth, I'd guess, is that no matter how inadequate she was at mothering, the real villain was the guy she married. I feel like I'm dumping on her for everything, and I don't think that's exactly fair, is it?"

DJ's response is interrupted by the flight attendant. "Something to drink?" he asks, and drops paltry packets of pretzels into their palms.

Both women request bottled water. Tuck asks for one for Kate as well, and DJ also wants two empty cups. Tuck is a bit puzzled by the cup request, but as soon as the flight attendant toddles off to the next row with his cart, DJ reaches into her purse again and pulls out a zipper bag of trail mix. Lowering her tray, she pours the pretzels into the bag, indicating Tuck should do the same with hers. She gives the bag a good shake, and then fills each cup with a tasty selection of nuts, raisins, granola chunks, pretzels and chocolate bits.

"Fantastic! In my book, chocolate can make just about anything bearable," Tuck says, picking through her cup for her favorite treats.

"Well then, perhaps we had better purchase a couple of pounds when we land," DJ says, as she drops a few of her own chocolate pieces into Tuck's cup. "And if all we need to make this trip endurable is chocolate, then it's on me."

"Sounds good to me," Tuck says, "and perhaps we can slide a few pieces under each of your rocks before we get down to business—you know, sweeten them up first."

DJ laughs.

"You have no idea what a great suggestion that is," she says, unfastening her seat belt and preparing to get up. "After all, these are my sisters we're facing this evening. I love 'em, and they're wonderful—but never underestimate their ability to complicate and confound even the simplest situation."

She looks at Tuck and shrugs.

"And we'll need about fifty pounds of the good stuff from Godiva if that's ever going to work on my mother."

DJ pulls at the seat in front of her and gets up.

"Now, if you'll excuse me, I intend to 'roam' my way to the rest room. Please send a search party if I get lost."

# NINE

THE CAPTAIN ANNOUNCES that Wake Forest is currently just barely visible through the clouds out the right side of the airplane, and that he is putting the Fasten Seatbelt sign on due to turbulence between here and the Atlanta airport.

Kate sits up, pulls the ear buds onto her lap and, to no one in particular says, "Hopefully not a foreshadowing of the turbulence we'll run into once we *get* to Atlanta." Tuck laughs, but quickly grows quiet when she realizes that DJ is asleep.

Kate clutches Tuck's arm as the plane suddenly navigates a series of turbulent bumps in rapid succession.

"I hate flying and this is exactly why," she says through gritted teeth. "And don't go telling me about how no planes ever crashed due to turbulence and all that blah-blah. It scares me and I don't like it. That's all that matters to me."

She looks over at DJ, who has slept through the entire episode.

"How she does that, I'll never know. She used to wake up every time the clock ticked in college. Now look at her. A bomb could go off and she wouldn't-"

"Okay, shut up with the bomb stuff, Kate, or we'll be in deeper shit than a few bumps," Tuck cautions and changes the subject. "So what do you make of all that?" she whispers, snuggling closer to Kate. "I know you weren't listening to that iPod. You do so love to eavesdrop."

Kate ignores the thinly veiled jibe.

"What has always amazed me has been how well grounded DJ turned out given all of what she's been through." she says.

"On a daily basis you and I both see people who have been leveled by less than half of what she experienced and have become emotionally crippled," says Tuck. "This gal has literally dug her heels in like a pit bull, and worked like hell to succeed. And all I can think now is that she deserves a god damned break. Enough already."

"I hear you, Tuck. What a mess she got born into. An emotionally disconnected mother and a father just this side of pathologically sadistic."

"Thank goodness she at least had her aunt Lena. It's nice to hear her talk about her. I can't imagine what it would have been like for Deej to have had nobody at all. She sounds like a remarkable woman. She's probably where DJ got a lot of her strength," Tuck suggests.

"I think you're right on target with that, hon," Kate says. "DJ told me once that Lena hated her father, thought he was selfish, advised her mother not to marry him. Evidently the feeling was mutual."

"What do you mean?" Tuck asks.

"No love lost either way, from what DJ says. She said after Lena told her this, it finally made sense to her why her father would get so furious whenever he was hitting her and she would cry and call out for Lena. And this was way past the time they had lived with her grandmother and Lena."

"Jesus, Kate."

"I remember her saying she knew he would hit her harder if she called for Lena, but she always did because she knew he hated it."

"Stubborn girl, but you've got to admire her spunk. And he sounds like some kind of raving lunatic."

"Yeah, all dressed up in a three-piece suit and looking like mister do-gooder civil servant. What a joke." Kate's knuckles are white.

"It's a wonder he didn't hurt her permanently—physically, I mean. He sure as hell hurt her emotionally."

"No question about that," Kate answers, solemnly. "Years ago, DJ told me that she finally stopped calling for Lena after one incident when he got so enraged he started shaking her by the shoulders. She swore she could feel her brain sloshing around inside her skull. That scared her into silence." Kate lowers her voice. "God, I hate that bastard. Almost sorry he's dead. I'd have relished the idea of marching *him* through the court process and right into the slammer."

"Oh my god yes," Tuck responds. She is energized by the thought. "Jail would be the perfect poetic justice for a guy like that, wouldn't it?"

"Well, DJ has broken that silence in a huge way with this new book, hasn't she? Won't be too long now before we all find out what happens next. And I'll tell you, Tuck, that dream she had about the rocks freaks me out just a tad, also," Kate adds. "Could be some nasty stuff under there."

As if on cue, the flight attendant announces that they are preparing the cabin for their arrival into Atlanta.

This time DJ stirs, raises her seatback, and looks at her friends. "That nap really helped a lot. I feel much better. How about you two?" she asks.

The reply is one word, uttered in unison. "Much," is all they have the energy to say.

"Well, then, brace yourselves, ladies-" DJ says, but is interrupted by a frantic Kate.

"Why?" Kate sits up straight and looks around. "What's wrong? What happened? Is the landing gear okay? Is it going to be rough? What?"

"No, no, relax, Katie. I didn't mean that at all."

"Then what?" Kate demands. "You know better than to do that to me on an airplane."

"I'm sorry. Yes," DJ says, barely concealing a grin, "I should have thought before I spoke."

"Jeez." Kate takes a deep breath and blows it out slowly, relaxing just a bit.

"What I meant was, get ready for the first game of this triple-header we're trying to pull off," DJ says. "Let me remind you again, that these are my sisters we're facing this evening."

"Arrggh, an evening with the tigress of-" Kate starts to say, but now DJ cuts her off.

"And you. Yes you, Katherine Brennan." DJ leans fully across Tuck so she can look Kate in the eye. "You need to back off Christine tonight. No matter what bait she throws at you, and we all know she will, you are not to bite. You hear?"

"But, Deej…"

"No buts, Katie. This is all too hard. Honestly. I don't have the energy to spare. We have to get right back on this plane tomorrow morning and go face my mother. Tonight will be a walk in the park compared to tomorrow, believe me. The only way I can handle all this and not freak out is if I can count on you both to back me up. This thing with you and Christine is two decades old. How it began and why, I don't know, and right now I don't care. We cannot waste time on that this weekend. I mean it."

Totally confident that she's been heard, DJ tightens her seat belt and puts her seat back into the full, upright position for landing.

# TEN

COLES MAKES A TOTAL of eleven calls in his attempt to contact the notorious Raymond "Zipper" Martone, leaving messages that he has an urgent matter to discuss. He is thwarted at each endeavor, however, because Mr. Martone is currently "unavailable", "out of town", "taking a sauna", "out of the country", "away on business", "not taking calls", "not interested", or "otherwise engaged". None of this distresses Cole in the least. He remains convinced that if even one message gets through to Martone, his call will be returned.

He has given his cell number for the callback, so Cole clears his desk for the weekend, packs his briefcase, and puts his own copy of the manuscript and the one he had the foresight to ask his secretary to reproduce for Martone under his arm. He leaves the office for home. He is halfway down the hall to the elevator when he remembers, returns to his office, opens the middle drawer of his treasured desk, removes the expensive cleanser and chamois cloth, and spritzes away the remnants of DJ's fingerprints. With a satisfied sigh of relief, he repacks and is on his way.

Cole obsesses about the phone calls as he drives to his weekend place in Rockport, leaving and revising message after message, until hit by a jolt of reality as intense as a mainline injection of caffeine.

*Holy shit. If the FBI has a wiretap on that guy, and why wouldn't they for Christ's sake, they sure as hell have to be wondering who the fuck I am and what I want. Eleven messages! What the fuck was I thinking? Stan is going to ream me out from here to Kansas. Crap, he'll probably banish me to Kansas, if he doesn't fire me first. What the fuck do I do now?*

Cole pulls his BMW into the first rest stop he can find and sits grip-ping the wheel, his knuckles white. Willing himself to relax and think, he takes several deep breaths and wonders if it's time to call his psychoana-lyst, then dismisses the idea almost immediately. He detests appearing this needy to anyone.

"Yeah, right," he mumbles to himself, "Friday evening of a three-day weekend. Have to work this out myself. Okay, think. The FBI will wonder what I'm up to, but they have no file on me or anything that ties me to Martone. So they run a check, find I'm clean. No big deal, right? Right. Good. Okay. Relax. Get out of town."

Cole is only slightly less anxious as he eases the car back into Friday traffic heading north. It is not until he drives into Rockport itself and turns toward the sea, spotting his home in the distance, that he begins the slow process of unwinding.

The one thing Cole did not lose in his divorce is the ocean front home he inherited from his grandparents. Cole's grandfather had made his mon-ey alongside the Kennedys, Cabots, and Lodges, and Cole was not about to let go of the prominent weather-beaten "cottage" that figures prominently in artists' renderings of the old fishing village turned tourist trap.

It stands off by itself, with just a narrow lane out to the massive rock upon which the house was built. The miracle of how the house survives hurricanes and massive winter storms contributes to its allure for him. He gave up much in his divorce in order to keep the place, but he has never regretted that choice. He is convinced that today, more than any other day, the covered three-sided porch, white rocking chairs, a good cigar, and a Glenfiddich on the rocks—okay, perhaps two —will ease his troubles away, if just for a while.

It's the final regatta weekend of the season in Rockport. Cole edges his BMW through the streets crowded with tourists, sailing junkies, and peddlers of anything emblematic of the sea, from the typical T-shirts and beach towels, to the rather obscure neon gardening clogs and nautical flag thumb tacks. Traffic is monstrous. Cole swerves to avoid a fish truck pulling sharply into a restaurant parking lot, and DJ's manuscript slides across the seat and *thunks* against the passenger door, shattering Cole's attempt at relaxing.

"Oh, don't worry. I haven't forgotten about you," he grumbles, glaring for a split second at the packet now threatening to disappear downward between the seat and the door. "Homework. I have always hated homework. I used to get Fs in homework. And now this homework might effing be the end of me."

As he turns onto the causeway leading to his home, he spots an unfamiliar pick-up in front of his garage, two men in the front seats. He slows, his hands suddenly wet against the wheel.

"What the… Oh, God, yeah, of course. Will. Jeez, I am such a wreck." Cole's brain takes these seconds to process what he sees, finally realizing that his caretaker has come to open the house as requested. "Must be he's got his son Ted with him."

Will has spotted Cole's car, gets out of the cab and leans his lanky frame against the fender, waiting as Cole parks, organizes his overnight bag, briefcase, and manuscript.

"Need any help there?" he asks.

When Cole doesn't answer, he continues, "Sorry we're so late opening up here, but it's been nothing but chaos in town today. Everything's all set, though, and I had Ted make a grocery stop earlier so the fridge has a few things in it. Fire's set to light, and we gassed up the boat for you, too."

Cole's eyes shift to the left, taking in his pride and joy rocking gracefully alongside his dock. It never ceases to fill him with the thrill of ownership. His beautiful X-41, the Editoria, winner of the most recent Marblehead to Halifax race, swings peacefully in her berth awaiting his hand at the wheel and a stiff wind to fill her spinnaker. A sigh of longing escapes his lips, and he realizes he hasn't been listening to what Will is saying.

"…and that should do it unless you have anything else. We still have two more places to get ready for tomorrow. Takes New Yorkers longer to get up here than you Boston folks. Give me a call when you leave and we'll close her up for you."

Cole has finally arranged his belongings, slinging the bag over one shoulder and freeing up an arm. He reaches to shake hands with Will and calls "hello" to Ted, who nods into the side view mirror and tips his cap.

"Had a hell of a time getting through town myself, Will. Hope the weather holds for the weekend. I appreciate your getting things ready here, as always. I should be good until Tuesday morning, and at some point we have to talk about putting the shutters up for the winter. Let me know when's good for you to go over things. Maybe next weekend?"

Will opens the door to the pick-up, slides in and tells Ted to add a meeting with Mr. Alexander to next weekend's schedule. Cole steps back from the truck.

"Thanks for everything. Have a good one," he says as he waves his hand in a semi-salute, watching Will maneuver the truck back and around his car.

The pick-up stops and Ted leans out the window. "Sorry, sir," he says, "Almost forgot. I bumped into Mitchell Sanders in town. Asked if I saw you to let you know he's available to crew for you if you're racing tomorrow. Said just to give him a call."

"Wish I could," Cole responds as he looks with longing at his boat, "but it's homework for me this weekend, I'm afraid." Cole slaps the manuscript for emphasis and moves toward the fieldstone steps to the porch.

"Better you than me. See you later, Mr. Alexander," Ted calls as his father steers the pick-up down the lane and across the causeway toward town.

Watching the truck until it rounds the bend, Cole turns to take in the sights and sounds of his beloved family home with its weather-worn shingles and white trim. On three sides of the property, waves are beating their rhythmic time against the rocks. The wind is up and pushing onshore. He can taste salt on his lips and realizes that his sun glasses are also glazed with spray. Moving the glasses onto his graying head, he counts five sea gulls perched on the peak of his house struggling to keep their balance in the stiff breeze. They are lined up, beaks facing east into the wind, spaced evenly like targets in an arcade game. Cole's smile at that thought turns quickly to a glower as he spots the ridge of white guano drippings along the roof. He wonders if anything can be done about that, and mentally adds it to the list of things to talk to Will about next weekend.

Unlocking the door, Cole steps into his own history and that of his father and grandfather. Solid oak surrounds him, from the flooring to the paneling and up the staircase and beyond. Thick ceiling beams of the rock-solid post-and-beam construction encase him, and he feels a sense of safety for the first time since DJ sat across from him at ten fifteen this morning. Family pictures, maps and sailing awards adorn the walls and he is—just briefly—overwhelmed with nostalgia for the days this house was full of people and laughter, including his ex-wife, son and daughter.

He places his paperwork and briefcase on the dining table in front of a set of four large windows that overlooks his dock and boat and the harbor of Rockport just off to the right. Three large J-boats, spinnakers out full, are passing just off the point light at the entrance to the harbor, and Cole allows himself the brief wish that he could race tomorrow.

*Ah, well. It is what it is,* he tells himself. *I have work to do.* He shoulders his bag, takes the stairs two at a time, and enters the master suite to change from his business suit to a pair of Dockers, boat shoes with no socks, and a mocha cashmere sweater. Thinking about his plans for a cigar out on the porch, he exchanges the sweater for a sweat shirt, and goes down to the kitchen to see what Ted has brought.

Cole's cell phone rings and he takes a long, deep breath before answering, mentally scanning what he needs to say in case it's the Zipper. He punches Talk and says "Hello".

"Hey, Mr. Alexander, it's me, Tony Panchetta. Finally found you. Stan Whitman asked me to keep an eye out for trouble. I'm parked down at the edge of the driveway here in full view of the house and anyone coming from any direction. Everything good up there?"

Cole is aware of the relief he suddenly feels. He looks out the kitchen window and down the drive, spotting what looks like a Pontiac Aztec on the widest curve of the causeway.

"Just fine up here, Tony, I see you."

"Okay, then, Mr. A. You might hear me walking around a bit during the night. I know you have shells in the driveway, so I'll be making some noise. Let me give you my cell number in case you need to call me."

Cole writes the number on a paper towel. Tony tells Cole he's in good hands and they both end the call.

Fortified with a sandwich of cold cuts, his Scotch bottle, ice bucket, and cigar, Cole pulls a rocking chair up to the porch rail on the right side of the house, out of the worst of the wind, where he can still find good light this late in the fall evening. He leans back in the chair, takes a few good puffs on his illegal Cuban, and picks up both his cell phone and DJ's manuscript. He takes a moment to enter Tony's number into his cell then peeks along the left side of the porch to get a reassuring look at Tony's car.

*Okay then,* he thinks, *time to get some work done.*

He opens to Chapter Eight and begins to read it for the third time.

# ELEVEN

## 8 • Peeling the Onion

*Perhaps more than anything else, it is difficult for me to write about my mother. She did not protect me, did not listen, and was not present emotionally—among many other things.*

*But, in spite of everything, she is still the only mother I have.*

*For some time now, I have had the image of her in my head as a tiny mouse that spotted a magnificent piece of cheese—my father—headed for it, had to have it, went for it with gusto, and with such a devil-take-the-hindmost ferocity that the trap surrounding the cheese never entered her focus.*

*Emotionally, she had little to work with. She was a child during the depression, born to Italian immigrants. Her father died from tuberculosis shortly after her birth, and in order for him to be allowed to die at home, she was placed in the home of a wet-nurse for some months. It is a sad testament to the level of communication in her family to say that my mother never knew this had happened to her until sometime in her sixties when her aunt told me and I told my mother.*

*She and her brother were raised by their mother and aunt in the household of wealthier immigrants for whom my grandmother worked as housekeeper, cook and seamstress. This situation was not as negative as might be imagined, however. They were treated with dignity within this new arrangement, and my mother and uncle were given educational and social advantages that they would not have had access to otherwise. My grandmother was eventually able to afford her own tenement house with an attached store in which she sold small necessities, sewed school uniforms and did alterations.*

*Perhaps these early years were the catalysts for my mother's inability to attach to her children in that loving and profoundly intimate way of mothers who truly bond with their babies and refer to this early experience as something akin to falling in love. Simply by nature of infancy itself, the vulnerability and dependency of a baby pulls at the desire of most parents to nurture and protect. My mother, quite sadly, came into parenthood absent this ability to connect in the most primal and necessary ways.*

*As a result, we five children remained vulnerable and unprotected in ways that, at times and for various ones of us, proved to be cataclysmic.*

*What did not change for the children we were, however, was the ever-present, visceral need for her protection, her attention, her love. For her to turn her eyes to us, to see each of us for the children we were—as individual as snowflakes, but lonely and alone within our little bodies and always, always, teetering on the brink of anxiety.*

*I wonder if it is significant that she now has macular degeneration and can no longer see much at all...*

*She was also beautiful.*

*Dark brown hair that was almost black, framed petite facial features and her Mediterranean coloring lent an exotic air to her quiet charm. In spite of the fact that she and her brother were two of very few Italian-Americans in a Catholic school dominated by children of Irish descent, and that they were often taunted and called WOPS, she was beloved by the nuns for her conformity and piety. She developed strong friendships that she enjoys to this day.*

*What she became, in fact, was an Italian-American princess awaiting the favors of someone bold and daring enough to carry her away from the destiny of a life like her cook/seamstress mother who could both pluck the chicken and cook it up in a pan. The family dreamt great things for her that did not include cooking for other people, cleaning their homes, or sewing their socks. Like most of the other girls in her high school graduating class, she went both off to work and in search of a husband.*

*She did, indeed, marry the man she would describe to us as the "catch of the day". Pictures of the two of them together in their dating days and early marriage are of happy times hiking and picnicking with friends. Her "prince", the handsome, popular athlete, had chosen her above all others. Over time, my brother and I would come to replace our mother's term of endearment for him with what we considered to be a much more appropriate sports metaphor, and often referred to him as a "foul ball".*

*Eventually she found herself with five children, an unfaithful husband,*

*and the prolonged experience of severe economic stress, necessitating her re-turn to work. She supplemented his income by doing door-to-door product satisfaction surveying, walking, talking, walking some more, then taking buses home and walking the mile from the bus stop. This was long before everyone had a phone, and even the best of science fiction hadn't yet pictured such a thing as an internet where this kind of work could more easily take place in the comfort of one's own home.*

*This was also in the days when we lived in a tiny starter house north of the city—having moved out of my grandmother's tenement when the third child was born. My brother JJ, sister, Rose, and I shared one bedroom, my parents and the twin babies, Margaret and Mary, the other. We had only one car, and the part-time working woman was a full time mother to five.*

*Brutal as he was with his children, my father never hit her. Complaints to her about his behavior with us were always met with suggestions about how we could be better children, although there were a number of times she made comments such as, "I don't know what gets into him", and, "I keep telling him you kids are going to grow up not liking him".*

*The strongest critical comment I can recall her making to him in our presence when he was being particularly rough on us, was a mild, "Don't you think that's a little too much, dear?"*

*There were times when he was so punitive that all five of us would be cry-ing, and she would threaten to leave us, running out the door, down the hill and around the corner. I can remember being so afraid of her not returning that I would go to my room, open the window, and holler as loud as I could through my tears and hiccups, "Mommy. Mommy. Come back, mommy. I'll be good, mommy. Don't leave me, mommy. Come home. Please."*

*Mommy wasn't much, but she was all we had between us and him.*

*Years later she would tell me that my crying made her come home. Not because it was clear we needed her. But because she could hear me even two streets away and she was embarrassed about what the neighbors would think of her for leaving.*

*This was, quite frankly, where she lived—in fear of what others might think. Of her as a mother. Of us as a family. We were Catholic school chil-dren. Our neighbors were not. If we were given a holiday from school that they did not have, we were not to say anything, for fear of making them feel bad. We were to behave. We were not to bring attention upon ourselves. Not to ask questions. Not to breathe too loud. Not to. Not to. Not to... We are still not to...*

*My mother's eyes were always searching, searching outward, catching the nuances of other's reactions. They rarely landed on us in tenderness.*

*As a baby, my brother was fed only every four hours, and grew up bone skinny with a big head. She thought people would think she starved him. So I was fed on demand, and immediately turned plumpness into fat. That I was and am so different from her has been, for her, an eternal embarrassment— so much so that during my adolescence and into my adulthood when I am being praised by anyone outside the family for anything I have done or won or written, her immediate response is to remind me that the moment would have been more special "if only you weren't a size sixteen. Dear".*

*Her head is full of oughts. To be a good and valued person, one ought to be a church-going, pre-marital-sex-abstaining, still-eating-fish-on-Fridays, Catholic. She categorizes people and situations into hierarchies of worthiness and doles out her attention, affection, and money according to where you appear on whatever scale she happens to be working from in her head at the moment.*

*The church factors heavily in her oughts.*

*For example, a relative getting married will receive a gift, the value of which does not depend upon the closeness of the relative, the need of the couple, or what she gave last year to the sister of the same relative. Instead, value will be determined by judgments: getting married in the church; getting married to another Catholic; getting married for the first time; getting married to someone who is also getting married for the first time; never had a child out of wedlock; never had pre-marital sex, etc. This person is entitled to the best and most expensive gift. A slight change in any category reduces the size and value of the gift.*

*This is not about love. It is not about money. It is mostly about parsing out affection based on her view of one's worth. There is nothing unconditional about it.*

*Each of the five of us received our parsing of affection according to her judgment of how well we measured up to her view of our conformity within the parameters of her hierarchy. It changed from day to day. We knew there was always a scorecard, and a score was being kept. We were never given the rulebook, but we grew to know the rules. Intimately.*

*Her rules never fit any of us. And, I, in particular, bristled with the rigidity of these senseless, unforgiving mandates and fought against them with a resolve that both amazed and horrified her. It became her mission to break my will. In response, I tried to save myself the only way I knew how. I dug my heels into any solid ground I could find under my feet and defended it with the tenacity of a Sherman tank.*

---

*I do not know if my mother ever longed for her own mother to be more than she was—to hold her on her lap, run her hand across her forehead and down her cheek, listen intently to the playground news of the day, or to sit with her when a bad dream tore her from sleep.*

*But I did.*

*I longed and longed and longed, far beyond reasonable to long for something that simply could not be.*

*I believed that in my stubborn resistance to her standards I could change her—that I could fill the emptiness within me with anger, and be satisfied.*

*I was wrong.*

*I spent years fighting for more of her, when what was best for me would have been less. I had been deserted emotionally by a mother incapable of anything more than that.*

*And it would be years before I became able to see that the longer I tried, the more in danger I was of becoming an emotional cripple myself.*

*The day I finally understood this to be the truth, I cried with a grief beyond measure.*

*I am my mother's daughter. It is recorded as fact on my birth certificate.*

*But mostly…*

*I have never really had a mother at all.*

# TWELVE

THE PLANE IS TOUCHING DOWN in Atlanta just ahead of a formidable thunderstorm, lightening scorching the skies to the west and the wind peppering the windows with driving rain. It bobs and bows under the force of the gale and lands with such a powerful jolt that the passengers break into cheers when it finally slows and turns toward the gate. The flight attendant reminds passengers to remain seated until the plane comes to a complete stop, adding "Now wasn't that landing something, folks? Let's hear it for Captain Corcoran!"

In the din of the second round of applause, Kate whispers to DJ, "Captain Corcoran has to be pooping his pants right about now. We got lucky with this one. They stick you into a seat like a sardine in a can, and in the end they have to shake the shit out of you just so you can get out of the damn thing. Oh, lord, how I love to fly the friendly skies!"

"Let's just grab our stuff and get out of here," DJ responds, pulling their carry-ons out of the overhead rack. "I've got to call my sisters and tell them we're in so they can set a time for dinner."

"And I need a pit stop before I can do anything else," Kate says as the passengers begin to move slowly toward the exit. "Let's eat fairly soon, too. I'm starving."

Tuck offers to run ahead and call for hotel transport, but DJ has a surprise. "No need for that," she says. "We should have a limo waiting."

"Now you're talking, my friend. I am finally being treated in the style to which I could become accustomed. If I didn't have to pee so badly, I'd kiss you right here and now. Grab this, will you, honey? I really have to run." Kate passes her bag to Tuck, calls "Wait for me", and enters the ladies' room.

Finding a fairly quiet spot along the far wall, DJ fishes in her purse for her cell and punches in her sister's number. Christine answers with a shrill, "Well, it's about time. Where are you? You're the one who called this meeting, and we've been sitting here waiting for two hours."

Choosing the higher road is always easier when dealing with Christine, so DJ ignores the tantrum and says, "The weather was just awful, but we're getting the limo to the hotel right now. We'll drop our stuff in our rooms and meet in the lobby. Did you make dinner reservations anywhere?"

There is a brief but telling pause before Christine responds, "Oh. No. I forgot. Let's just eat here anyway. They have a great restaurant and, besides, it's way too crappy to go out. We're under a tornado watch."

DJ hears her sister Sarah say something into the phone. "What was that?" she asks.

"Sarah says we don't want to wreck our day's work," is Christine's response.

"I thought the two of you came in early to go shopping?"

"We did, for a short time. But then by noon it started to pour, so we came back here and spent the rest of the day in the spa. You ought to try it. It's wonderful. Wait 'til you see us. We're gorgeous!" Christine's testy mood of a moment ago has melted away with the memory of her cucumber facial. "Oh, and thank you, by the way. We charged it to our room, since this little trip is on you."

DJ catches sight of Kate coming out of the restroom. "Glad I could make you both so happy and do my part to beautify the planet. Goodness knows it needs it. Look, got to go. We'll be there soon and we're hungry, so get a reservation for five of us."

"Sounds like you brought Fric and Frac with you too, huh?"

"Yes, I did. And you behave yourself." DJ snaps the phone closed and begins walking toward baggage claim.

"What was that about?" Kate asks. "Was that Christine?"

DJ's answer gets vacuumed into the air as they enter the steep escalator with its glowing overhead neon rainbow lighting. Too steep to talk, too noisy to hear. A short tram ride delivers them to the baggage area where they are greeted by more than a dozen limo drivers in uniform. The tallest, thinnest, and perhaps oldest amongst them holds a sign boldly announcing BRAVA in black block lettering.

They follow him to the sheltered curb where, one by one, they enter the limo under the protection of his oversized black umbrella. Once the bags are installed in the trunk, they head toward the hotel, making small talk about the weather and learning that there have been a series of tornado watches over the past few days.

"Pretty routine for us around here," the driver assures them.

Tuck responds with a shudder. "Too scary for my blood," she says, and engages him in a conversation about what to do in case the warning develops into reality.

DJ turns to Kate. "Is it just my imagination or does she really get off on this preparedness stuff? Or maybe she just likes talking to people? She's amazing."

"Both, would be my guess," laughs Kate. "She'd know exactly what to do if we were invaded by alien space warriors. Then, once she'd bent them to her will, she'd chat them up to the point they'd be begging to be taken to their space ships with a promise never to return. It's a skill. Admirable, isn't it?"

They are interrupted by the driver. "Excuse me, Ms. Brava. If I may be so bold. Might I have your autograph? My wife has been reading you for years, and I took the liberty of getting her your latest book in the hope you would sign it for her. Recognized your name when they gave me today's pick-up schedule. If it's not too much trouble?"

"No trouble at all. I'd be pleased to do it." DJ searches her purse for a pen. "What's her name so I can address it to her?" she asks as the driver passes the paperback to her.

"It's Doris," he says. "She's been quite ill and is in a rehabilitation center. Tonight when I go and read to her, this will really cheer her up. Thank you so much. It means a great deal."

DJ completes the dedication and returns the book to the driver, noting his name above the passenger side visor.

"Perhaps I can ask you a favor then, Mr. Travers? Would you be able to pick us up again tomorrow at eleven and take us back to the airport? I neglected to make the limo service round trip when I called yesterday."

"Certainly Ms. Brava, I'll call it in to my agency as soon as I drop you off." He turns the limo into the circular drive of the hotel, parking just out of reach of the driving rain. "Here we are."

With the help of the hotel valet, the three travelers and their things are moved into the lobby and out of the weather. As DJ tips the driver, he takes her hand in both of his and again speaks his gratitude for helping to bring some joy to his wife. "And I will personally pick you up tomorrow at eleven," he reminds her as he turns to leave. "Enjoy your evening."

"Excuse me, Mr. Travers," Tuck calls him back. She closes a bill into his palm and quietly says "Take this and buy Doris a teddy bear to keep her company when you aren't there. Strange request, I know, but trust me, it will help."

The driver stands for a second in stunned silence, then smiles, tips his hat, and leaves. DJ has heard the exchange, and Tuck winks at her, "Hey. Always pay a good thing forward," she says. "Now let's get signed in here. I'm starving."

# THIRTEEN

DJ HAS SURPRISED THEM AGAIN, this time with the Presidential Suite, accessorized with flowers, fruit, champagne and—best of all—chocolates. "I thought we could all come up here and talk after dinner," she suggests. "Big living room and lots of couches and chairs."

"I just love it when luxury cuddles me in her lap like this." Kate has sprawled herself across one sofa in a diva-like pose. "I'll have the bonbons, please."

"You'll get freshened up and have dinner first," Tuck calls from the far bedroom. "Come on in here and help me unpack."

"Ah, you're such a harsh mistress, my dear. You could leave me to my fantasy for just a bit longer. After all, I am off to do battle with the notorious Christine Martone Springfield. I need fortification." Kate slouches into the room and plops herself down on the bed.

"You're not doing battle with anyone tonight, Katherine. And you will, I repeat *will*, get along with Christine for this one night. I don't know what it is with you two, but you're both firecrackers with too short wicks if you ask me. Here, put these on." Tuck tosses a clean blouse and pullover to Kate.

DJ appears in the doorway. "I'm heading down. Meet you in the dining room when you get your you-know-what together. And, Kate, please listen to Tuck and try to act right with Christine, OK?"

"It's not 'you-know-what', DJ. It's called shit. S-h-i-t. And mine is very well put together, thank you very much. It's that sister of yours…"

DJ plugs her ears. "Not listening," she sings and waves a dismissal, leaving the other two behind.

Tuck aims a pillow at Kate. "I love it when your maturity slips below the pre-school level. It's so charming. Now, let's get moving."

WHEN KATE AND TUCK CANNOT FIND DJ or her sisters in the dining room, they split up to look for them. Kate finally spots DJ leaning against the door to the bar area, watching her two sisters having a drink together, their backs to the door. She places an arm around DJ's shoulder.

"What's up, toots?" she asks, "everything okay?"

"Oh, you know, just thinking. My sisters weren't abused in the same ways JJ and I were. We were all mistreated, and all suffered from the daily damage of just being in the family. But in many ways they were treated differently. My mother used to say it was because she and my father were so worn out by my brother and me that they were just too tired to care when the other three came along."

"So how was it different?" asks Kate.

"I don't even know if it matters. But they got things when they asked for them. We didn't. Otherwise their behavior was pretty much ignored. And in the end, what did it matter anyway? We all suffered."

"And that's the bottom line, DJ. You all suffered."

"Watching them now... Christine hasn't stopped talking and Sarah hasn't stopped smoking. Sometimes I think we're all just so wounded. It wasn't always like this. We had all been doing so much better until Maggie got sick. It's been harder on Christine than anyone else, I think, because of them being twins. Used to be one of them would start a sentence and the other would finish it. They were so much a matched set. Now, I think Christine rambles on because she's not sure where the ending is any more. The boundary that held her in, held her together, is missing and she just spills out all over the place sometimes. It's like her regulator's broken. There's no 'time to stop, now' button. It makes her so hard to be with."

"Well, I told you it wasn't me," Kate does a Groucho move with her eyes and flicks an imaginary cigar.

DJ smiles weakly. "And Sarah, she's always been the lost child, the middle kid. My brother and I were older so we ignored her, even though she and I shared a room until we were in our teens. The twins had each other but they also tortured her, so Sarah became this quiet, anxious, mousey kid who was very much a loner and frowned all the time. We used to call her 'Our Lady of Perpetual Pout'. And she still does that thing with her mouth. See? You can see it from here."

Kate looks with such intensity that Sarah turns, scanning the room. She spots them and taps Christine on the shoulder, smiling at DJ.

"There you are," she calls, dropping her cigarette ash onto her lap and then scrambling to brush it off.

"Lord, have mercy. If the two of them don't look like they walked right out of a Lord and Taylor's flyer. I'm going to find Tuck. Be back in a minute." Kate flutter-waves at the two sisters and heads back to the reception area.

DJ opens her arms and gathers both sisters in for a hug.

"You two look terrific," she says, standing back and looking at them closely. "Something's different, though. Don't tell me. Let me guess. God, how long has it been? You can't have both changed that much, can you?"

Sarah and Chris are wagging their heads back and forth, taunting DJ who willingly plays along.

"Ah, your hair," she says, delighting them. "Both of you got great cuts." *But neither of you have noticed mine*, she is judicious enough to not say out loud.

Christine is practically dancing.

"The spa was having a special and I've wanted to get this mop cut short for the longest time," Christine says, as she runs her fingers through what little is left of her former shoulder-length hair. "I was reading an article about how short hair is now the 'in' style for the over-forties like us, and then Carla and Meredith both e-mailed me that they had theirs shortened last week, which left me being the only one of my old friends with long hair. And now they're both talking about letting it go gray. I'm not sure I'll go that far, but this really does look good on me, doesn't it?"

DJ and Sarah share a quick look and interrupt Christine by insisting it's time for dinner.

"And yours looks great, too." DJ admires Sarah's cut, now flecked with blond highlights. "Not ready to do the gray thing yet, either, are you?" she asks as they enter the dining area and wait to be seated.

"My hair's way too thick. It'll corkscrew all over the place and I'll look like a box spring on acid. Besides, now that I'm starting to have grandkids, I'm determined to at least look young. I have no desire whatsoever to be reminded how old I am, thank you very much. Speaking of which"…

Sarah removes a cell phone from her jacket pocket and keys up pictures of her kids and grandkids.

By the time all the "adorables" are said, the three women are sitting at a round table overlooking the courtyard.

"Still pouring, and that lightning is frightful," comments Christine. "Let's order right away in case we lose electricity."

"Oh, please, Christine. Can you just relax for a minute and not have to see everything as a crisis? Just chill." Sarah reaches for her cigarette pack, then realizes where she is and replaces it in her pocket.

"Well it happens," Chris says with a barely concealed whine. "Our old neighbors, Pete and Linda, were at their club last week for a wedding and they lost electricity. A wedding! And no way to cook. So, don't tell me to relax, because you never know around here, especially with tornado warnings."

"Look. We've had a great day. We're going to have a great dinner. And it's not costing us a dime. Just enjoy it," chides Sarah. She turns to DJ. "Where's Tuck and Kate? I thought I saw one of them with you just a minute ago."

"Kate went to find Tuck. They'll be right here."

"Still joined at the hip, I see," says Chris.

Before DJ can respond, Sarah cuts into her. "Just what the hell is your problem with Kate, Christine? I happen to think she's wonderful, and her partner is too."

"Well, I suppose, for a less-be-ing," she drawls, stretching out the syllables until they are about to snap.

"Was that you calling me, Christine?" Kate leans over her shoulder and plants a kiss on Christine's cheek. "Still have your droll dense of humor, I see. But do try to move yourself up into the twenty-first century when you get a chance, will you?" She and Tuck give Sarah a warm hug and seat themselves on either side of DJ.

While Christine makes a great show of wiping her face with her napkin, Tuck apologizes for being late. She explains that the front desk night clerk is a social worker she met recently at the Children's Advocacy Center's conference in Huntsville, Alabama.

"Her husband was killed in Iraq and she's trying to raise two youngsters. She can't do it on a social work salary, so she moonlights here. Tough life for her. However, she did tell me we shouldn't worry about the weather too much. Storm's almost over and tomorrow should be beautiful."

Moments after that glib assurance, a blaze of light and immediate crack of thunder set the lights flickering. The women startle at the strobing images of each other, their movements caught in millisecond blinks, like actors in an ancient silent movie. Sarah throws her head back, Christine clutches her purse to her lap, DJ's open hand spreads across her chest, Kate and Tuck reach for each other. It ends abruptly and, after a mutual intake of breath, the five women break into laughter.

"Well, so much for the weather report, Tuck. Don't quit your day job any time soon," quips DJ when they have regained their composure and the lighting has returned to normal. "Let's order before things get worse. Right, Christine?"

Before Christine can respond, the waitress appears with menus, introduces herself as "Brandy", and offers to take drink orders.

"How about we order a bottle of red and one of white for the table? That okay with everyone?" DJ doesn't wait for an answer, but confers with the waitress and settles on two wines guaranteed to go well with fish and beef.

By the time the wait person returns with the wine, everyone is ready to order. Brandy patiently deals with requests to repeat various items on the evening's special menu and explain the contents of sauces and sides. Eventually that feat is accomplished to everyone's satisfaction and Brandy heads to the kitchen.

Wine in hand, Christine leans across Tuck and toward her sister. "Okay, Donna, what's this all about? We don't hear from you for months, other than a quick, 'sorry, I'm writing', and now you call us in from all corners of the earth for a major confab. And you bring your posse. What's going on?"

DJ takes a deep breath, reaches for the red, buying herself a moment to reflect by pouring half a glass and taking a sip.

"Okay, here's the thing," she says. "Just this morning I delivered my new book to my editor. My guess is that I'll hear from him within the next few days about whether or not they are willing to publish it. So…"

"So this is a book wrap party you invited us to? Is that it?" Christine has jumped right into the breathing space DJ tried to give herself. "Funny you never invited us before and you've written, what, ten, twelve?"

Sarah doesn't miss a beat, either. "Oh, hush up, Christine. Listen, Donna, what do you mean when you say '*if*' they publish it? They've published all your books. What's going on? What's wrong with this one? You didn't kill off Serpentine Lancaster did you? Because you know I'm not ready for her to be gone at all. You know I live vicariously through that woman. I love her and I need my yearly fix. Tell me now, because if you did, I'm gonna need a cigarette."

Sarah sees that Christine has her mouth open, ready to leap, but she isn't quite finished. "And you know you feel exactly the same way," she says, shaking a finger in Christine's direction. "Hell, you know how much mileage we both get in our social circles because she's our sister. We can't let her do this."

She turns to DJ. "You simply cannot do this. You cannot kill Serpentine. We," and now she draws a circle with her forefinger, drawing them all in, "we are decidedly not ready to lose her, period, end of discussion. Kate, please pass me the wine, red. God," she exhales, and sets her face in pout position. "I need a cigarette."

DJ feels the comfort of Kate's arm across the back of her chair. "If you two would just give me a minute to explain, I think you'll see I did not kill off anyone. And, trust me Serpentine has many more hearts to crush before she gets hers. She's my bread and butter character. I still need her."

DJ fingers the flowers in the small vase on the table.

"I did do something in this book that I want you to know about, however, and I want to tell you in person so we can discuss possible fallout."

She has their attention now. Sarah, who had unwound herself as soon as she heard Serpentine will live to love another day, is back to gripping her pack of Marlboros. Christine has folded her arms across her considerable chest and screwed up one side of her mouth, biting on the lower section of lip. Her 'don't-give-me-any-bullshit' pose has leveled more than one innocent storyteller. DJ, however, has seen it all before and is well prepared.

*Here goes*, she thinks. "Look, for quite some time now I've wanted, no, *needed* to write about my life—the things that happened in our family, as well as the things that happened just to me. This feeling pulled at me stronger and stronger each time I thought about it over the past few years. This time around, I couldn't ignore it any more. I wrote about it and delivered it to my editor this morning. That's why I've been so self-absorbed these past six months and pretty much unavailable to you. I'm sorry about that, but this is just what I had to do."

Sarah is the first to speak. "So this is like what, a biography? About all of us? Growing up? Are you sure this is a good idea?"

"More like an autobiography, meaning it's about my life. Our lives," DJ offers, "and whether or not it's a good idea is still up for grabs. I just know I absolutely had to write it. And I wanted you to know that I did, because it involves you as well."

Christine has now pursed her lips into sharp points. "But you didn't stop to think that maybe you should have talked to us *before* you wrote the damn thing, did you? What kind of bullshit is this, Donna Jean? And where is the book? Do we get a copy? What the hell did you say in it, anyway? No wonder you had to bring your bodyguards. I swear to God, you really do know how to piss me off."

Kate leans into the table, ready to take Christine on, but DJ's soft hand upon her leg moves her back in her seat.

*How in hell do they both do that thing with their mouths?* DJ thinks. *I have to ask Kate if I do that, too. I hate it.*

"Look," DJ says. "I know it's difficult, but let me explain this so you can understand. This is the story of my life in our family. Mine. People who don't know your relationship to me won't know it from the book. You're both married and have your husband's names. And it's so much more about Uncle Joey and Uncle Eddie, and JJ, and our parents, such as they were—well, *exactly* as they were—than it has to do with you anyway."

About to wriggle out of her underpants, Christine pounces again. "Oh, so now we're not even good enough to be in the damn thing, is that it? You're about to splash the family name all over the world, and we don't even get a mention? How many languages do they print your books in, all of them? Thanks a lot. Thanks a whole damn lot."

Tuck has her mouth open in amazement, watching the family dynamic—something she would never do with her client families. The scene is mercifully interrupted by Brandy, bearing salads and soups. The small group falls into an uneasy silence, with the exception of a muted "thank you" repeated each time a plate is set down.

Kate catches Tuck's questioning look, but she simply shrugs one shoulder and raises a palm—a 'don't ask me' gesture they often use when confronted with puzzling situations. This isn't Tuck's first encounter with the Brava tribe in full tilt boogie, but she is always slightly in awe watching DJ's sisters swing from pillar to post and back again.

DJ attempts to restore calm. "How about we try to enjoy dinner and finish the conversation later? We have a great living room in our suite, and can go up and have coffee or a nightcap together. I'll try to explain more about all this. How does that sound?"

There are no murmurs of assent, just Christine speaking barely above a whisper. "Oh, yes, do come up to our suite later. You'll love the view of the city from our penthouse. And I'll have the butler arrange hot toddies for us as well." She stabs a cherry tomato with such force the seeds squirt across the table and land on Kate's sweater.

"Nice shot, Shaq," Kate wipes the mess into her napkin and dips one edge in water to rub into the reddish smear. "I'll send you the bill."

"Oh, just give it to your fearless leader," is Christine's response. "She's running this show. She might as well pay for it, too." Christine takes another stab at a tomato, and again sends up a wad of seeds, this time into her own wine glass.

All four women lower their forks and glare at Christine—then crack up laughing.

"Enough, already, people," chides DJ, "time to assault our food."

*I don't know what the hell is up with Christine,* she thinks. *She's usually pretty bitchy, but this is way off the charts even for her. This can't be just about Katie. Can it?*

# FOURTEEN

COLE HAS LOST THE LAST of the evening's light and grown chilled in the deepening shadows of the porch. He gathers the evidence of his past few hours—empty Scotch glass, cell phone, pen, highlighting marker, reading glasses, plate with two spent cigar stubs rolling lazily close to the edge, DJ's manuscript—and heads inside to the warmth of his fireplace and just a chapter or two more before retiring for the night.

He gives the well-laid fire a chance to grow a bit while he brings his dishes to the kitchen and places them in the sink for the morning. Before settling into his easy chair, he adds two substantial logs to the fire and re-sets the cinder screen. Only then does he gather up the heavy manuscript and read some more.

## 10 • Peeling the Onion

*I lived in four different houses in my childhood.*

*Only the first one could really be called a home.*

*When my parents married, they lived with my mother's mother and aunt in Evans Hill. We lived there until I was three, when my first sister was born. My brother and I were cherished and loved and protected in this circle of family where the older nurtured and supported the younger, where the youngest could safely toddle, wobble and fall, and where caring hands would reach out to hold and soothe.*

*With the birth of our sister, we moved out of the city to a suburban start-*

*er-house—affordable, but far and away too small for an eventual family of five. Economic stress and distance from previous sources of support ignited the flames of anger and discontent that, over time and in subsequent houses, led to the firestorm that eventually destroyed our family and smothered my burgeoning spirit.*

*We moved again when I was nine, back to Evans Hill and into a three-story tenement so that my father's mother could live with us after my grandfather died. My mother made another move back to the suburbs with my siblings when I was away at college, although I knew nothing of this move until summer vacation, when a classmate dropped me off at the house, only to find it empty. A neighbor told me where they had moved to and, when I finally arrived at the new ranch house, it was only to find that there was no room for me. My mother had purchased a roll-away cot for me to use in the basement family room. Message received.*

*All of these were houses, not homes.*

*But I never stopped longing for the home I had as a very small child.*

*You see…*

*I've heard it all. What they all say. Both sides, actually. Those who think that home is the place you go where they have to take you in. And those who say you can never go home again. They're both wrong, of course. And, oddly enough, it's equally true that they are both right.*

*We carry it with us. For good or bad, we carry the home we grew up in, were loved in if we were lucky, were tortured in if we were not. It's barnacled to us, fastened to the underside of our souls, hanging on for dear life no matter how we try to run from it or replicate it.*

*We can start a new one, a better one. Make a home with a heart for roofing and substance for floors and walls. We can dance on hardwoods or be cushioned on Persians. We can scent it with jasmine and color it with rainbows, and it can rest us and cherish us and hold us safe. We can invite in only the blessed, the reverent, the loved and loving ones. We can grow old in the sanctity of its embrace.*

*We can grow old, older, oldest, rest sacrosanct in the well of our creation, and still, still, yearn for what was, could have been, or should have been in that first place called home. It truly makes no difference what the original experience was—the longing, pulling, magnetic force of memory never leaves us.*

*Even in mid-life, there are days when I still plow through the memories of those early times with the fierceness of a farmhand behind a horse—upheaving the clods of circumstance and events, trying desperately to stomp* them into something other than what they were. Wanting, needing, a different mural of my early days. A softer, safer watercolor of my life.

Please understand, what I do not want is for these memories to be my memories. I do not want them to have actually been the reality of my life or to tally the days spent in fear and despair and have them be mine. It is unfair, you see, to really be sliding down the other half of my life when, in truth, most of the first seventeen years should not be allowed to count at all. And I do not mean this in the frivolous way some middle-aged beauty laments the crow's feet around her eyes and hastens to schedule the first of many "lifts". I say this truth because I spent those years hiding anywhere I could, escaping, quite literally, to a hole in the wall of a barrier foundation out our back door and across the alley from our house on Evans Hill.

I would inch along the edge, gripping the underside of a rusted gate to shimmy into the space where ancient cement had worn and cracked and fallen away. With just enough room for my behind, I'd tuck my legs up under me and gaze across the city of Providence from one of its many hills. I'd ignore the calls to come help with dinner, do my homework, or watch my sisters. And I would dream of running away.

I would become the bear that went over the mountain to see what she could see.

Home may, in fact, be where they have to take you in. It may also be where you can never go again.

I cannot willingly describe that house, my room, the kitchen, bath, or living room. Ask me, instead, to tell you about making friends with daddy long legs, letting a baby garter snake wriggle in my pocket, or how it felt to have chickadees light upon my shoulder and peck crumbs from my palm.

Ask me these things and I will tell you how the sunset blazed in me a freedom to believe in something better than what was, how the birds sang to me a sweetness I could hold within my heart, how the wind lifted hope into my chest, and the snow blew the blackness from my soul.

All of these made more of a home to me than any house I ever knew— with the sole exception of that earliest home with my grandmother and her sister.

From them I learned how to make my own house into a place of love and generosity and safety.

A home with a heart… and a soul.

———————

COLE IS CHILLED AGAIN, to the very bone this time, and is suddenly aware that only one log has burned. *That other one was probably too green to have caught hold,* he thinks. *I should have checked it first.*

The weariness of his long day overtakes him, and he decides he's had enough. He banks what's left of the fire, locks the doors and turns off the lights. The Zipper has still not called, but he takes his cell phone upstairs with him just in case.

Thoughts of Martone have unnerved him again, and he takes one last look out the bedroom window and down the drive. While he can't quite make out Tony in the total darkness against the backdrop of the night ocean, he is reassured by the glow of a cigarette being inhaled.

As for the manuscript, he leaves that open to Chapter Eleven on the lamp table next to his favorite easy chair.

# FIFTEEN

"OH, WOW, TO HELL WITH going back to San Diego. I could spend the rest of my life living in this place. There's a Jacuzzi in here and even one of those heating racks for your towels. I mean, Christine and I have a nice room, but this is heaven." Sarah gushes after exploring the suite. She grabs a love seat and lies back to enjoy the luxury.

They have opted for coffee and dessert in the suite, and the room service attendant is placing caf and decaf, and desserts of steaming peach cobbler and chocolate molten lava cake, on the dining room table. "The ice cream is in the freezer, ladies," he says with a slight bow. "Will y'all be needing anything else?"

When he has been tipped and sent on his way, DJ turns to the others, bows, and in mocking imitation, says, "And now, ladies, I will remove that ice cream from the freezer, and slather it all over this hot peachy thing that has been screaming my name since it walked in the door. If y'all would like some, I heartily suggest y'all grab it now."

Three of the five head for chocolate, ice cream on the side. DJ reluctantly shares the cobbler with Tuck. By the time they have each settled into their cozy nest for an evening of talk, they are armed with coffee and their chosen treats. The dessert platters have been scraped clean enough to pass for fresh.

Christine is the first to speak. "You know, I have to hand it to you, Donna. This is pretty nice. Thank you."

Sarah's "Mmff ttffuu," said with a mouth full of chocolate and accompanied by a head nod, seems to mean 'me too'.

"You're both very welcome," DJ smiles. "But I don't just want to wine and dine you into a sugar coma. I honestly want you to understand what I wrote in this new book and why." She glances at Kate for moral support and receives a *go-for-it* thumbs up.

Before DJ can begin, however, Sarah interrupts. "No, wait," she says, plopping her empty plate down hard on the coffee table. "First of all I want to know what name you give me in the book. If no one will recognize us, what are we called? I want to be called Rose. I've always loved that name. We tried to get the kids to name the baby Rose, but no luck. So, if I'm in this book, it has to be as Rose. Got that?"

DJ's chin is resting on her hand, and she slowly wraps a forefinger across her lips. "Okay, but at this point I'm not sure I should name anyone other than JJ and Maggie. If I change that, I promise to call you Rose."

"Good."

"And, you?" DJ turns to Christine, "any requirements?"

"Nope, don't really care one way or the other. It's your party now, isn't it?"

DJ gives Christine a long look. "Yeah, it's a party. Or not."

She shakes her head, takes a deep breath, and continues.

"You both know what happened to me with Dad and with Ed and Joey. You know how long I worked on it. Even to be able to talk about it was sometimes excruciating. But I did. Hell, I'm still doing it to some extent. And now I need to take it to the next level. This book has been in me all these years. I can't write any more of my so-called *money* novels until I tell this story—my story. I don't know how else to explain it to you. All I know is that you have both supported me in every other thing I have ever tried to do, no matter how hard, no matter how long it took. And now I need you to support me in this, too. Please?"

DJ looks at Sarah and Christine, pleading with her eyes for them to hear her. To her surprise, Christine is the first to respond.

"What do you want us to do?" she asks. "Sarah's in San Diego. I'm in Ann Arbor, for Christ's sake. It's not like we're at home any more. What can we do?"

"And what does mother have to say about all this?" Sarah pipes in.

"That's just it. I haven't told her yet. You're the first. Because you totally know she's going to be calling each of you the minute I leave her place and try that splitting us off from each other thing she's so good at."

"Yeah, you're right. She will." Christine is sitting up now, cake plate and coffee set on the floor at her feet. "But, don't you dare sell us short, DJ. That crap of hers never worked before and it won't work now. She might be old and pissy..." She laughs at her own joke. "Actually, last time I saw her she really was quite pissy. Oops, that's neither here nor there, is it? What was I saying?"

*Just how much wine did she have downstairs, anyway?* DJ wonders.

They are all laughing now, with that somewhat hysterical laughter that is both relief and release. And again, the tension in the room is broken. DJ envisions herself this day as a rubber band, pulled and stretched to the snapping point of anxiety and then released back into the comfort zone of support and caring. This is what she can always count on from Kate and Tuck. This is what she has been praying her sisters would also be capable of providing her. And they are.

*So far, so good,* DJ thinks. *Chris is still a prickly pain in the ass, and Sarah simply cannot let any little thing slide on by without some kind of cryptic remark or two. Life as usual with the Martone sisters! But I'll take what I can get tonight.*

As the laughter diminishes, DJ's sigh of relief is audible. Kate and Tuck are on the couch holding hands.

"You girls are simply awesome," Kate says. "You're naughty little devils, the lot of you," she adds with a grin and a bit of a brogue. "But I do so love a naughty girl."

Tuck gives her a friendly elbow jab in the ribs.

"I haven't been called naughty in quite some time, Kate. Thank you very much." Christine raises a coffee cup in salute. "I rather like it."

It's Sarah who pulls them back on track. "So what's next, DJ? You have to tell mom sometime, don't you?"

"She's next on the list. Tomorrow afternoon, late. We have a flight to Providence at one. You should expect to hear from her just about the time you'll both be sitting down to dinner, so be prepared. Then we'll see Raymond on Sunday and I'm done, for now anyway."

Christine cuts in. "Uncle Raymond? What the hell are you seeing him for?"

"I need to find out where Eddie and Joey are. At some point I'm going to want to confront them and I'm long overdue for that. They might be the most affected by the book, come to think of it, but I don't care about that one way or the other. I just need to do whatever makes sense for me. I never got the chance to give them hell before and I want to do it soon."

Christine and Sarah share a look of concern. Sarah moves to sit next to DJ. "I wouldn't pin my hopes on Raymond giving you too much help in that regard, DJ," she says.

"Why not? Raymond must have known what they did. He got them away from me. He gave them jobs in his business and told them to stay out of New England. And they have. Now I want to talk with each of them. Kate and Tuck are coming with me."

"Help me out here, Christine," Sarah pleads.

Christine groans aloud.

"Okay, here goes… DJ, what the hell planet do you live on anyway? How many years has it been and you still haven't figured this out yet? Raymond didn't give Joey and Eddie 'jobs' in his business." She makes air quotes with her fingers. "Raymond 'disappeared' Joe and Ed, as in m-o-b disappeared. No one has heard from them in more than forty-some years. Jeez, DJ, that ought to be a clue. Try Googling them in Baltimore and Philly, which is where he supposedly sent them, right? They aren't there. They never were there. Poof! Disappeared. Dead. End of story."

"Jesus, Christine, how to finesse bad news," Kate is watching DJ digest this new information and can see she is upset.

"Talk to us, DJ. What's happening in your head right now? Sarah, let me sit there will you? Thanks." She slips into the small space between them.

Sarah moves over reluctantly. DJ is her sister. She should be the one comforting her, but this situation is too big for her. *Better let the pros take over,* she thinks. *Probably a good thing she brought them with her.*

DJ seems to be in shock, but internally she's rallying her troops to deal with this new reality.

"And Dad?" she asks her sisters. "What about Dad?"

"Him, too, we think," responds Sarah.

Christine nods in agreement. "Yeah, him too."


DJ's BODY TWISTS SIDEWAYS from the blow, and she falls back against the sofa cushions, mouth open, eyes fastened upon the rotating ceiling fan. Her mind, however, has retreated to some distant longitude and latitude totally unknown to humankind. She is doing what she had learned to do decades earlier to escape, to numb, to protect—if only in her mind. And she is now crawling into a tiny cave carved out of cement.

*Help me. Help me. Help me. I can't breathe. I've got a cement truck on my chest. Get it off. Get it off. I can't freaking breathe.*

She begins grabbing at her clothes, pulling the cardigan away from her throat, sweating along her neck and brow. She is panting, and spasms shake her arms and legs.

*I will kill him. I will kill him. I will kill him. Oh, sweet Jesus, get this cement truck off of me. I can't breathe. It's killing me.*

Kate continues speaking calming, reassuring DJ.

"DJ! DJ! It's okay. You're okay. We're here with you. It's Kate. I'm holding you. It's okay. Take a deep breath, slowly. Breathe out. Good. Take another breath, slowly, slowly. It's okay, I'm right here and I'm holding you and you're okay. Keep breathing. Slow it down. Slow it down. We're in the hotel room and you're okay."

DJ is resisting being pulled back into herself.

*I will see him and I will kill him. That shit! Oh, god, I cannot take more of this. My father and my uncles! I try and try but I cannot shake them off me. I'm covered with them. I'm covered with their filth!*

DJ frantically wipes her hands, rubbing something only she can see off the front of her clothes, swiping at her mouth. She has no sense of where she is or who might be with her. She believes she is lost once again in a time and place where she is unable to help herself.

But this time she is not alone. Kate continues to hold her and speak calmly, calling DJ back to the present, into the room, onto the couch. And slowly, mercifully, DJ is able to allow herself to be called back.

She is done. DJ releases her coiled muscles and slumps against Kate, lets herself be held for a moment and then pushes upright. Tuck hands her a damp facecloth and towel, and DJ wipes away her sweat and tears.

"Sorry," she mumbles, "thought I was past doing that."

Her sisters are still wide-eyed with fright.

"What the hell was that?" Christine asks. "Are you all right? I thought you got therapy. I thought they cured you of all that stuff. That's the same thing you used to do when you were a kid. What the hell is going on?"

"She dissociated," Tuck says. "Happens sometimes when a person hears or experiences something that's too hard to deal with all at once. It's called a defense mechanism. Kids do it when they can't handle trauma. It's a way to kind of escape from the pain. DJ learned it early on. Problem is people who learn it early tend to use it later in life when hard things happen. That's all."

"That's all? That's all? She scares the crap out of us and all we get as an explanation is 'that's all'?"

"What more do you want, Christine? This is just the way it is. I'm sorry." DJ's weary voice slips into silence.

"And now I suppose you're going to blame me, aren't you?" Christine asks, clearly gearing up for a fight.

Sarah jumps in. "She's not blaming anyone, Christine. You just close that mouth of yours right this minute."

"DJ," Sarah shifts her focus away from Chris, "is writing this book even good for you, or is it hurting all over again? I think that's the question you need to ask yourself."

DJ's answer is a long time coming. None of the women know what to expect. DJ has had her arms wrapped around her stomach, but now she slowly sits up straight.

"No, Sarah," she says, "the question I actually have to ask myself right now is what the hell am I doing in a hotel room in Atlanta hearing this crap for the first time from people I have lived with for years? That's what I'm asking myself." DJ's fists are clenched. "And, you know what? I don't have an answer to that question. Do you?"

She looks at her sisters. They can see the hairs on the back of her neck standing so upright she might as well have her finger plugged into a socket.

Sarah speaks calmly. "It's not crap, DJ. It just is. And if you let yourself think about it the way we have, you'll see there's no other explanation. I'm sorry."

"Sorry?" questions DJ. "Sorry they're dead, or sorry you two never told me? Which is it?"

DJ is up and pacing, walking behind the couch. Four sets of eyes are moving with her.

"You," she says, pointing at Christine. "You get all pissed off because I didn't tell you sooner I was writing a book. What bullshit! How long have the two of you known about Dad and the other two? Huh? And no one thought of telling me? Well it's *about* me, damn it, isn't it?"

She strides once, then twice, around the dining room table, finally coming to a stop on the far side by the window.

"And here's the answer to your question," she says, now pointing at Sarah. "Writing my book was helping me heal. Notice I said was. Now I don't know what the hell to do with this information about Raymond. I don't know what to think, and I sure as hell don't know what to do. So, all of you, just let me be. Please."

She looks at all of them, shakes her head and stalks out.

Sarah and Christine stare at the closed door, mouths agape.

Kate places her hands on her knees and rises slowly from the couch. She looks at the others.

"That went well, don't you think, darlin's?" she says to no one in particular, sarcasm leaking Irish timbre into every word.

# SIXTEEN

SARAH IS RAMMING THE KEY CARD so hard into their door mechanism and wrenching it out so quickly that she has to repeat the procedure three times before it works.

"I don't know what the hell you were thinking, Christine, but I asked for you to help. I definitely did not ask you to drive right in with a load of crap and dump it on her head. Sometimes you make me crazy." She slaps the card on the table next to the TV and turns on some lights.

"Oh, give me a break. She's smarter than the two of us put together. Maggie, you, and I figured this out years ago all by ourselves. You mean to tell me she couldn't do the same thing? All the damn therapy she's had? And all her so-called friends. This is what they do for a living." Christine opens her suitcase, grabs her cosmetic kit and heads for the bathroom.

"Look, Christine. All I'm saying is that she was traumatized. More than us." Sarah raises her hand when she sees Christine put down the cold cream she's using to remove her makeup. "I know, I know. We all were. But we didn't get what she got and you know it. I don't know why. Maybe we were just luckier than her. So maybe it was easier for you and me and Maggie to look at things in ways DJ can't, or couldn't, because it looks like she's doing that now. And this has to be really hard for her."

"She was going to figure it out sooner or later anyway, Sarah. I'm fine with what I said. I did her a favor."

"Yeah, some favor. Remind me never to cross you." Sarah rummages in her own suitcase for a nightie.

"Besides, she's got her lesbian guard up there. What does she need us for?"

Sarah throws her nightgown onto the bed and returns to the bathroom.

"Is that what this is about, Christine? Is that what this is really about? Really? Because if it is, you are way out of line here." She plants her feet just inside the room, one arm across the doorway, blocking Christine's egress. "Talk to me. Now," she insists.

Christine closes the lid of the toilet seat and plunks herself down.

"Not for nothing, Sarah, but they're lesbians. Lesbians! She's been hanging out with them for years."

"And?"

"And what? Isn't that enough? It's just not right."

"For heaven's sake, Christine, it's not as if you've never seen one before. You lived in Boston. Now you live in Ann Arbor. Don't they have lesbians there?"

"Don't be an ass, Sarah, of course they do. They're just not hanging out with my sister. Maybe she's one, too." Christine stands and removes the cap from the toothpaste tube, smearing a line across the top of her red brush.

"She's not. And so what if she is? It's none of our damn business, either way. What I wish for her is for someone to love her the way she deserves to be loved, and I don't give a rat's ass who that might be. She's our sister no matter who she chooses to love." Sarah's agitation is palpable, the room vibrating with its energy.

"Well, that's just the point now, isn't it?" Christine jibes back. "She is our sister, but who does she go to when she needs help? Not us. You saw how Kate wiggled her way between you and DJ after I said what I did. It's always them, not us. When Maggie was so sick, every time DJ came to help, Kate had to come with her. It's like they're joined at the hip and we're the leftovers or something."

Sarah is taking her frustration out on her bed linens, pulling out the tight corners and releasing sheets and blanket from their confines.

"Don't you ever get tired of seeing yourself as a glass-is-half-empty person, Christine? Honestly. I loved it when Kate would come with DJ to Maggie's. Your husband never came with you. Mine never came with me. Helping Mags live and then die was the hardest thing I've ever had to do. You, too. Maybe you, especially. And yet our men were not there, not one time. Kate came with DJ every time."

Sarah enters the bathroom again.

"Do you know what I'd give to have a partner or a friend like that? Do you? Kate and Tuck could be ninja zombie hobos for all I care. She's damn lucky to have them and I'm glad for her. You need to get over yourself and act right. And soon." With that, Sarah retreats, slamming the door to the bath behind her. *You are such a bee-atch, Christine. You really are.*

She stops outside the bathroom door, then turns and opens it again.

"And Maggie would chew your ass all the way back to Ann Arbor if she heard you talk like this and you know it." She repeats the door slam.

The pair is silent as they wind up their preparations for sleep. Christine finally finishes with the bathroom and gets into bed with a book.

Sarah showers and then has to rearrange the bed linens she pulled out when arguing with her sister. Finally able to crawl into bed, she pulls the covers over herself, but cannot resist one more attempt to reason with Christine.

"Listen, Chris," she says, lowering both her tone and temperature, "you and I, we have our husbands and our children and now grandchildren to love and to be loved by. That's a whole lot of wonderful. And in many ways it's a miracle, given how we grew up." She takes a breath. "DJ has us. She has us and Kate and Tuck. And for her that's also wonderful and miraculous. She has her writing and, yes, that's made her famous. But being loved by her fans is not the same thing as having love in her life. That's got to come from us—you, me, Kate and Tuck—all of us. Okay?"

Christine turns away from Sarah, face to the wall, deep into her pillow.

"Humph."

"Humph? That's all you have to say?"

"Humph. Humph."

"You know, Christine. Upstairs you asked what planet DJ's been on. Down here I wonder what century you're living in. And you'd better be careful. You're getting more like mother every day."

And she is startled, but not really surprised, when a flying pillow wallops her full in the face.


TUCK, KATE, AND DJ have not made any attempt to ready themselves for bed, although they are, each in her own way, more than needful of sleep.

"So what are you thinking, toots?" Kate asks as gently as she can. "This is some damn hard news."

"That's the thing, Katie. I don't know what to make of it. Don't know if I should be angry or relieved, or sad, even. Don't even know if it's true. Don't know what it would mean if it were true. And if it's not true I'll wring both of their necks for messing with my head like this."

"And I'll help you do it," offers Tuck. "Hell of a kick in the head, I'd say. But you were right about one thing, Deej."

"What's that?" DJ and Kate both look at her.

"There really is a bucket load of shit under those rocks you dreamed about. Shit and secrets and maybe even bones. Damn!"

"I could not have scripted this if I'd tried," DJ says. She slaps at a couch pillow and stuffs it into the small of her back, squirming to get more comfortable. "Not even for the most outrageously twisted of my novels. So what do you two think? Could they be right?"

Choosing her words carefully, Kate looks directly at DJ.

"There are so many ways that Christine is a loose cannon that, under ordinary circumstances, I'd treat the whole thing lightly, coming from her. However," she pauses for emphasis, "you both know I'd be voted most likely to holler fire in a crowded theater under the most benign of circumstances. And," another pause, "Christine and I are not exactly bosom buddies. But," one more pause, "this time I really think she's on to something. It sounds right to me. People don't just disappear any more these days. Not like your uncles did anyway."

"And my father, he died of a heart attack at work, for god's sake!"

"That's another issue altogether, I think. I don't know what to make of that. I really don't." Kate looks hopefully to Tuck, "Any suggestions?"

"Only one and I don't think you'll like it any more than I do," Tuck says. "Much as I hate to say it, DJ, it feels like you have to see Raymond about all this. Turn over that rock and see what crawls out."

DJ slumps forward with her head in her hands.

"This is making me nuts. I'm right back to how I felt when I was in therapy. Like my body is at war inside myself, the left and right sides attacking the part in the middle that's trying so hard to just stay sane. And I'm exhausted from it all. I'm tired from a hell of a day, anyway. But this... this is threatening to knock me on my ass."

From her sitting position she uses both hands to pitch the couch pillows across the living room and into the bathroom door, each satisfying thud reviving her just a bit more.

"Well, here's some news, ladies," she says mid-throw, "I refuse to end up on my ass."

This last statement is punctuated by the loudest thud of all.

"Would a plan help? What do you want us to do?" Tuck asks.

DJ looks at both of her friends, seeing their worry as well as their tiredness. Pulling herself up and off the couch, she heads for her purse and then the phone.

"You're right," she says, "time to get organized and make a plan. The heck with my mother for the time being, I'm changing our tickets. We're going back to Boston to talk with Raymond. You two, go to bed. I'll check in with you when I get this done."

"Oh, and one more thing," she says, rubbing her forehead above her eyes. "Before we leave in the morning, I've gotta mend some fences with the girls."


KATE AND TUCK are snuggled in bed together when DJ taps on their door and lets herself in.

"We're all set for the two o'clock flight direct to Logan, and I left a message for Raymond that we want to see him around six. We can have breakfast with my sisters as planned and then the limo will take us to the airport. Is this still okay with you two?"

"Come here, you," Kate says with arms reaching to pull DJ between them under the covers, "time for a cozy."

They sink deeply into the bed, wrapping DJ in their warmth and affirming their commitment to walk this path with her.

"I'm going to fall asleep right here if I don't get out now," DJ says, throwing the covers back and crawling over Kate. "I need to pee and shower and brush my teeth. You sleep. I'll be fine. I love you both. Good night and thank you. You are my heart, both of you."

She blows them kisses from the door and leaves.


LATER IN THE NIGHT, Kate awakens to the muted sounds of crying from DJ's room. She considers then rejects an urge to go and comfort her, turning instead to wrap her arm across Tuck. She lies awake in the dark for quite some time until the sobs from the adjoining room subside.

# Saturday

*"There's a hole in the middle of the prettiest life, so the lawyers
and the prophets say.
Not your father or your mother or your lover's gonna ever make
it go away…*

# SEVENTEEN

A WEATHERED HAND REACHES for the manuscript, left open by the hearth. Settling into an easy chair, the curious interloper places a finger in the open chapter and turns the cover over to read title and author. His body gives an involuntary start, as if stung. Wounded, he bends to the unexpected task, and begins to read.

## 11 · Peeling the Onion

*My father anointed himself Pope of Evans Hill, with all the infallibility and omniscience assumed by the person in Rome who held that position. We were to be obedient, respectful, humble, and grateful in his presence. He woke us with a yardstick on weekend mornings, and lined us up in the living room to do calisthenics in the evening. We polished his shoes and leather gym bag, scrubbed his whitewalls, gave up our money to him. We were schooled to do as he said and not to think about it. To do it immediately, without question.*

*"I didn't ask you to think. I'm telling you what to do. Now do it," was followed by a swift backhand to the face. Always the face. The head. To question, to process, to inquire, or to be curious was anathema. Dangerous.*

*In our house, making a mistake could start an avalanche. And it could end by being slammed so hard in the side of the head that brain matter sloshed to the other side and back again.*

*He was short and solid, the oldest of four boys, an athlete in his youth*

*and a lover of sports. He skated and golfed, refereed football and umpired
baseball. That my brother would not play was embarrassing to him. In a
childhood-long gesture of attempted appeasement, I tried to make that up to
him. I skated and played basketball and softball, and spent hours in the yard
after dinner playing catch with him. Safer to be up close and know when the
avalanche would hit, than to be caught unaware and leveled just the same.*

*In the end, even this did not matter enough.*

*The summer of my tenth birthday, before the beginning of fifth grade, I
was busy making friends in our new neighborhood and watching the pears
grow big enough to eat on the tree just outside our back door. Living in the
city was painful to me, the closed-in feeling of being surrounded by tene-
ments and fences and yards only large enough for trash cans hurt my soul. I
ached for space, for the distance I needed to see what was coming and prepare
for it. In the city there were too many people, too much chance I'd miss something hurtful coming my way. I was forever on the lookout for peril, believing
my vigilance would keep me safe.*

*In the end, I did not see it coming at all. My father delivered me up to
the pain, and had I been wrapped in steel and sealed with golden rivets, my
innocent body could not have been offered up more purposefully. Nor could I
have prevented what happened.*

*It was quite simple, actually. My father needed the house sided. My un-
cles were in the business. We had no money. So I was bartered.*

*My body was my father's share.*

*There would be no more visible asbestos on our house when they were
done. There would be no visible sign of what they had done when they were
through with me.*

*My father drove me to their apartment, dropped me off outside and told
me to go in, that he would be back for me in two hours. I did as I was told.
That was all I was told, and I knew better than to ask.*

*Uncle Eddie had seen me coming and hollered to come in, they were in
the den. Both Eddie and Joey were on the couch in front of the tiny black and
white TV. We didn't have one, so I was excited to be able to watch with them.
Joey asked me to get him a beer from the fridge and when I returned they had
taken their shirts off, their curly dark chest hairs sticking out of the necks of
their sleeveless undershirts. Eddie pulled me onto his lap, telling me to give
my old uncle a kiss. His hands were on my chest, and unbuttoning my tan
seersucker blouse.*

*"Still not wearing a bra yet, are you Donna? Watch this," he said, and*

turned me toward him, placing his mouth on my nipple and sucking. "How's that feel, baby?"

When his hands pulled down on my shorts, I realized that this was all too familiar and that I was in trouble. They had been drinking. I was alone. JJ was not here. No one was here for me.

When they were done with me they fell asleep. The both of them. Right there on the couch. With their clothes off. When my father came to get me, he saw all that. And all he said was "Get dressed". And we went home.

I was a good girl. I did not tell my mother. I did not tell my brother. I crawled into my bed and curled up into a ball and did not cry even one tear. I did not expect anything to happen to them. And it didn't.

When Saturday came around again, my father told me to get in the car, and I did. We drove to my uncles and on the way I tried once, just once, to get him not to do this to me. "Please, daddy. Please, daddy. Please don't make me go there."

My father took his right hand off the steering wheel and snapped it into my face in one swift move. "Shut up," he said. "Shut up. Now."

He pulled up in front of the apartment, told me to get out and that he would be back in two hours. I doubled over on the doorstep, gripping my sides to keep from throwing up, a low moan of "noooooooooooooooo" escaping my lips. Joey came to the door and said, "Get in here, kid, now."

This time, when they were done, my uncles put me out on the steps to wait for my father. I peed in the back seat and sat in the wet until we got home. "Clean it up," was all he said. "Now."

I lived in silence. I prayed in silence. I stood before the crucifix in my room and could not make sense of any of this. In school and at church I had learned to honor my father and my mother. I was not yet ten years old, but I knew that this was not honor-able. Not worthy of honor. Not worthy of respect.

I lived in fear. I prayed to be delivered from my pain. I prayed that Saturday would not ever come again. I prayed to die. I found a hole in the wall in the alley out back and I planned to live in there and never be found.

But life, once again, went on around me, past me, through me. Nothing changed. My father never took me there again. But now I was damaged goods to him, and so he took their place. And he did not have to drive me anywhere or leave me. He lived here and so did I. And he controlled my universe.

How invisible was I that no one could see my fear? That no one could see my pain? Could not see me pull into myself even more tightly than before?

*The sight of Vaseline, even toothpaste, made me nauseated. I felt dirty, showering often to cover imaginary smells. I stole pennies from my grandmother's store to buy the sugared candies I craved to rid my mouth of seared-in tastes and textures.*

*Living in anticipation of evil is terror.*

*Living in spite of evil is a miracle.*

*It was only the summer before fifth grade, but it would take decades for me to gain this knowledge and believe again in the miracle of living.*

# EIGHTEEN

COLE HAS SPLEPT PEACEFULLY and deep in his Rockport home, the cool salt air blowing softly through his open window alongside the bed. But it is the aroma of fresh-brewed coffee that coaxes him from his dream of captaining the *Editoria* through a fierce storm and into the lead of the Newport to Bermuda race. In the dream he is cold and wet and feels himself deserving of the mug of hot brew his cook is handing up to him from the galley.

Cole certainly does not expect the very large man in a dark suit, turtleneck, and buzz cut, offering him coffee in one of his own mugs when he opens his eyes.

"Time to rise and shine, Mr. Alexander, you have company and breakfast is waiting downstairs." The big guy speaks gently, as if he were Cole's major-domo, and this their morning ritual.

Cole almost wets the bed. He throws the covers back, knocking the hand holding the coffee, and thereby soaking his Tresse blue D. Porthault luxury French sheets a murky brown.

"What the eff..." he starts to yell getting up, but then stops himself and sits back down quickly, landing right on the wet spot. "Damn it. How did you people get in here? How did you even know where I was?"

"Mr. Martone will explain all that downstairs, sir. He has arranged a breakfast meeting. Please dress and join him." The big guy is very patient.

A sheen of sweat covers Cole's body. He needs to pee. He needs to cry.

He needs to get the hell out of here. "I want to shower first," he manages to say. "I'm soaked with coffee."

The big guy takes this in stride. "Very well, sir. I'll tell Mr. Martone to expect you in ten minutes."

When he has gone, Cole turns the shower on, giving it time for the water to warm, and leans against the sink trying to figure out his options. On the one hand he needs to talk to Martone. On the other, he is scared to death of him. He can call for help and that will be the end of coming to some agreement about DJ's book. If he doesn't get help—well, he refuses to let his thoughts take him there. He is, after all, all alone out here and, oh, *God, I'm in deep shit* is all he can think. *Where in hell was Tony—all that 'protection' Stan got for me?*

In the bathroom, he opens the window and sticks his head out far enough to see down to the causeway. There is no Pontiac Aztec in sight.

*Son of a bitch! That guy left me to hang. What the hell do I do now?*

Time is passing. Cole takes a quick rinse in the shower, towels off, dresses, and goes down to face the Zipper. *If I'm a dead man, I might as well eat first,* he reasons. And then he sends a prayer out into the universe. *Please help me stop shaking and please don't let me cry.*

Cole pauses at the bottom of the stairs. There is an old man hunched in the easy chair, his back to the stairs, manuscript open on his lap. He appears not to be reading, but is staring out the bay window watching the fog bank blow billows of gray across the point. The rising sun challenges the fog, alternating light and dark in the room, creating an eerie, Twilight Zone-like aura.

There is movement to Cole's left and the same big guy who awakened him clears his throat and announces, "Mr. Alexander is here, sir."

The man in the chair seems to shake himself loose from his thoughts as the big guy steers Cole toward him. "Mr. Alexander, this is Mr. Martone."

Martone extends a fragile hand. "Ah, Mr. Alexander," he says. "It's been quite a while since we last spoke. And now there seems to be some urgency to your situation. Yes?"

Cole reaches to shake hands. He is stunned at the changes he sees. The man in front of him is dramatically different from the one he has held in memory for almost twenty years and whom he has made all the larger and more powerful by his belief in the threats made on his life.

The hand he grasps is cold but seems charged with electricity. Cole backs away quickly, stumbling on the edge of the rug. Grabbing the table for support, he manages to right himself without falling. *Please don't let me pee my pants. Please.*

"What...? How did you...? You can't just walk into my house..." he begins, but each sentence trails off into the ozone. Realizing he is shaking, Cole again leans into the table and notices it is set for two. He turns to Martone.

"Will you join me for breakfast?" asks Martone with a smile. "I took the liberty of assuming you are a gentleman who would prefer his eggs benedict-style, and I also stopped in the North End on the way up for fresh rolls and ricotta pie. Anthony has prepared a lovely meal for us."

Martone has moved from the easy chair to the table and seated himself at the head. Cole, mouth agape, arms out with his palms up, looks around the room for help from someone, anyone. But there is no one.

He sits.

"Mr. Martone," Cole begins, "I realize I called you. But that still doesn't give you any right-"

"Please," interrupts Martone. "Call me Raymond. And would you prefer Cole, or Coleman? I myself do not care for Ray. It's too abrupt, too sharp. But Raymond, being a two-syllable word, has the edge taken off it, don't you think? What's your preference?"

"No. Yes. No. Wait a minute. No. Cole is fine. This is making me nuts. What are you doing here, Mr. Mar... Raymond?"

*What the hell happened to my god-damned protection? I swear to god, if I live through this I'm going to kill Stan. I swear...*

Cole is finding it difficult to sit still, but his attempt to rise and move is met with a firm hand upon his shoulder, pressing his body back to the sitting position. The big guy is behind him.

"Ah, but it is you who has been seeking my attention. I assume it is about this," he says, all but caressing the manuscript on the table beside him. "We will attend to that later. For now, Anthony will serve us and we will talk of more pleasant things."

*Wait a minute!* Cole thinks. *What in hell was the name of that guy Stan called for help? Tony? Anthony! No way. Now you're being crazy, Alexander. Stop being a jerk. Don't let your guard down here, man, you're in a bucket of shit.*

The swinging door to the kitchen opens and another big guy—with a white chef apron tied snugly across his rather formidable torso—enters carrying a tray of juices, coffee, eggs, rolls, condiments and of course, the ricotta pie which he places in front of both men.

Martone thanks Anthony, then turns to the first big guy and says, "Why don't you and Anthony relax on the porch for a while, Vincent? Cole and I are quite comfortable here, aren't we, Cole?"

"Oh, yes. Yes, of course," Cole responds distractedly. His thoughts are elsewhere. *Maybe he's going to poison me. I'll only eat what he eats. Jesus! Vinny and Tony. How stereotyped can this get? I can't believe this guy. Raymond, Tony and Vinny! I'm in a god damned B-fucking movie and he has me by the balls! Again! What the hell did I do to deserve this?*

Cole picks up his knife and fork, then leans his wrists against the table and looks at Martone. He is impeccably dressed in an Armani silk suit, replete with gray silk shirt and matching tie. There is one gold chain around his neck and another on the right wrist accenting a gold and onyx ring on his left middle finger that looks to weigh more than his hand. Age and perhaps illness of some kind, have clearly not sucked the self-assurance of power and money out of him.

"Please," Martone gestures with his fork, "enjoy your breakfast. Anthony is quite the accomplished chef. He was sous chef in one of Emeril's restaurants in New Orleans and also at Tavern on the Green in the Big Apple."

Martone lowers his voice as if including Cole in a secret. "Had a touch of trouble with authority figures—nothing I can't handle, I assure you. And, there's nothing he can't prepare. I've been trying to get him to join my staff for years. Today, I succeeded." Again he gestures with the fork, "mangia."

For the first time, Cole looks down at his plate. The lobster benedict looks superb, dripping with just the perfect accompaniment of hollandaise, and the grilled asparagus spears have been peeled to promise exquisite tenderness. *Poison or no poison, I'm eating this. I've been a food snob all my life, and if this is my swan song, I'm going out in style.*

"Good, no?" asks Martone when he sees Cole has eaten half his serving. "I told you he can cook."

"This," Cole speaks with his mouth half full and fork ready to deliver more, "is the very best benedict I have ever had. Why isn't he on Food Network or something? Where did you find this guy?"

"Much to my delight, Cole, he was sitting at the end of your drive in a car watching the house. We had a talk, and now he works for me."

Martone shrugs, smiles at Cole, raises his palms and turns them outward. "What could I do? I've wanted him for years. So now I'll pay him more than your guy will. It's just business. You understand?"

Cole's fork drops onto his plate, splattering sauce across his shirt.

*Jesus shit. I knew it!* "Welcome to my parlor said the spider to the fly," Cole mutters under his breath. *I'm dead meat.*

# NINETEEN

HEN DJ HEARS KATE AND TUCK stirring next door, she pops her head in to say good morning.

"Look, why don't you two just relax this morning? Order room service. Sleep in a bit. I'll stop at the media center and print our boarding passes and join my sisters for breakfast. We can meet up in the lobby around ten when the driver's due to pick us up. I'm packed already, and if you'll take my suitcase down I'd appreciate it."

Kate and Tuck have propped themselves against the headboard, sheets pulled up.

"I'll get the boarding passes, DJ," offers Tuck. "Just leave me the flight number."

"Sit for a sec, why don't you?" Kate pats the bed next to her. "How are you doing this morning, girl? It sounded like you had a rough night. And do you really want to take on your sisters without backup?"

DJ flops on the bed and groans.

"Oh, Katie, those are two tough questions. I didn't sleep much, that's for sure. I felt like I was riding a wave all night, surfing my way up and across fury and curling down into just plain old sadness. Kicking myself for not being sharp enough to figure this out for myself, and then not even being sure it's true. Frankly, I got sick of that real quick."

"Well, you always could ruminate with the best of them, as you well know, darlin'" says Kate with a grin.

"But it never gets me anywhere. I have to do something. Change something. Find out the truth and then decide what to do with it." DJ begins to shake. She looks at both Tuck and Kate, eyes wide with distress.

"Dear God. Could this really be true? Could it? Could Raymond have killed his own brothers, and my father? What kind of a monster does that?" She is wringing the end of the sheet, pulling it in two directions at once.

Both Kate and Tuck are silent.

"And why? To protect me? That's probably what he'll say, isn't it? He did it for me? What does that make me? What did I start by telling him? Did I even tell him? I don't remember if I did. He just seemed to know. Shit. This is driving me nuts." She lets go of the sheet and begins worrying a piece of paper.

"It's when I start thinking about what to do if this really does turn out to be true, that I start freaking out. Know what I mean?" DJ looks down to her hands which have been methodically tearing the note paper where she has written the flight number for Tuck. It is now shred into tiny little squares. She lets the pieces fall onto the bed and reaches for the pad and pen on the nearby nightstand.

"This might be the stupidest thing to ask right about now," says Kate, "but have you given any thought to what it means for your book if this ends up being true?"

Tears fill DJ's eyes and she raises a hand to cup her forehead.

"That's the thing. I can't even go there. I try and I hit a wall. If this is true... *if* this is true, it changes everything." The tears have breached their boundaries and she reaches for the edge of the sheet to wipe them away.

Kate takes DJ's hand in both of hers. "Here's what it doesn't change, my friend. You are a survivor of some terrible shit, stuff that was done to you. Stuff you're not responsible for. Whatever Raymond did or didn't do related to that stuff, is not on you. You did your work. You picked yourself up when you were as fragmented as these pieces of paper." Kate throws a handful of DJ's tattered note in the air and watches as pieces fall dizzily to the carpet like seed pods from maple trees. She looks up at DJ.

"You struggled and worked at it and put the pieces of yourself back together. You are a woman with courage and power. This will not destroy you. I promise."

"Right now I feel as if my pieces are cracking at the seams, Kate. I really do. Like I only fit myself back together with putty and it's all coming apart." DJ is shaking her head.

Kate scans DJ's worried face, then notices she must have bitten her fingernails during the night. Tuck gives Kate a nudge and glances at DJ's wrists where several old scars from self-inflicted wounds look reddened from recent rubbing.

"Let me tell you something, Deej." Kate runs her own thumb across DJ's wrist. "You are not put together with putty. Crazy Glue, perhaps, but not putty. There is much more substance to you than that. And you are well beyond needing the behaviors you used in the old days that helped you cope with what happened. And... and here's the biggie, darlin', you are not alone this time. You have let us in and we are staying for the long haul. Got that?"

"Yes," DJ whispers, still teary.

"And just one more thing," Kate adds. "We will help you see that your book is published, no matter when and no matter in what form. If that's what you want, then we will help you make it happen, with or without this new information from your sisters. Got that, too?"

"Yes. I... I need a tissue. Please?"

Tuck leans in and gives DJ the box of tissues. She cleans up, and then closes her eyes, clearly spent.

"I do not know what I did to deserve you two in my life. I truly don't. It fills me with wonder sometimes. I am so grateful. Thank you."

DJ opens her eyes to see Kate and Tuck making silly faces at her and reaching to tickle her toes.

"Love you right back," says Kate, as DJ swings her feet off the bed and out of range. "It's about time you received what you deserve rather than what you were dealt. Just never forget that all that stuff was what happened to you. It is not who you are. It is definitely not who you are or who you have become. You have a life, and a good one. You did that. You made that. That's who you are. Not because of what happened, but in spite of what happened. You are one impressive woman. And we are proud, proud, proud, to be your friends. So there! Now, that is all from this side of the bed, ladies, good night, ah... morning." With that, Kate sticks her tongue out at DJ, slides down in the bed and pulls the covers up over her head.

"Ditto from this side," says Tuck, jerking the sheet from Kate. "But we're not done yet."

"We're not?" Kate asks, popping her head up. "What did we forget?"

"Breakfast with my sisters, right?" DJ looks at Tuck who nods in agreement.

"I think I can handle this one myself," she says. "They deserve some one-on-one with me at any rate. I probably scared the heck out of them last night, so I do have some cleaning up to do."

DJ places the note pad and pen on the dresser. "This is the flight number for you, Tuck. Thanks for taking care of that. My bag is just inside my room. See you in a couple of hours. Get some rest."

Kate reaches for Tuck as DJ opens the door. "No rest for the loving, my friend. We are about to do that thing that we do so well. Good luck with the barracudas, and please put the Do Not Disturb sign on the door on the way out. Thank you."

DJ pulls the door closed and hangs the privacy card as requested. She smiles briefly then gives herself a good shake when she remembers her mission and heads for the restaurant to face her sisters once again.

# TWENTY

"WHAT WAS THAT?" questions Martone as he slips a large wedge of ricotta pie onto his plate.

Cole's eyes are closed, and he is rolling the skin above his nose and between his brows with the precision of a baker kneading bread. "Huh?"

"That nursery rhyme thing you just said, about the spider." Martone washes the pie down with a sip of coffee, unaware of the crumbs on the left side of his chin and lip. "Where've I heard that before?"

Cole looks at Martone and has to restrain himself from reaching across with a napkin and wiping the man's chin. "Oh, uh, it's from a poem, by Howitt, and a song by Paper Chase. And also a picture book by DiTerlizzi."

*Will you listen to me? I'm an idiot! Shooting my mouth off about books to this asshole. Grow some balls, Alexander. You've got nothing to lose.*

"Look, Mr. Martone, I-"

"Please. Raymond."

"Yeah, okay, whatever. Raymond. I feel like you're jerking me around, here. Let me explain something." Cole starts pushing his food around the plate with the back of a knife. He is aware of his heart kicking a tango against his chest wall.

"I called you. Against my boss's wishes, I called you. It was a courtesy call. Based on our last…um…meeting or encounter or whatever you might want to call it, I thought it important that you found out from me what was going on, before you found out some other way. That's all I wanted to do. I even brought you a copy of the manuscript. But now I'm sitting here thinking you've got some plans to hurt me, and I still don't have any freaking clue what any of this is about. I didn't sixteen years ago, and I still don't today. So, for the love of God, man, either tell me what the hell is going on or, or, I'll have to ask you to leave. Please."

Cole is only aware that his voice has risen in pitch and volume when Vinny opens the screen door. "Everything okay in there, boss?" he asks.

Martone raises a hand. "We're just fine, Vincent, thank you." He smiles at Cole. "You really need to relax a bit, young man, before you have an aneurism. Nobody wants to hurt you. Here, have some good ricotta pie. Best of the North End. You'll feel better."

Martone cuts a large slice of pie and pushes it toward Cole.

*I cannot effing believe this guy,* thinks Cole, as he pushes the pie back toward Martone.

"I'm trying my best to be hospitable," Martone says, picking up the plate and placing it against Cole's chest. "The least you can do is be courteous in return. And, just so we understand one another. I will tell you what I want to tell you when I'm good and ready to tell you. Got that?" he adds, slapping a fork on the plate.

The pie feels like gravel in Cole's mouth. He has no saliva and tries washing it down with orange juice, the whole mess curdling instantly in his stomach already full with acid born of fear. But he eats it. He eats it while Martone smiles and cuts himself another piece and drops crumbs across his chin and onto his silk Armani suit. Cole could not have picked up a napkin to swipe at the crumbs if his life depended on it.

"Know what I'm thinking?" asks Martone, gaze focusing out the bay windows and down toward the dock. "I'm thinking this would be a great day for a sail. How about you treat us to a day on the water? Call it a thanks for this wonderful breakfast. I haven't had the pleasure in years. What do you say?"

Cole struggles to swallow the last piece of pie. "No. No sailing," he says, regretting it immediately as Martone's face takes on a red hue from the neck upwards.

"I mean, I have no crew. It takes at least four to run the boat, and my usual guys are crewing for other people in the Regatta today. It's a forty-one footer, a racing boat, not a day sailor. No seats. You won't be comfortable. Besides, it takes a lot of people. Sailors. People who know how to sail..." Cole runs on, his mouth flapping open and shut way ahead of his brain.

His brain is on another plane altogether.

*What the hell? My bones will wash up on the shore, picked to death by fish. I can't do this. This is crazy. This is two thousand fourteen for God's sake. Who still does this to people? Oh, obviously. People like this guy...*

Cole's conversation with his own head is interrupted by the sound and vibration of his cell phone deep within his pocket. He reaches for it and fumbles, dropping it onto the table. Desperate to grab it before Martone, Cole slaps at it, knocking it against his coffee cup, cracking the porcelain and releasing the contents across the linen tablecloth. Martone pulls back from the table to avoid the spill and Cole rescues his phone.

"Stan! Stan." *Thank God. It's Stan.* "Listen, boss..."

"First of all, why the hell didn't you tell me you were going up there for the weekend? Do you have any idea how long it took our guy to find you? And now I can't even reach him. What the hell is going on, Alexander? Have you seen our guy? Have you set up a meeting with Martone? I don't have time for this bullshit, Cole. I really don't. Talk to me."

Stan is on a roll and Cole is desperate for him to take a breath.

"Stan. Listen. Just listen, would you please? You won't believe this. I woke up this morning and Martone is in the house, and your guy, Tony, who's now Martone's chef by the way, is cooking us breakfast. You were supposed to get me a bodyguard, Stan. But you got me a chef. A chef! Actually, Stan, you got Martone a chef. Now, Martone—excuse me, *Raymond*—wants me to take him out on my boat for a friendly sail. That's what's going on, Stan. I'm not up here having a party. Frankly, I'm pissing into my socks. That's what the hell's going on."

Cole is pacing and gesturing and only stops short when he notices both Vinny and Tony watching him from behind the porch door. He turns back to the table where Martone is smiling and slowly extending his hand, indicating he wants the cell.

Puzzled, Cole looks at the phone and back at Martone. "You want to talk to Stan? Is that it?"

Martone nods.

"Be my guest," Cole responds and hands him the cell.

"Mr. Whitman, a pleasure to make your acquaintance. I've been enjoying Cole's company, although we have yet to discuss our mutual problem. We were just heading out for a sail on this splendid morning. Would you care to join us?"

Martone covers the cell with his hand, and whispers to Cole, "I assume it would be fine with you that I invite him? Yes?"

*I do not effing believe the balls on this guy,* Cole tells himself for the tenth time this morning and runs his hands through his hair. "Sure. Whatever. Yes. Of course. Good idea." *Please, God, let Stan say he'll come. I might have a better chance if there're two of us.*

Stan is in high gear. "Listen, Martone, this has to end now. My man there is a wreck and no real good can come of this. He didn't do anything wrong. And we all just need to calm down and talk about this."

"He certainly is a wired one, Stanley. I'll give you that." Martone is finding some pleasure in watching Cole pace around the table mumbling to himself, and occasionally stopping to realign place settings and silverware or sop up some of the recent coffee spill.

"Let me assure you that I wish no harm to either one of you," he continues. "I simply desire to have a sail and do some more reading of my niece's manuscript before making any decision about my next move. And I would like to get out there before the sun gets too warm. Looks like an unusual scorcher for so late in the year. You know, global warming and all. But, if you are unable to join us, Stanley, I will have to end this conversation now." He snaps his fingers to get Vincent's attention, and waves him into the house.

"No, I can't join you and that's a big boat. You'll need an experienced crew. That's a bad idea, Martone. Someone could get hurt. And by the way, what's this about you stealing my bodyguard? I hired that guy to watch out for…" The last of Stan's comments are lost as Martone dramatically presses End and turns to Cole.

"Now, Coleman," he says. "I'm sure a proficient sailor such as you would have extra boat shoes or sneakers and perhaps a shirt or two for my friends here. Why don't you go get them set up. And, please, don't forget the sunscreen. SPF 35 or more will do nicely. Thank you." Martone picks up both the manuscript and the phone which has begun ringing again and retreats to the porch.

It takes a hand on his back from Vinny to get Cole moving from the spot where his feet have frozen to the hardwood floorboards. He watches his phone—his only source of hope for assistance—go out the door, slipped deep within Martone's suit jacket.

# TWENTY-ONE

ONCE AGAIN, DJ PAUSES at the door of the restaurant to observe her two sisters. They have ordered coffee and busy themselves with cream and sugar. *Nope, I'm wrong. That's skim milk and the stuff in the yellow packet for Christine, and black with about one tablespoon of cream for Sarah, if I remember correctly.*

They're dressed for a day of shopping. Almost identically, it seems, and right out of either J. Crew or Land's End in tops and slacks. Sarah is sporting another in her amazing array of handbags, this one by Vera Bradley. And Christine, the foot maven, is wearing a pair of shoes that DJ wouldn't last in for five minutes without breaking all ten toes, never mind walking from store to store. *I really do have to ask my mother again if I was adopted,* she thinks and gathers her courage to join them at the table.

"There you are," Sarah trills, clearly having some anxiety about how this morning meeting will go. "We were getting a bit worried, weren't we, Christine?"

Christine is having difficulty making eye contact with DJ. She busies herself with her coffee until Sarah nudges her under the table. Christine gives a start and glares at Sarah.

"God," Chris says, glaring right back. "I'm in the middle of drinking here. I can't do anything until I've had coffee. You know that."

Sarah huffs and nods her head in DJ's direction, poking Chris again with her foot.

"Oh, all right. Good morning, DJ." Christine's mocking tone is punctuated with a fake smile. She looks at Sarah. "Happy now?"

She picks up the menu, buries herself in it and mumbles, "What's good here?"

"It's breakfast, Christine, breakfast. Not the *Bon Appetite* nine-course brunch," Sarah is in rare form. "They can hardly damage an egg now, can they?"

DJ resists a formidable urge to scream for help.

"Give it a rest, you two. This is an awesome start for a day of shopping, but you won't make it to noon if you keep this up." she says instead. "Actually, Chris, the Southern Special is supposed to be great. Might even carry you through to evening from what I hear." She picks up her own menu and scans the choices.

"I think I'll do the breakfast buffet," says Sarah. "I like the variety. Where's the waitress? Are you two ready to order?"

"Aren't we waiting for your sidekicks?" asks Christine, doing that thing with her mouth again, puckering it to one side. She snaps open her napkin and lays it across her lap.

Sarah glares at her sister. "Do not, I repeat, do not start that again or I swear I will push you down the first escalator I can find. I mean it." She faces DJ and rolls her eyes, exasperated.

DJ can't help herself. She leans across the table toward Christine and whispers, "They're in bed having sex, kiddo. Sex. Lesbians do that, you know."

"Yeah, and I'm surprised you're not in there with them," Christine spits back. "For all the time you spend with them. They're not your family. But you tell them everything, go everywhere with them. You're like stuck to them for dear life or something. I don't get it."

"Wow. Okay, so that's what this is about. Finally." DJ sits back in her chair and looks at both sisters.

Sarah reacts to the look by backing away, her hands up. "Don't blame me," she argues. "I'm not the one with the problem here."

"I get that, but this is important for both of you to know. Kate and Tuck mean the world to me. And, yes, I tell them most everything. And we've been through a lot together since college. Frankly, I'm not sure I could have made it without them." She feels her heart rate begin to rise, fueled by anger at having to do this again and again.

"You two both married after college. You have partners, good ones, and kids—and kids who are now having kids. I don't. I've got lots of great friends and two very special ones. They have actually become family to me. But, in the end, that's still different from you two." She looks at Sarah.

"I was the very only person you trusted to babysit your first child,

Sarah wasn't I? And I never babysat anyone else's kids at Disney World but yours, Christine, or knelt on the floor and prayed the night dad's girl-friend showed up drunk and started breaking things in the living room and screaming at mom. That was with you and Maggie. Remember?" She's looking at Christine.

"All the friends in the world can't change what we went through to-gether or what we mean to each other. And really great friends never take you from your family. They just add to it—if you'd only let them."

Christine has tears in her eyes. "Yeah, yeah, yeah, okay, I get it."

"No she doesn't." Sarah is leveling Christine with a scowl again. "Tell her what you told me last night." She pauses. "No? Okay, I will." She turns to DJ. "Christine thinks you're gay and not telling us. You know, because of what happened with dad and the uncles."

DJ shakes her head and laughs. "Oh my god, Christine, really? Just imagine. If every female that ever got hurt by a male ended up gay, the world would be exploding with lesbians. Sorry, no, it just doesn't work that way. And as for me, well, the jury's still out, so to speak. I'm fully wrapped up in my writing, so not much sizzle going on right now. Hope-fully that will change. And then we'll see."

*Liar, liar, pants on fire!* thinks DJ. *Okay, but it's only an itty bitty lie. Marsh and I just went out to dinner twice. No way am I going to say any-thing to these two piranhas and get eaten alive. Not yet anyway.*

"So... you're saying, what? Maybe?" Christine asks.

"I'm saying why does it concern you one way or the other? Your sexual relationship with Garret is none of my business, and who I might choose to love sexually is also none of yours. And if this question is really about Kate and me, then get real. If anything was going to happen there, it would have happened long ago. We love each other. We are not in love with each other. We are not attracted to each other sexually."

She stares at Christine.

"Are you following any of this? Here's a newsflash for you: gay people are not attracted to every person they ever see who is the same sex as them." *Am I really having this conversation with a forty-six year old woman?* "You're attracted to Garret, but you don't throw yourself at every male you see just because you happen to be heterosexual, do you?"

Christine looks away and turns a bright red.

The reaction does not escape Sarah's critical eye.

"Oh my god, Christine, you're cheating on Garret." Sarah says, about to have a heart attack, slapping her palm against the table. She turns to DJ. "She is. She's cheating on him. I can tell."

DJ is stunned as well. *Okay… so now we're getting down to what's really bugging her,"* she thinks. *This ought to be good!*

Sarah swivels back to Christine. "You are. And you're guilty as sin. Oh, this is just too much. I need a cigarette. And all this stuff about her," Sarah points to DJ, "is so we won't talk about what's going on with you. You are a snake, Christine, a snake."

"Excuse me." A strange new voice joins the group. The waitress is poised above DJ's shoulder, pad and pen in hand, eyes wide and brows raised. She has obviously heard every word of Sarah's rant. "Um… Have y'all decided what you'll have?" she asks.

All three heads bury themselves again in the menu, too embarrassed to look at the woman directly. They each order the breakfast buffet. Sarah asks for a fresh carafe of coffee, while DJ opts for green tea. Christine rises quickly and heads for the food line.

Sarah looks at DJ and shakes her head sadly. "Well. There you go. I knew something was up with her, but I had no idea what. This explains a lot. She's been miserable since Maggie died and about as charming as a rattlesnake. This is turning into a hell of a weekend."

"It's sucking the air out of my news balloon, that's for sure," DJ responds. "I'm going for food, and I think we need to give her a chance to explain when we get back. I have to leave in an hour, but this latest installment in the soap opera of Chrissie's life could take a week to get through. Coming?"

"Are you kidding?" asks Sarah, pushing her chair back and standing. "I can only handle this on a full stomach. And I have to spend the rest of the weekend with her, too." Quite dramatically, she slings her Vera Bradley bag over her left shoulder, grazing DJ's nose, and heads for the buffet.

CHRISTINE IS THE FIRST ONE back to the table with her food. She has her head down and keeps it there when her sisters return. Aside from an intermittent 'huff' from Sarah, the small group starts to eat in silence.

*Okay. Time to bring in the compassionate big sister,* thinks DJ. She pours herself the last of the tea, and adds a squeeze of lemon. She lifts the cup to her lips then replaces it in the saucer without drinking.

"Chrissie, I know you must be feeling pretty embarrassed right this minute, but I'm so glad this is out and on the table." She speaks calmly and deliberately.

"I can't imagine how hard it must be to be carrying all this around and feel you couldn't really talk about it. My stuff has been taking up all the space. I'm sorry. I bet you thought we'd all be together this weekend and you could just, you know, let it all hang out."

"You two have no idea how lonely I am out there," Christine is tearful and bursting with the need to be heard. She blots her mascara with the ends of her napkin, looks at it and realizes she has stained the cloth.

Sarah pulls her shoulder bag from the back of her seat and removes a tissue from a small travel pack. She smacks the packet in front of Chris with a self-satisfied grunt.

"Can you just explain to me how you can be lonely in Ann Arbor, Michigan, for goodness sake, Christine?" Sarah harps. "The place was one rocking town when I helped you move. There were plays and lectures and all kinds of activities and free classes. I thought we had pulled together a whole plateful of things you wanted to do."

Christine flicks her wrist at Sarah, dismissing everything she has just said.

"I don't know what I was thinking, agreeing to sell the house after the kids were gone and move to the frozen mid-west with no ocean and nothing resembling fresh fish other than something called sturgeon, for God's sake. Garret and his mid-life crisis, and his wonderful new job at the University, I'm so sick of it and sick of him loving it so much. I hate it. I hate the place. I hate the people. I just hate it."

"What's to hate, Christine? I mean it," Sarah is unrelenting. "What exactly is to hate in a place that has everything you could possibly want in terms of things to do? I'd love it there."

Chris turns on Sarah.

"Oh, who gives a crap what you'd love, Sarah. For goodness's sake, you've got a husband who's moved you from pillar to post all over the place whether or not you've wanted to go. And, okay, to your credit, you've adjusted everywhere, made friends easily, found lots of things you like to do."

She takes a deep breath, but continues before Sarah can respond.

"But I'm not like you, Sarah. Or you, either, DJ. I'm not good at change. I just don't fit in easily anywhere—at least not for a long time. I never wanted to move. Garret did. And now, damn it all to hell, he's as happy as a clam and I'm miserable. And I don't even have the kids to take care of anymore." She rips another tissue from the pack and dabs at her mascara.

DJ places her hand on Sarah's arm to stop her from making a remark she might regret.

"Let her finish," she says for Chris's benefit.

"And then I met this guy at the supermarket, no less. And he looks like George Clooney."

"Uh, oh," mutters Sarah under her breath. Chris raises her eyes, but continues.

"And he's a professor, but he's from the east coast too, and we just talked and talked over coffee. Oh, you know, one thing led to another. It's the same old boring story of an affair that you hear every day. And I'm so ashamed and so afraid Garret will find out. And I totally know I don't love this guy. I love Garret."

"Well, *that's* good to hear," Sarah can't stop herself this time. Her cynicism has been let loose and it's swooping across the table and dive-bombing her sister.

Christine purposely ignores her and continues.

"But I can't tell him, and I can't tell anyone out there because then he'll find out, which he just might anyway because they're all so 'tight' as Garret says. What he means is they're all like a little clique of teenage girls, talking amongst themselves. It surprises me they don't all burst out into giggles in their little groups. Ugh! And I don't have any friends there anyway."

"Well you'll never have any if you keep this up," Sarah starts, but stops short when DJ says her name sharply.

"And then we all show up here, you with friends you talk to about everything, and you, Sarah, with all those pictures of the grandbaby you can see every day if you want to. I just… I'm just so jealous of both of you."

*Well. This explains a lot,* thinks DJ, but before she can respond, Sarah chimes in.

"Jealous? Of what? Look at the mess DJ is in for starters. She's-"

"Thanks, sis, that's a real help," DJ says to Sarah with all the sarcasm *she* can muster, then turns to Chris.

"What did you hope to get from us? I mean, what do you need us to do? Just to listen? Do you know?"

Chris is almost through the entire packet of tissues. "I want you to be my best friends. I want you to tell me to stop seeing Rafael. I wa-"

Sarah cuts in sharply. "Oh my god, his name is Rafael? *And* he looks like George Clooney? I'm coming to visit. I need to meet this one. This could be great for one of your novels, DJ." Sarah is practically bouncing up and down in her seat.

"And you have the nerve to ask me why I didn't say something sooner?" Chris asks, boring her eyes into DJ. "You're not being helpful, Sarah. This isn't one of DJ's stupid romance novels. This is my messed up life and I want you to listen to me. I love Garret. I do. I really love him. I just hate Ann Arbor and I miss my friends. I miss Maggie. I miss my old life."

DJ sneaks a peek at her wristwatch. *Twenty minutes. I've got twenty minutes to deal with this and get out of here. If I had a nickel for every trage-comedy I've gone through with these two I'd never have to write another book. And did she just diss romance novels? Mine, in particular? Okay, she did, but I'm not going there. She needs to be in counseling with Garret. But if I tell her that, there's a good chance she'll whack me with one of her heels and then I'll never get out of here. Oh, what the hell…*

"Look, sis," DJ says to Chris. "You might not want this advice right now, but you really sound like you feel terrible about the bind you're in and want some relief. And I mean more relief than just talking to us about it. So, yes, I do think you should end the affair. Right away. And… I know you'll hate this part, but I think you need to be in counseling. With Garret."

"DJ, I simply cannot tell him what I've done. I can't," Christine's tears have sent Sarah looking frantically through her purse again for more tissues.

"Let me just finish, Chris. You and Garret need to be talking about how lonely you feel and what the change in moving to Michigan is doing to you. He doesn't need to know how far it's gone, but counseling will never work if you're still involved with George, um, Rafael. You know that, right?"

Sarah, for once, has nothing to add and simply nods her head at everything DJ has said.

"I have an idea," DJ continues, "two, actually. I can ask Kate and Tuck to recommend someone in Ann Arbor who's a good marriage counselor. It's where they did their graduate work, so they should know someone. You can start working things out with Garret and see how things go. And, how about I rent us that place at the shore in Rhode Island where we always went when Mags was so ill, and we can all get together for Thanksgiving there? My treat, airfare and all."

Now Sarah comes to life again. "Me, too? I mean, us too? Rob, and the kids and the baby?"

"The place is huge, remember? So, yes, all of us. And Chris, if you can even find your two kids and pull them in from whatever ends of the earth they're on these days, yes. All of us. Kate and Tuck, too." DJ herself is getting excited at the prospect of a large family gathering. "And, hopefully, the edits of my book should be just about over by then and it should be on the way to publishing. I'll have it for you then."

DJ grows quiet for a moment, and then looks at her youngest sister.

"None of this makes up for the fact that you're feeling all alone out there, Christine. Sarah and I can both do better with calling more often and just staying in contact with each other all around. I know when I get into my writing I close myself off from most everyone, especially with this most recent one. I apologize for that. I don't ever want either one of you to think you can't get what you need from me." She looks at both sisters. "Are we okay? All of us?"

"I still miss Maggie, you know. She was my best friend ever." Christine says it flat out as a statement and Sarah and DJ simply nod their heads.

Sarah raises her coffee cup. "To our sister Maggie, beloved, and gone too soon," she says, and they repeat as they clunk cups. "To Maggie."

A full minute passes in silence and then DJ checks her watch. "Whoa. I have to get moving. And I haven't even touched any of this food." She wraps a scone in a napkin and bolts down a few mouthfuls of yogurt. As she turns to remove her jacket from the back of her chair she spots Tuck waving the boarding passes at her from the lobby and pointing at her watch.

"There's my posse," she quips, smiling at Chris.

"And I suppose you're going to tell them everything, aren't you?" Christine asks.

"Oh, you bet your buns I am. This is entirely too good to keep to myself. We have the whole plane ride to dish on this one."

DJ holds a finger up to Tuck, asking for another minute even though she sees the limo driver approaching Tuck.

"Listen, you two, I love you both very much. I'm going home to confront Raymond today and-"

"You're still going to see that creep? Even after everything we talked about last night? Do you have some kind of a stupid death wish or something, DJ?" Christine tosses her napkin on her plate and grips the tablecloth. "Don't you get it yet? He's dangerous. He freaking kills people."

"Why do you think neither one of us has gone anywhere near him for years, Deej?" Sarah asks. "Rob would have a fit if I even thought of doing what you're doing. You're nuts to do this. Honestly, there's something seriously wrong with you."

"Perhaps there is, Sarah, and perhaps you're right Chris," DJ says, looking from one to the other, "but if I don't go, I'm never going to find out, am I?"

"Find out what?"

"First of all I want to know if he really did kill them. And then, if he did, I want to know why," DJ says. "Just why. I need to know why. And he's the only one with the answer to that isn't he?"

Out of the corner of her eye she can see Kate holding up her suitcase and waving that they have to get going. She looks at her own watch and then nods that she's seen them.

"Look," she says to her sisters, "I'll be careful. Those two will be with me and I'll call you as soon as we leave his place, okay? But I am going, and now I really have to leave or we'll miss the plane."

"Well, I still think you're nuts," Sarah says as she pushes back from the table just a bit.

DJ raises her hands in a surrendering gesture.

"That may well be," she says, "because I'm going to see mother tomorrow as well. Where all that takes me next in terms of the book, I have no idea. But in the meantime, I promise to let you know and I promise to be there when you need me, and even when you don't."

"Oh, god," says Sarah, trying for levity, "big sister will now smother the hell out of us. Be careful what you ask for… and all that." Her voice trails off as she notices tears in both sisters' eyes.

DJ stands and gathers her things. She wraps her arms around Sarah and gives her a hug. "Take care of her," she says, with a slight tilt of the head toward Chris. "Oh, and I've taken care of the hotel bill, so knock yourselves out."

"No worries there, DJ," Sarah reassures her, "none at all. Thank you."

Chris's hug is more like a death grip and goes on for longer than usual. She whispers into DJ's ear. "Please be careful at Raymond's. I love you. Thank you. And tell Kate and Tuck they're lucky to have you as their best friend, too."

# TWENTY-TWO

THERE'S A COOL TEN-KNOT WIND on the water this morning, but it's causing Cole to sweat. It would be just fine for his usual crew. But one look at the three clusterfuckerteers hanging on for dear life is enough to convince him he won't venture far.

'Vincent' and 'Anthony', my ass, he thinks. They're thugs for god's sake. A matched set of mobsters, not some characters out of Julius Cesar! It's Vinny and Tony in my book and this guy Tony's a real asshole, jumping ship like that. How in hell did Stan even know about him in the first place? And what the eff is all this about anyway? I do not have a g-d clue.

A buoy race is underway well off his starboard side, but he steers in that direction to have other boats in his vicinity, just in case Martone and his men have ideas of hurting him. Cole has no intention of raising a sail, either, nor does he have any qualms about taking a wave from the side instead of head on in order to shake the boys up as much as possible.

He takes a good look at his 'crew'. Vinny and Tony are struggling to stay upright as they help Martone onto the cockpit bench. They are obviously uncomfortable in their topsiders which barely fit them, but closer to comical in polo shirts that roll at their midriffs, exposing hairy stomachs and belly buttons. A bona fide Patriot cheerleader drag show, he thinks, and allows himself a smirk. Their Bermuda-length shorts are cut-offs created with scissors Cole found in a drawer below deck. It's the first time all day they aren't wearing guns. Martone has those in his jacket pocket closest to the rail.

"Experience tells me this ride need not be so rough, Coleman," says

Martone with an edge of warning. "I would suggest you turn us into the waves and head away from boat traffic. Perhaps raise a small sail and allow us the pleasure of a peaceful run on the water?" This last is posed as a question, but Cole takes it for the directive it is meant and turns the wheel accordingly.

Martone is finally settled on the bench, slathered in sunscreen and sporting a Panama hat. *That'll last about two minutes once we get into the wind,* Cole smiles. *Better take my satisfactions where I can.*

He asks Vinny to take the wheel and hold it steady as he makes his way to the bow to raise the jib and then back to raise the much more difficult mainsail. When he relieves Vinny, Cole cuts the motor and turns the boat slightly to fill the sails. They feel a slight tug and the boat tilts to port as they catch the wind and head toward open waters and into the chop, swells all around them. Out of the corner of his eye, Cole watches Martone steady himself on the slick bench and reach for DJ's manuscript. He begins to read.

## 13 • Peeling the Onion

*I wonder if it is possible for a normal person to understand what it is to live in a constant state of confusion. Or to understand why children who experience abuse at the hands of adults who purport to love them and are charged with their intimate care, can never be quite sure of those adults, or of what they might do next. Of the difference between what they say and what they do.*

*I know there are some people who are truly evil, and that even they are capable of fooling some of the people some of the time. But I think it important for me to be as clear as possible about this: in spite of everything, I do not think that any of the people who used me so violently and hurt me so deeply, both emotionally and physically, were evil.*

*None of them—not my father, or my uncles, or my mother for that matter, were abusive or unfeeling or ungiving of themselves all of the time. Mine was not a twenty-four-seven type of abuse. It is true that I never knew what would happen next. Or when. And because I did not know, and because I had no yardstick to measure what it was about either me or them that could set abuse into motion, I existed on some plane that I can only describe as a foggy nether-world of confusion and shame. And I did not trust a single one of them.*

*I did not, however, stop living with them or learning from them. Good things. Things that I am proud of now in my adult life.*

*My mother loves the ocean. Loved to swim. She entered the water as if it were a baptismal pool, reverently, transported away from time and re-sponsibility. Watching her in the water, watching her carve her way through the surf and across the swell, arms pumping rhythmically, legs churning up the wake behind her in perfect scissor kicks, was the purest of pleasures. We jumped and clapped and cheered her along from the safety of the beach, thrilled with what our mother could do.*

*She had five children. At the beach, she sang, "Five little water babies, all in a row. Put them in the ocean and watch them... gooooooo." And she would slide her hands out from under our bellies and launch each of us into the swells. Laughing. Joyful.*

*At home, she never sang.*

*Or touched us with such grace.*

*I rarely remember her without a book. We were library stack stalkers, searching for anything new, different, challenging. "Go outside, or read a book," became her summer mantra, and there were times when three or more of us were vying for the cooler spots in the house in front of a fan, or outside under the pear tree to sit and read. All of us grew into passionate readers. Those of us who are still alive, still are. And I, the writer!*

*For all of her emotional detachment, she has a sentimental streak wider than a four-lane highway, and has saved every card and letter and home-made art project we ever produced. She's as close to being a hoarder as a per-son can get without really crossing over into that twilight zone of suffocating from one's possessions. My own collecting comes nowhere close to hers, but I have been known to buy two or three of the same item—just in case—or to buy something I adore and then put it away somewhere safe—saving it for good.*

*And as for my writing... She saved the first story I ever wrote in cursive. From third grade:*

>   *My Cat*
>   *I have a cat. His name is Mittens. He is all black but he has white on two front feet and one in back. His feet look like tiny mittens. I love to hold my cat and make him purr. He had four kittens but we had to give them away.*

*I found the lined and wrinkled paper, yellowed with age and faded pencil, words wobbly written, deep in a box when we moved her to assisted living. She saved the first story I ever wrote, she said, because she loved the pure childish certainty it contained: that I indeed had a male cat that miraculously had given birth to kittens.*

*In truth, we never had a cat. What she had endearingly saved was third grade fiction at its finest—the first bright budding of the fiction writer into whom I would struggle so diligently to blossom and mature.*

*To my knowledge she has not fully read even one of my fourteen novels. Nor would she love them if she did. My belief is that she would stop reading at the first "vulgar" word or sexual innuendo. My stories no longer contain the purity of third grade fiction. I no longer carry within myself that kind of purity. But my mother does.*

*She was, just like the rest of us, molded in the shape of her environment. To stand out in any way was to invite attention, perhaps even scorn. She had to strive to be not so Italian in an Irish catholic school, not to be perceived as fatherless in a community of church-going families, not be one of the girls who smoked, or swore, or wore clothes that were too revealing. Unlike many of us, however, she has never been able to morph into a different shape of herself—over time and with information and experience. Her social anxiety simply prevents her from doing so. And the words I say, the images I use, the passions I suggest in my writings are far too much for her to negotiate. That I am not still writing about male cats having kittens is, I venture to say, a great disappointment to her.*

*She spent hours with her women's magazines, culling stories and poems, prayers and recipes, exercises, housekeeping, antique and fitness advice, filing them in folders, then placing folders into boxes. She saved Easter Seals and stamps and soda pull-tabs and postcards. During the move I found a postcard she had saved, addressed to me from my father when he was away for a month the summer I was eleven. It read: "I will be home at the end of next week. You and JJ had better be toeing the line or you're going to catch it. Dad."*

*I actually do realize that two people do not fall in love and decide to marry and raise children with the intent of hurting those children. But it happens. It happens far too often. It was not until I found this postcard that I truly understood the power my father had over me. The power one person can have over another—especially a child. Power that could be used to terrorize from hundreds of miles away with so few thoughtless words.*

*I see that I have chosen to describe his words as thoughtless, rather than* cruel— intending them to hurt. In truth, it could have easily been either. Why she kept this card in particular, I do not know. I will choose to believe that her need to collect it as a postcard overrode her judgment about the meaning of its message and its capacity to hurt me again, even in adulthood.

Once a summer we each had a shopping date with her where we spent the day in the city, picking out patterns and cloth and other sundries, underwear and school shoes or even the occasional store-bought dress. It was a day out of the house, an adventure that was often boring, actually, but that always ended with a stop at Shepard's Tea Room, where elegant ladies often dined, and where children who behaved nicely could have cream cheese and date nut bread sandwiches along with an ice cream soda. This was a day close to Heaven!

For all of her emotional distance from us children, she valued and cultivated her friendships the way collectors care for rare orchids. To this day, she still has a cadre of wonderfully gracious and thoughtful women friends who follow my professional accomplishments with notes and words of both encouragement and praise—things I rarely receive from her.

Throughout my childhood, this group of women met often at one another's houses—once a year at ours. My sister and I shared a bedroom off the living room and I would lie awake for hours listening to their stories and laughter, thinking this was just the grandest thing in the world. They referred to themselves as "the girls". And when I reached high school, I began having my own "girls" over during summer vacation to talk and laugh and eat.

This small act that gave my mother such pleasure in her otherwise difficult life left a lasting impression on my soul. For all the unhappiness and deceit that I shielded myself from on a daily basis, there was a tiny island of safety and hope that I was exposed to once a year.

I carry this gift from her.

I cherish my friendships for the precious jewels they are. Because in so many ways, my friendships saved my life.

My mother showed me how.

And I doubt she even knows or could understand how this could mean so much.

---

My uncles are another thing altogether. There are four in all. My father had three brothers and my mother had one.

*I am at a loss to even entertain what two of them could have contributed to my development in any ways even remotely positive.*

*My father's two middle brothers were my abusers. As alike as a pair of socks, they rarely functioned as other than a unit. They worked hard at their trade during the day and drank themselves into the next morning. When they visited us they brought a party with them, loud and vivacious, full of laughter and beer and gallons of ice cream for us kids. They danced my grandmother around the kitchen, leaving her breathless with giggles and charmed into a false sense of them as wonderful, dutiful sons. We children followed their tidal wave as it moved through our house, swelling the rooms with good vibrations that burst out into the yard and down the street, sucking the neighbors into its power.*

*But that did not last. Not long after they abused me they packed up and left, separating from each other with all the pain of conjoined twins following surgery. The last we heard was that they had taken jobs in different cities working for their youngest brother.*

*They never visited. Not once. And they never danced my grandmother around the kitchen again.*

*The truth is, I did not miss them.*

*The other truth is that I want to see them one more time.*

*Because now I no longer fear them.*

*And because they have some explaining to do.*

---

MARTONE SHUDDERS and lets out a moan, attracting the attention of Cole's crew. Vinny goes to him immediately, bending close to speak privately. Martone's hat has, indeed, blown out to sea, and Vinny removes a handkerchief from his own pocket, ties a knot in each of its four corners, along with nickels to add weight, and places it over his boss's head.

"That's ridiculous," Martone says as he pulls the odd covering off his head. "Very creative, Vincent, thank you. But, no."

"Give me your hat," Vinny says to Anthony who has been looking pretty close to being seasick for over an hour. The poor guy struggles to get the hat close enough to toss to Vinny without having to let go of the rail he has been furiously clutching.

Vinny asks if there is water and Cole points down into the galley. "There's a fridge full of cold ones on the left," he says.

Anthony is told to bring up a few bottles and it gives Cole a small thrill to watch him weeble his way to the gangway and down. His momentary inattention has caused the wind to go out of the sails, and the boat rocks and dips into a strong swell.

"Sorry," yells Cole and swings the boat back into the wind about ten degrees. "Are you okay over there, Raymond? We can head back at any time. The breeze is really starting to pick up out here and your guy in the galley is looking a bit green around the gills."

"I assure you we are all just fine, Coleman. Please proceed with what you are doing. Thank you." Martone's voice has lost some of its strength, and Cole can see Vinny remove pills from a vial and place them in his boss's palm. Amazingly, Tony has managed the gangway steps with four bottles of water without a mishap and is passing them around. Martone swallows the pills with half a bottle of cold water and returns to the manuscript.

––––––––––––––

*Raymond, my third uncle is the enigma of the family, so different from his brothers that he most likely teleported here from a galaxy far, far away.*

*To their boldness he brought sincerity; in the wake of their harshness he was gentle. Quiet and introspective, younger by almost twelve years, he excelled at school and was on track to be the first in the family to attend college. Although he might have pursued a deferment, he chose to serve in Vietnam and, like so very many others, after three tours he returned a broken and bitter young man.*

*He did so poorly on the shooting range that he was assigned to assist the medical corps. His job was to prepare the dead for return to the states. Hundreds of bodies times hundreds of days fed his own fears and angers. Again, like so many others, he found relief in the mind-numbing coma offered by the readily obtainable drugs his unit used to treat the wounded, and in the plentiful and wide varieties of local illegal drugs as well.*

*My siblings and I adored him, both before and after Vietnam. With us he was patient, listening to our adventures and answering our endless lists of questions, most of which began with "Why?" His knowledge was exhaustive, and if he did not know something, he would return the next day with books, or take us to a museum, or find someone who knew the answer. Drugs or not, he was to us a small island of sanity and constancy in an otherwise unpredictable existence.*

---

*After my father died, my mother's grief was such that we were slowly devolving into feral children, with my brother in the role of lord of an annoying and out of control pack of house flies. Our uncle Raymond stepped in and supported my mother and grandmother and, twisted as it might sound, brought us all our first real experience of peace. He made sure we stayed in school and paid for each of us to attend college, and when my brother died, and much later, my sister, he was the one who took care of the tedium of details and arrangements.*

*Although I never told him, I believe he knew what had happened to me at the hands of his brothers. I believe he knew what they had taken from me, had tried to destroy in me. And to this day, I believe he thinks he can make up for what they did. He wants, I believe, to find some way to right their wrongs.*

*I have come to understand, however, that even God doesn't have enough power to right those kind of wrongs.*

---

THE WIND HAS NOT PICKED UP, as Cole had just predicted. In fact, the wind has failed altogether and the sails are flapping listlessly against their lines. They are becalmed and therefore much more at the mercy of the swells. Cole is about to tell Martone that he needs to use the motor again, when he notices that Raymond has stopped reading and is staring out into the open ocean.

As an editor, and as a statement of exactly who he is as a person—especially according to his ex-wife—Cole knows himself to be better at reading books than he is at reading people. So when he sees Martone as he is now on the deck of his boat, slumped over DJ's manuscript and staring at the empty horizon, he is reminded of a description he read many years before.

*"He is involved in a struggle with a familiar sadness and a raging anger that swirls and churns within him like milk poured into cold coffee."*

"Holy shit," he blurts aloud, remembering the source of the line. It is from DJ's very first novel.

Cole's outburst has aroused Martone from his trance. "What is it?" he asks, startled.

"Oh, ah, nothing really, just that we have no wind and we'll have to motor again. Otherwise we'll be bobbing in the swells all day. Not the most comfortable way to sail, especially with you trying to read over there. Okay with you if I tune her up?"

"Fine," Martone says and returns once again to the tome on his lap.

---

*To speak of my father as having given me lifelong gifts is complex—complicated. Some are outright genetic traits that I would have inherited no matter how he behaved, such as my stature and the fair skin that burns rather than browns even in the winter sun.*

*Some are the result of time and attention and repeated exposure to the things he valued. My proficiency at and love of sports, my preference for anything having to do with the outdoors, including camping and adventure travel—all these are gifts from my father. I hold the steering wheel with my right hand and flop the left out the window when I drive on a warm day. The way he did. Rub my chin when I'm deep in thought. Run my hand through my hair just before putting on a hat. Love coffee ice cream. Still use the hunt-and-peck method of typing on my keyboard even this late in my life. All very much like him.*

*Most of the things I received from him, however, were born of my need to be different from him. He was a man of prejudice. A man who ridiculed people on welfare and called people of color names not worthy of paper and ink. He teased and taunted and poked us to the point of tears. But even these ugly traits affected me, triggering deep within me an angry counter reaction that came to full blossom during adolescence.*

*With my brother, I marched against the war in Vietnam even as my uncle fought there and we worried about him daily. I honed my passion for social justice issues on the back side of the same knife my father used to shred to pieces ideas and ideals held by those whom he deemed lesser than he. When I dared to stand up to him and defy him, the backhands to my face and head cut my lips and bloodied my nose.*

*He ridiculed my body, the fat I grew in order to make myself less attractive to men like him, the way I spoke, the things I read. He called me names, refused me the treats he bought my siblings, prohibited my mother from making clothes for me, embarrassed me about my weight in front of other people.*

*He ridiculed me. He ridiculed me, and what it did in the end was teach me tolerance. He ridiculed me and it taught me respect. I learned tolerance and respect for others, for their pain, for their difference. I learned all this from the disrespect and intolerance and abuse from my father. He did not mean it as a gift. But it is one of the most profound and long-lasting gifts I have ever received.*

*He could be a monster who invaded my dreams, my room, my body. But he also locked the doors and windows at night and kept us feeling safe from outside unknowns. When I won a science fair award, he greeted me with applause when I returned home. He took me to buy my first bike and first really good sleeping bag. I spent Saturdays in winter skating on ponds in the woods while he played hockey with his friends. He umpired my softball games. And more, and more, and more…*

*He died. And when he was gone, I was glad.*

*He died. And when he was gone, I missed him.*

*He died. And with him went the chance to grow into the place where I could even try to make him tell me why he did those things to me.*

*He died. And I still do not know the answer.*

*I will never know the answer.*

———————

*Confusion is not an arbitrary result of abuse to a child. It is a constant, a given. It ferments in the secrecy with which the abuse is bound. But the life of that family, and of each of its members, simply continues.*

*My mother sewed clothes for our bodies and for our dolls. She cooked and cleaned and talked with the neighbors, just like every other mom. My father worked, played golf, umpired baseball, refereed hockey and football and coached a pee wee team pretty much like any other dad. We kids went to school, got decent grades, played sports, had friends, went to church and said our prayers at night just like most other kids.*

*But we were not just like most other kids. Because, when we weren't looking. When we least expected it. When we had finally started to let our guard down just a tiny bit…we would be slammed right back into the reality of living in a family that kindness had forgotten.*

*And, if you were an extended family member, or a friend or neighbor on the outside looking in, you would have no way of knowing, nor would you believe, what life was really like for those of us on the inside desperately looking out.*

*Abuse happens in some families. And children are hurt by abuse. These children are often desperate to know why. Why them? Why me? The answer, of course, is because it can. Abuse happens in some families simply because it can. Those who experience it take no solace whatsoever in this answer. Many will spend their lives in search of a better answer to the question.*

*I have found that I am one of those people.*

---

THE SEA HAS TURNED TO GLASS. Without the wind, and not enough sail to provide good shade, the sun's high noon heat has become intolerable. Martone has shed his jacket and closed the manuscript, placing it next to him on the bench. Sweat beads line his forehead and neck. He had removed the tie at the start of the trip, but now his silk shirt is sticking to his back, revealing the outline of a sleeveless undershirt. He finishes the last of his water and asks Anthony to bring him another. To Cole, Martone is looking even worse than he did a half hour ago.

Earlier, Cole had tried unsuccessfully to see exactly what chapter the guy was reading. He has spent most of his time at the helm trying to figure out just what problem Martone could possibly have with DJ's manuscript. Cole has read most of it four times now. As devastatingly profound an autobiography that it is as a whole, DJ has painted a very positive picture of Raymond—in fact, the only positive picture of any of her uncles. *And it isn't as if the entire continent doesn't already know what the guy does for a living, either,* Cole thinks. *Heck. It might even work miracles for his image. Here's hoping that reading it will help Martone realize he has nothing to fear.*

Cole decides he can stay out on the water and motor these guys around in circles until the boat runs out of fuel if he has to. *If that's what it takes for Martone to allow me to publish the novel,* he thinks.

Cole's moment of fantasy fades quickly when Martone calls his name and tells him it's time to have "a little talk". Cole has Vinny take the wheel and points at the harbor entrance lighthouse, only the tip of which is visible on the horizon.

"Keep that lighthouse at one o'clock, just off the tip of the bow," he instructs, giving Vinny a pat on the back—a gesture he instantly regrets when Vinny pulls away and stares Cole in the eye.

"Sorry," he mutters, and slides behind him. Trying to avoid settling too close to Martone, Cole drags a large sail bag across the cockpit deck and sits facing the man he fears. The instant his behind hits the bag, however, Cole flashes to Martone's thugs forcing him into it and tossing him overboard. His muscles suddenly weaken at the thought and he grabs the gunwale to stop himself from collapsing onto the deck. The sensation of sinking turns his stomach on end.

*Oh, Christ, I'm a dead man. What in hell does this guy want from me anyway? Really, Alexander, are there any more ways you can prove you're a wimp? I don't know if I can even talk to him. My mouth is like sandpaper. I have no spit...*

Cole's obsessive thoughts are finally penetrated by Martone's question.

"What did my niece tell you about this book of hers?"

"Aside from the fact that she wouldn't bring us another manuscript until this one was printed," Cole is puzzled by his question, "absolutely nothing. She walked out. Why?"

Martone leans forward and places his hands on Cole's knees, speaking just loud enough to be heard.

"Because, Mr. Coleman Alexander, Mr. Editor-in-Chief... because you are not going to publish this book."

Cole looks at him, frightened, and totally confused.

"But, why?"

"Why? Because I say so, that's why. And if you do, you have my word that it will be the last book you ever publish. Do I make myself clear?"

For emphasis, Martone presses his thumbs into the flesh on the inside of Cole's knees, surprising him with the power of his grip.

"Ow," he groans and reaches to remove Martone's hands. The pain increases. Cole tries to pull his legs away.

"Do I make myself clear?" Martone repeats, squeezing tighter.

Defeated and hating himself for his cowardice, Cole hangs his head.

"Yes," he whispers. Tears well in his eyes. "Perfectly."

Cole slides sideways on the sail bag, leans well over the rail and retches into the sea.

# TWENTY-THREE

LUCAS TRAVERS, THE LIMO DRIVER, is packing their few pieces of luggage into the trunk while DJ, Kate, and Tuck make themselves comfortable in the back seat, ready for the short drive to the airport.

"Well, well, well. You two look positively blissful," DJ teases.

"One can only try, Miss Scarlet," drawls Kate. "One can only try one's very best to rid the world of lesbian bed death. Isn't that correct, my darling Audre?" She lays her head on Tuck's shoulder and swoons. "Ah, but we have achieved nirvana. Now, if we could only save Tara as well."

DJ rolls her eyes and laughs. "I'd better get you out of the south before you get too attached to that accent, my friend. Your poor clients will be so confused. Only Tuck and I know you can carry on like this for weeks. I'm thinking Ireland, Italy, France… remember? And we were there for a month, then. You haven't even been here for twenty-four hours and listen to you."

Kate grins. "It's my precious musical ears, darling. Can't be helped."

"No, it's your warped sense of humor, my friend," DJ says with a smile. "And, thank goodness we've all got one. I certainly could never have made it this far without mine, could I?"

Travers starts the engine, then turns and slides the glass enclosure open enough to ask the ladies if they are all set.

"We are indeed, Mr. Travers. Thank you. It's the same terminal as yesterday." DJ responds.

"Please, call me Lucas, if you will. And I am so grateful to you Miss

Brava, and you too, Miss Tucker. My wife was just thrilled with the book and it surely lifted her spirits like nothing else has seemed able to do."

"You're so welcome, Lucas. I'm glad it's a help to her. And if you give me your address, I'll send down a copy of my next book in that series when it's published, as well."

"That would be a blessing, thank you. And Doris loved the bear as well, Miss Tucker. The nurses have told me that she cries most nights, and they try to sit with her when they can. They think she's lonely. You know, we've been married forty-six years and, except for my service years we've never even slept apart 'til this happened. That bear will keep her company and remind her of me and give her some comfort at night 'til I can get her home again. So, I thank you all from the bottom of my heart and I will pray for you every day."

He turns back to the wheel and says, "Now, let's get you where you're going." He pulls slowly into Saturday mid-morning traffic in downtown Atlanta, and heads for Hartsfield Airport.

"What a sweet man," Kate says, moved by his sincerity. "And I hope you remember to bring me a teddy bear, too, when we've been together forty more years." She smiles sweetly at Tuck.

A cell phone rings and all three women rummage for theirs until the unmistakable refrain of Ode to Joy is recognized as Tuck's. She has a text message from the airlines that their flight has been delayed for two hours.

"Oh, groan," DJ says. "I hate sitting around the airport bored to tears, especially today when I'm dying to sink my teeth into Raymond. This is going to set everything back a few hours on the other end too. Damn."

Kate asks DJ if she wants to tell Lucas to take them back to the hotel.

DJ's reaction is strong. "Absolutely not," she says, "we have to keep this moving forward."

"Besides," she continues conspiratorially, "wait until you hear what happened at breakfast. And, speaking of breakfast, I'm starving. I never really got to eat anything. We'll have time now for me to get something in the airport."

Both Kate and Tuck are looking at her.

"What?" she asks, smiling slyly, fully aware that she has dangled a huge carrot and will hold it out there as long as she can.

"What?" she asks again, aiming for innocent but landing solidly in guilty. She laughs. Both friends glare at her.

"Give. Give it up right now or pay the consequences," Kate threatens, laid back southern drawl giving way to south Boston rigid resolve.

"Okay. Okay. You'll never guess what most of Chrissie's whining was really all about," DJ teases. She turns a bit sideways in the car in order to be able to see both of them at once.

"Probably that underneath all that blatant hostility lies an unrequited adolescent crush on me?" questions Kate, sarcastically.

"Ha," Tuck responds. "Of course it would have to be about you, wouldn't it? No way. My guess is that she finally admitted to being a self-centered jealous pain in the ass who-"

Kate interrupts Tuck's comment. "Hey, are you calling me narcissistic? I am so not," she crosses her legs and flips her wrist at Tuck. "What I am, my dearly beloved, in case you haven't noticed, is unerringly accurate."

"And, once again, you prove my point. But, alas, all is not always about you," Tuck places a finger against Kate's lips. "Now, shush. How about we ask the person who was there to tell us exactly what Chris was whining about? All this speculation is-"

DJ interrupts. "Hey, forget that for a minute, you two. I've got a great idea." She taps on the glass partition to get Lucas's attention. He presses a button on the dash and the panel slides left.

"Yes ma'am?"

"Lucas. Our plane has been delayed by a couple of hours. How far out of the way would it be if we made a stop at your wife's nursing home and went in for a quick hello? Could we do that without too much trouble?" asks DJ.

She turns to her friends. "That okay with the both of you?"

Lucas is having trouble keeping his eyes on the road and is instead checking DJ out in the rear-view mirror. "You'd be willing to do that?" he sounds uncertain that she means it.

"I can't think of anything that would give me more pleasure right now, Lucas. Do you think we would be permitted to stop in for a few minutes?"

"Oh, yes, of course we would. They like it when folks come in, and I need to tell you this will have Doris up and doing the two-step in a sweet second. Lord, she is just going to fall out when she sees who I'm bringing in. I'll just turn around here, take a few minutes on 104 and we'll be right there. God bless you, miss. God bless you." Lucas attends to the driving once again.

"You wouldn't be trying to rack up some points with heaven by doing this, would you?" Kate questions. "You know, in case it gets tough later today dealing with Ray, or tomorrow with your mother? Maybe?"

"Maybe," responds DJ. "It can't hurt. And, besides, it's such a simple thing. And look how happy it's already made one person."

They sit quietly for a few moments. "Sometimes," DJ adds, almost to herself. "Sometimes that's all that really matters."

"What's that?" Kate isn't sure she heard what DJ said. She leans in closer.

This time DJ speaks in a forlorn whisper.

"Sometimes making one person happy is just enough all by itself."


THE HOUR THEY SPEND at the nursing home is one of pure delight. Doris has all she can do to stop from dancing, which, of course, would do more damage to her hip. But DJ is allowed to push her from room to room in a wheel chair, teddy bear on her lap, and then into the recreation room to show off her new, and very famous guest.

Turns out DJ Brava is a big hit among the readers. She's even more popular with those who listen on tape. A staff member rushes to pull all their copies of her books from the library shelves so that she can sign each of them. DJ borrows Doris's copy of her most recent book and does a brief reading, then spends half an hour answering questions about writing, and of course, discussing the strange and romantically star-crossed life of her heroine Serpentine.

Lucas, Kate, and Tuck soak all this in from the sidelines. Lucas has not taken his eyes off Doris, and grins with gratitude at DJ for the enormous boost this has given to his wife's morale.

Both Kate and Tuck are themselves awestruck. The change they see in DJ as she careens around corners pushing Doris, full of joy and delighting in this simple pleasure is fascinating to them. But it is the self-assurance, the confidence and poise as she stands in front of the small group and talks about her writing, the creative idea process, and of her nemesis Serpentine that has them mesmerized.

DJ has always, always, hated the part of her contract that involves book signings, interviews and interactions with the public of any kind. She does it, of course. It is required. But she is unremittingly nervous and abrupt and so very much out of her comfort zone that it is hard for her friends to watch, especially when she is on TV.

But here, in this place where she has impulsively chosen to come, where her presence and her work are being celebrated by octogenarians and recuperating injured elderly, here DJ has found a moment of pure inner peace with herself. She laughs, and dances Doris around in circles. She's wired and energized, kicking up her heels and having a ball. Happy. Carefree.

"Something is finally letting go in her," Kate whispers to Tuck. "And I think it's a very good thing. The book, this trip, her sisters, and what we still have to do in Boston and Providence—somehow it is setting her free."

"About god-damned time, too," she adds, as her eyes brim with tears.

"WHEW," DJ flops back into the seat of the limo and pulls the belt across her chest. "That was fantastic. Exhausting, but wonderful. I had a ball. And I'm starving." She rummages through her purse. "I thought I had a scone in here somewhere. Ah, here we go."

The napkin-wrapped scone has been mashed to crumbs for the most part, but DJ manages to scoop up what she can salvage and enjoy a few hearty bites.

"Anyone have anything to drink?" she asks, brushing crumbs from her lap. "I still need to get something more substantial at the airport."

Lucas directs her to a button on the rear side door. A false front slides upwards to reveal a small mini-bar complete with ice and chilled water bottles.

"Ah, relief." DJ downs half the bottle. "Want anything?" she turns to her friends and sees they are smiling at her. "What?" she looks down at her jacket. "Did I spill it?" Finding no apparent water stains, she shrugs. "Okay, what? What did I do?"

"What you did, my dear," Tuck reaches over and ruffles DJ's hair, "was make a whole bunch of people a whole lot happier than they ever expected to be this morning. That's what you did. And it was beautiful to watch."

"You think they liked that we stopped in?"

"Liked it? They loved that you stopped in," Kate says. "And look at Lucas. He's had that grin on his face for the past hour."

DJ shifts a bit in her seat to catch Lucas in the rear view mirror. Sure enough, he's beaming. Lucas spots her and gives her a quick thumbs up and mouths a 'thank you'.

"You were just the cat's meow in there, Deej. You rocked their world.

You made Doris Queen for a Day and gave them something great to talk about for weeks." Kate pumps her fist and offers DJ a high five.

DJ thinks quietly as they move slowly through traffic on the Airport Parkway. "You know," she finally offers, "I'm beginning to believe that something good happened inside me when I dumped that manuscript on Cole's desk. I don't think I ever realized how plugged up I was with my past. I literally feel as if I pulled the stopper out of the bathtub and a whole bucket of old stuff is starting to drain out. Finally."

She pushes out a huge breath. "Not that it didn't open another whole spigot of poop that I now have to deal with. But, it's such blessed relief to finally have written it down and gotten what was on the inside, out. I didn't expect it to feel quite like this, but I think I like it."

Kate says nothing more than "Hum" and a peaceful silence falls around them. DJ closes her eyes and feels herself relax, swaying just a bit with the rhythm of the road.

Within a minute she sits up, startling Tuck and Kate. "Whoa, I almost forgot. Would you believe that Christine is having an affair?" DJ slaps her knee and laughs. "Damned if that one didn't take me by surprise."

Both Kate and Tuck explode with a resounding "What!"

Kate practically chokes on her laughter. "That stinging nettle of a sister of yours actually found someone besides Garret who is willing to spend time with her? *Quelle surprise!*"

"Oh, stop it, Kate. She's in quite a mess and I told her you'd be willing to get a referral for her, and then for her and Garret to get some counseling. She's really in a lot of pain over this, first of all. And, second, I think the move to Ann Arbor has been pretty difficult. She left everything familiar behind. Too much, I think, and she's miserable with nothing to do or no one to do it with. Garret is so absorbed with his new job. I think she wanted a chance to talk to Sarah and me about that last night, and then I come in full of my own stuff, dragging the both of you along, and, I don't know, she just got overwhelmed with feeling jealous or something. It was too much for her."

When DJ stopped to think and take a deep breath, Kate jumped right into the space she left open.

"She's living in Ann Arbor, one of the most happening college communities on the planet, and she can't find something to do except have an affair? What the hell is wrong with that girl? If she were in South Bend, or if she were in Champagne, I could almost see her point, but she's sitting in the middle of art and music and theater and politics, to say nothing of world class sports. What *is* wrong with her?"

She looks at Tuck. "We absolutely loved it there, didn't we honey? Hell, if there hadn't been so many damn social workers per square inch in town, we'd still be there. And if Chris wasn't doing anything or going anywhere, how did she meet this guy anyway? He's not a colleague of Garret's is he?"

DJ's face reddens. "Um… no," she says, looking at the floor. "She met him in the grocery store, in the produce department, no less. They were comparing asparagus, and…"

"Ach," Kate cackles. "You are making this up. This cannot be true. It's way too Serpentine-what's-her-name."

DJ raises her right hand. "God's honest truth. And even Serpentine is not that cliché. Which you would know if you ever read one of my books."

"Wait a minute. Wait a minute," Kate protests. "Don't make this about me. We're talking about your sister, not about me." She stops, then starts right up again. "And besides, I have, too, read your books, most of them anyway. And you've always known they just aren't my style. Until right this second, you've always said you didn't mind," Kate bristles.

Tuck intervenes. "You know what, Katie? DJ really doesn't mind. She's just pressing one of your all-too-visible buttons. And do you know why? Because you are absolutely right. This *is* about Christine, so let's see what we can do to help, okay?"

"And now you're patronizing me, Tuck, and you know I hate when you do that," Kate responds by glowering at her partner.

"It's exactly what you need right this minute, so be quiet." Tuck pats Kate's hand and turns to DJ. "We know a number of really good therapists in Ann Arbor. Give us a few minutes when we get back to the office and we'll put together some names for you to give to Chris."

"That would be great, thanks. I'd like to get back to her as soon as possible so she'll at least feel as if I really heard her.

"So you think that she was being more needy than vicious last night?" Kate asks, then whispers, "Because, she really was a total piss-ant."

Tuck can't believe that Kate is still being so obnoxious.

"Will you just stop? Thank you." She turns to DJ. "Does it change what she said about Raymond at all?"

The response is firm. "Oh, no, there's no doubt that Sarah and Chris both agree about what they think Raymond did. And they sure as hell had something to say this morning about what a jerk I am to go see him. But, no, what I mean is that Christine's hissy fit was really about her own life and what a mess it is. It just all got to be too much. In fact, this morning, she told me to tell you how grateful she is that you two are my friends."

Kate's response of "Yada, yada, yada," was drowned out by Lucas's announcement that they had arrived at their terminal.


TUCK ALL BUT DISAPPEARS as they line up to go through security, until Kate spots her waiting patiently three stations away.

"Yoo-hoo," she waves frantically. "Tuck", she hollers, pointing to the shorter line she and DJ are in. This, of course, prompts a stampede to Kate's line by seventeen other people. But not Tuck. She smiles happily, shrugs her shoulders, and moves forward in her own chosen line.

They meet up again at the gate, Kate anxiously waiting to question Tuck.

"What happened to you, hon? I thought you were right behind us. Is everything okay?"

The Boston passengers are jammed into every available seat on the concourse, limiting privacy, so Tuck leans in to Kate and DJ and whispers, "I wanted to be wanded."

Kate pulls back. "You wanted *what?*"

"Wanded. I wanted to be wanded by Kendra's sister. You know, my friend the bartender from last night? The one who said the storm was over? She has a sister who's a TSA here and told her I'd be coming through. She's one of us. And I thought it might be fun," Tuck is enjoying the astonished look on her lover's face.

"Turns out I was right," she adds. "It was lots of fun. And the pat-down was the absolute best," she teases, grabbing her heart and pretending to swoon.

DJ looks at Kate and sees her sporting a pout far exceeding anything her sister Sarah could produce on her best, or worst, day.

Tuck continues. "And don't you go thinking I have one of your so-called 'wandering eyes'," she says to Kate, "because I do not. What I do have, however, is a highly refined, goddess-given appreciation for the female form. Especially yours, my dear," she adds, with a smile meant to soothe the savage beast beside her.

It works—almost. "Well then, how come you didn't tell me? You always tell me," Kate whines. "I could use a good pat-down, too, you know?"

"Sometimes, my darling Kate, it's good in a relationship for each person to do some things on her own. It's what all the best straight magazines say at any rate. And, besides, I'm more than willing to share her technique with you when we get home. How's that sound?"

"Oh, yum, okay then. Good idea," Kate finally smiles.

DJ shakes her head and mutters quietly. "You two are something else."

They find the nearest Arrival/Departure board and discover that their plane is delayed yet again, so the three women stroll the concourse looking at things they neither need nor want. When DJ's growling stomach begs to be attended to they find a Yummy Wraps near their gate and make themselves comfortable with iced tea and sandwiches.

"At the risk of starting trouble," Tuck says between bites, "I think we need to strategize before we go ahead with this foolish plan to see your uncle, DJ."

DJ stares at her. "Foolish? I thought we settled all this last night. Besides you're the one who said it was the only way to find out the truth."

"I know, I know," Tuck says, "and I'm sorry but... Hell, no, I'm not sorry."

She drops her wrap onto the paper plate.

"Look. You both know I'm not an alarmist about stuff, but this whole situation is creeping me out. DJ, I don't know what your sisters said to you this morning, but if they told you it's a dumb thing to do, I say right on, because it is. If it was my idea, then it was a stupid one."

"What brought this on, Tuck?" Kate asks. "You never mentioned this to me."

"What brought it on was an attack of good old common sense. Why in hell isn't this scaring the crap out of all of us?" Tuck looks at DJ. "Seriously, this isn't any longer about some image of turning over rocks you woke up with yesterday morning. This is real life crazy shit."

Tuck picks up her sandwich, looks at it, then drops it again. With it, she drops her voice so low she is now whispering. She moves her chair closer to the table so they can hear her.

"This is about murder, for god's sake. Real bones and skeletons and secrets. What the hell are we thinking, going in there and accusing him of killing people? *That* guy? We'll be lucky if we get to walk out of there."

"He won't hurt us," DJ says. "He has never hurt me." She is adamant.

Tuck cracks her knuckles and rubs her forehead. Kate reaches to still her hands, but Tuck pulls away.

"Oh, really," she says to DJ. "You're so sure he won't hurt you." She leans as close to DJ as she can get and takes aim with her words. "Suppose he really did do this, you know, killed all three of his brothers? All of them. What makes you think you're any safer than they were, huh?"

Tuck looks at them, but DJ and Kate are staring at their plates.

"The truth is," she says, "we have no idea at all what he may be capable of. Not even you, DJ. You know and love him simply as your uncle. This other part of him, the one that controls a monumental empire that in all likelihood does have the mob connections your sister suggested, we know nothing about. Absolutely nothing. Maybe his love for you is enough so that he can hear your accusations and not react in a way that hurts you. Maybe not. All I'm saying is that we don't know. And because we don't know, we have to be cautious."

Tuck sits back and lets the barbs hit home. They can hear the first boarding call for their flight, but no one makes a move to respond. They simply sit, stunned, looking at their plates.

"I'm scared, okay?" DJ finally says, still not looking at either of her friends, "but I really, truly, must do this. And I'll do it alone if I have to."

"Whoa," Kate says, "no one is saying anything about deserting you." She glares at Tuck. "Are we, Tuck?"

"No, we're not. But the truth is that we're all scared. And doing things scared is not a safe way to do them," Tuck says. "If I hadn't learned *that* working the inner city as a social worker, then I wouldn't be sitting here now, that's for sure, and neither would you, Katie."

"Well, then, what do you have in mind?" DJ asks. "Because you need to understand, I'm going one way or the other."

"Yes, I hear you," Tuck says, "so I'll tell you what we're going to do. We do what we learned to do years ago. When we get home, we call our answering service, Kate, and we tell them where we're going and when we expect to be back, and we ask them to call us twice this evening at hours we specify. We tell them what to do if we don't respond."

She turns to DJ.

"And we leave a detailed note at the house about where we're going and why." Tuck leans on the last word and repeats it. "*Detailed*, DJ. Agreed?"

DJ and Kate look at Tuck. The second boarding announcement startles them both.

"Agreed?" Tuck asks again, "'cause, if not, I'm not going."

There's a sad overtone of resignation, and relief as well, in the way DJ nods her head.

Twenty minutes later they board the Boston-bound plane where they settle into first class seats, each woman in her own way mentally preparing for the confrontation with Raymond.

# TWENTY-FOUR

COLE HAS MADE HIS WAY DOWN to the galley where he has cleaned up a bit after his ordeal. Face washed and teeth brushed, he now sits on the lid of the head, fingers massaging his aching temples. He is engaged in a one-sided, silent war with himself, and his self-esteem is taking a serious beating.

*You're an idiot. You know that, don't you? You just made an absolute ass of yourself, puking on your own boat like a crybaby creampuff. And what the hell were you thinking, anyway? They can't get rid of you. They need you. All three of them. Laurel and Hardy up there couldn't get this boat back to the dock by themselves if it was ten yards off shore, floating on a tether and had a winch pulling it in.*

He could feel the boat pitching hard with the waves and wondered what was going on above deck, but was not yet ready to face Martone and company.

*All right then, game on. I owe it to DJ to try one more time to find out what this is all about. Hell, I owe it to myself. Damned if I'll stay out here another three hours and still not have a flaming clue what this is really all about. Nothing about this makes any sense to me.*

The boat hikes over hard to starboard and Cole slides halfway off the lid.

*Damn. Now they're screwing with my boat! I'd better get up there. Okay, Alexander, be firm, but don't be stupid. And stop acting like such a disgusting wimp. God, I hate myself.*

As he comes up the gangway, Cole can see the sails hanging as limp and empty of air as they had been when he went below. Tony is now unsteadily at the wheel and Vinny is again attending to Martone and talking into his cell at the same time.

Cole checks the horizon, searching for the lighthouse. He can barely make out its tip, well off to starboard at about their four-o'clock position.

"What the hell!" Cole explodes, giving Tony a shove and grabbing the wheel. He swings the boat around, taking dead aim for the light. Tony ducks, barely in time to avoid being swept overboard by the boom.

"I said to keep the lighthouse at one o'clock. Can't you idiots tell time, or do you only do digital? Morons. Where the hell were you trying to get to anyway, the North Pole? Christ!"

Tony has taken umbrage at Cole's rebuke and the near miss by the boom. He reaches to grab Cole by the collar, but a raised hand from his boss stops him short and he drops onto the cockpit bench.

Cole's actions have oddly managed to calm his nerves, and as he maneuvers the boat toward shore he feels his confidence growing. He turns to address Martone and notices that the man is smiling at him.

Fighting a sinking sensation once again in the pit of his stomach, Cole grips the wheel tightly and stares straight ahead to avoid Martone's look.

"I'm taking my boat back to the mooring, Raymond. This little pleasure cruise is over. And once and for all I want to know what the hell is going on here?"

Cole doesn't wait for an answer, just charges on.

"You wanted to scare the piss out of me? Well, congratulations. You did. Hope it made your day. Hell, you've been haunting my dreams for twenty years! That ought to make you positively orgasmic."

He pushes out a breath almost strong enough to fill the sails then keeps right on ranting.

"And here's a bulletin for you, Raymond. Stan and I have every intention of publishing that manuscript, whether you like it or not. You know why, Raymond?"

Again, Cole neither waits for an answer nor does he look at Martone.

"No? I'll tell you why. Because none of this is about you or what you want, Raymond. It's about DJ. It's about her and what she wants. It always has been. That's what you just don't get, isn't it?"

This time, Cole turns to look directly at Martone. "I don't know what your problem is and frankly I no longer care. DJ has written an amazingly powerful autobiography that she wants us to publish. And we will. And,

here's another thing: you can threaten me and my publishing house until the cows come home or until we give in and give up—whatever may
come first. But the bottom line is that DJ is determined to get that book
published. Given who she is, you can bet your ass that sooner or later
someone will publish it. Good luck trying to threaten all of us, Raymond.
But DJ is our author. She's given us many great novels, and we will give her
this. So the sooner you get over yourself and get out of her way, the better.
Is all this clear enough for you to understand?"

Cole is sweating again. Exertion from his outburst has raised his blood
pressure and turned his face the color of ripe plums.

"Now," he says, "as captain of this vessel, I am going to lower the sails.
Vinny, would you please take the helm and hold her steady on this course
while I make my way to the bow?"

Out of the corner of his eye, he sees Martone give a small nod of assent to Vincent who changes places with Cole at the wheel. This time Cole
intentionally places one full hand on Vinny's back and points toward the
lighthouse with the other.

"See that, dead ahead? Aim there. That's all you need to do." Cole ends
the comment with a strong slap to Vinny's back and heads along the side
to the bow, trying valiantly to ignore the rapid quivering of the snake tattoo on Vinny's right bicep.

When Cole has secured both the jib and the mainsail, he stows the sail
bags in the galley, grabs four beers from the ice box and comes back up on
deck, doling out a bottle to each of his crew.

He sits next to Martone on the bench and says, "Gets kind of hot out
here without a good breeze. Have to stay hydrated. Nice to have a brew at
the end of the trip."

Martone's smile of amusement has not changed. Now he shakes his
head slowly.

"My, my, my, Coleman, you certainly do have a bit of a backbone after
all. I was wondering just how long it would take you to give up the spine-
less jellyfish routine and grow some balls."

Cole stretches his legs out in front of him and takes a long pull on his
beer.

"So, all this has been just to amuse yourself, then? How very noble
of you. And here I was thinking you actually were a gentleman after all.
More's the pity, I say."

"It is totally unnecessary to get sarcastic. And it would be most unfortunate if we find we cannot work this little problem out together, now wouldn't it?" Martone asks.

"See, now, Raymond, this is the part that confuses me." Cole puts his beer on the deck and opens his left palm to Martone.

"On the one hand, you seem like a totally decent guy with a great command of the language and some measure of refinement. That's on the one hand. However," and here Cole lays open his right palm, "on the other hand, you threaten and terrorize and act like a goomba leftover from the days the mob ruled Boston."

Cole looks at Martone and hunches both shoulders. "So, which is it? I really would like to know. And what does any of it have to do with your niece? I know you've been reading what she wrote. Jesus, Raymond, I've been an editor for thirty years and I've never read a more painful or powerful piece of work. Don't you think she deserves her day in the sun after all the years she's spent underground with all this? I admire her. I admire her courage and tenacity. She survived stuff that would crush most people's spirit. She survived, and look at what she's been able to achieve in her life. And she credits you with helping her. How can that be a problem for you? For God's sake, man, can't you see how important this is to her?"

Cole has removed his hat and is working his fingers around the brim and across the red B applique. This time he speaks gently to Martone.

"Listen, Raymond. This woman is nothing short of a miracle. I want… I need to help her get this book published. She deserves no less from me. I'm her editor. I owe her the respect. It's… it's… I don't know. Just respect."

Martone places a hand on Cole's knee, causing him to flinch and quickly move his legs away from the old man's reach.

"You're in love with my niece, aren't you, Cole?" Martone asks, suddenly quite serious.

"Do I love her? You bet your ass I do." Cole is twirling his cap between his legs with one finger hooked into the sizing band in the back.

"Am I in love with her? No, I'm not." He looks at Martone and shakes his head sadly. "I floated that boat past her a long time ago, but she wasn't interested. Can't blame her really. I'm not what she wants. Or what she needs, for that matter. As you can tell from our encounters, I'm not enough of a stand-up kind of a guy. Put another way, I seem to lack the courage of my convictions in some major ways that women in general find off-putting. Or so I have been told. More than once."

Cole wipes his brow before replacing his cap. He tastes his beer and finding it too warm, pours it over the side and tucks the empty bottle between two cushions on the bench.

"I'll tell you one thing, though, Raymond. Come hell or high water, or you, I'm going to do what any good editor would do when given a manuscript of this quality. I am going to fight like hell to get it printed, even if I have to fight you. And then I am going to arrange the largest and most prominent book tour that we have ever organized, and I am going to see to it that her book sells well into the millions of copies."

Cole turns and faces Martone. "You can't stop me. I won't let you. Dead or alive, I will see to it that this book is published."

Vinny calls Cole's attention to the fact that the full lighthouse is now clearly visible just off the bow. Cole rises to take the wheel once again. He remains surprised that Martone has said virtually nothing in response to his comments.

*In for a dime, in for a dollar,* Cole thinks. *Might as well turn it in and twist it.*

"And just one more thing, Raymond, while we're on the subject. You need to take this up with DJ. Whatever your issues are—and I have asked and not been answered enough to believe you're never going to tell me—whatever your issues are, you need to deal with her. If she says to pull the book, then no matter how much I want to publish it, I won't. I can promise you that much. That's what I mean by respect."

Still nothing from Martone, who is once again staring across the water.

"Just do me one favor first," Cole continues. "Before you speak with her, read Chapter Twenty. I know you haven't read that far yet. If you can read that chapter, and still think it shouldn't be published... Well, there's something seriously wrong with you. That's all I can say."

At the rate they are motoring toward shore, Cole figures they'd be out about another hour. Plenty of time for Martone to finish that chapter and then some, if he were only so inclined.

Ten minutes or so pass before he notices Martone pick up the manuscript and flip ahead to open it at what Cole can only hope is Chapter Twenty.

# TWENTY-FIVE

## 20 • Peeling the Onion

*I do not quite understand how it is that most children survive abuse. That some do not is tragic. That so many do, and go on to do so well, is nothing short of miraculous.*

*I know there were many days I could not even see myself as having a tomorrow, never mind a future that spanned any further than the grade I was in in school. The question frequently put to me by my parents' friends about what I wanted to be or do when I grew up was so far beyond what I could contemplate that I might as well have been asked to believe people could walk on the moon.*

*And yet...*

*In my external life—the one where I lived with my family, went to church and school and suffered abuse—I could not envision any other reality than the one in which I felt myself bound as surely as if my legs were caught in a game trap, and I the unlucky fox.*

*In my internal life, however, I somehow gained the capacity over time to believe in better. Perhaps because there was always some form of force used, something that resulted in pain or fear of pain, that I was able to perceive some small fractures in the foundation of my experience. Enough, at least, to allow me to embrace a belief that what was happening to me was wrong, and that I not only deserved better, but that if I could just survive long enough, I myself was capable of behaving better than I was being treated.*

*The fractures were events that happened outside of me, outside of the daily events of my home life. They were often small things such as a word here, a smile there, an action or correction—a series of things that began so slowly as to be almost unnoticeable, like a thin trickle of water working its way into a tiny fissure in a house foundation that, over time and with heat and cold, expands and cracks the foundation open to receive even more copious amounts of water.*

*It is a fact that I have survived. It is a fact that I am well, and doing well. And perhaps this can be attributed simply to the fact that I was born with a determined constitution, an innate sense of resilience, or a strong survival instinct. This is entirely possible.*

*And yet…*

*I cannot discount or overlook the dozens of ways the world outside my house gave me messages about my value and worth—messages that ran so counter to those I received inside my family, that in spite of the fact that I initially rejected them with the thought of "You wouldn't say that if you really knew me", eventually I could not help but consider them.*

*They began to happen at a time in my life when I believed right down to the toes of my white Ked sneakers, that I was alone in the world and that there was no one who was for me. Many, many years before I understood, or even heard the expression "If I am not for myself, who will be for me?"; many, many years before I had learned to believe in myself, before I relearned how to trust others; many, many years before I would come to understand the role my brother and sisters, my relatives, my teachers, and my friends played in my survival—small things were happening that helped make my survival possible.*

*Of all the women in my family, the one whom I would come to understand loved me unconditionally was my great-aunt Lena. Along with my grandmother, who was her sister, she left the hill country of Italy for a better life here in America. She never married, and my grandmother was widowed early, so Lena worked both outside the home and inside as a babysitter and housekeeper.*

*As a young child, she was my best and only friend, and the weekends I spent with her in my grandmother's first floor tenement provided me with safety and a chance to simply be a kid. We'd take the street car to Federal Hill where we shopped in stores with windows hung with bulging gourds of provolone and salami, and where the streets were pungent with the smells of ba-*

sil and oregano and simmering tomato gravy. Our last stop of the day would be at Caesar the Butcher who would wring the neck of the fattest chicken and wrap it for us to pluck at home. As we said goodbye, he would pass his hand alongside my head and pull a quarter from behind my ear. "How did you do that?" I shyly asked each time, my eyes wide in wonder.

I was duckling and Lena was duck, as I helped her turn soil for her garden, followed her with clothes pins as she hung laundry, stirred the batter for fried yellow zucchini blossoms, sweated as she cooked and jarred bottles of tomatoes.

She worked as a candy dipper, and her hands held that deliciously sensuous chocolate smell throughout the weekend, from the time I ran to the corner to meet her bus on Friday evening, until I reluctantly returned home on Sunday afternoon. She would hold my face to say goodbye and I would breathe in the milk chocolate scent of her as a promise of next weekend and a confirmation of how much I meant to her.

When my father beat me, when the pain was so much I cried out for help, it was always Lena's name I called. I would quake in my bed, as far from him as I could get, trying to force myself into the crack between the bed and the wall, and I would cry for her.

"Lena," I would wail. "I want Lena. Please come, Lena. Please come." And he would hit me harder, enraged that I would call for her—of all people.

Could I have survived without the reprieve my grandmother's home and Lena's love and attention provided me?

I do not know.

There were occasions at my grandmother's when my uncle, her only son, was visiting that my safety even there was uncertain. I came in through the back way one Sunday after church, stepping into the kitchen and the familiar rich smells of garlic and chicken and ziti, to be quite suddenly grabbed by him and pushed up against the fridge where he ran his hands over my breasts and forced his tongue into my mouth. He shoved me away when he heard Lena calling from the living room, "Is that you, Donna? Come, I show you something."

I made every effort to avoid him after that. But I was still just a child, and one day was startled by him as I ran into the basement to find Lena. He blocked my passage on the stairs, and when I tried to duck under his arm, I accidently stepped on his foot. He swore at me and raised his arm to hit me. I cowered and waited for the blow, but Lena appeared from around the corner and grabbed his arm, twisting it back and away from me. He practically fell *down the steps, but she held on and put her face in his and said, "You no hurt the child."*

*"You no hurt the child."*

*Until that moment, that precious, unscripted moment in time, there had never been anyone in my life offering a message that was so clearly the opposite of how I was being treated, that to this day I can feel the pleasure of it wash over me like a spring rain full of promise.*

*"You no hurt the child."*

*I mattered to someone.*

*Lena was for me.*

---

*I learned early on that my home was not a safe place. School all week, church on Sundays, and frequent weekends at my grandmother's house were the only refuges for me when I was very young. It was by watching my brother, however, that I soon discovered two very effective alternatives to which I fled with all the force of a ballistic missile seeking its target. Sports and friendships.*

*Unlike many families in which abuse occurs, mine was not isolated or removed from people or places where the internal machinations might be discovered. Both of my parents had solid friendships and they socialized often in small intimate gatherings or multi-family events. It simply never occurred to us to say anything about how we were being treated.*

*I believe that my parents expected and encouraged us to have friends, and to have friends to our home. At one point I realized that most of my friends had no siblings—or just one—and while I relished spending time in the quiet of their homes, they frequently begged to spend time in mine because there was always some kind of action going on, better known as chaos.*

*As very young children we played outdoors almost exclusively, with whoever was available, with whatever toys or tools we had or could pretend we had. It could be cold enough to freeze bacon or hot enough to fry it on the sidewalk, but we would stay out, pretending we didn't hear the calls to come in, until the urgency in our parent's voices threatened physical harm if we did not respond.*

*Two of my girlfriends had no fathers, one due to death and the other to divorce. I loved having them over, because they respected no real boundaries with my father. They sat in his chair, they sat on his lap, they gave him lip* when he told them to move—things far too dangerous for me to even contemplate. And they got away with it.

In so many ways, these young women were my salvation. We walked, we listened to music, and we talked. But never, ever, about what we were experiencing at home. I had friends who had mothers addicted to prescription drugs, and fathers addicted to alcohol. Only later in our lives would we find the words and cautiously share them with each other in spite of the years of reality we so consciously ignored day after day.

And then there was the friend whose home I went to after dinner one evening so we could walk together to softball practice. I had no sooner entered their tenement than her father came home, picked up his dinner plate, threw it at her mother, slammed her against the wall and began hitting her. How dare she give him the same thing he had for lunch! We simply picked up our gloves and ball, and left down the back stairs. Not one word was spoken between us about the incident, nor do I remember having any feelings of worry about her having to go back home when practice was over.

I do not know if this was some form of code of silence, or just that each of our particular home lives was all that each of us knew because, back then, we had no information that would have led us to believe that whatever particular hell we lived through every day was anything other than ordinary.

And yet…

Each of my childhood and young adult friends bears some responsibility for my survival. They offered reprieve without even knowing, holding without touching, and healing without condition.

They were my safety net.

They were for me.

———————

Because my father loved sports, my brother hated sports. But when JJ found that sports could get him out of the house, he played. And when he could no longer bear to play, he volunteered to act as team manager. Anything to be out and stay out.

Because my father loved sports and my brother did not, and because I saw that sports got my brother out of the house, I played and loved sports. I cannot remember a time my father refused to allow me to go to practice or to a game—other than the time I dislocated a finger playing basketball about an hour before a softball game. When an x-ray confirmed fracture as well, *he insisted I forego the game. I was slated to pitch that day and, in my own mental universe, not being able to do so ended my one chance to be discovered and be recruited by the famous Connecticut women's softball team, the Raybestos Brakettes. I added to his long list of faults.*

*The one exception to my father's love of sports was basketball, but while he endlessly derided the game and its rules and players, all four of us girls played and practiced and used the two-mile walk to the gym as a ready excuse to leave home right after dinner and be out well past nine a few nights a week. Neither snow, nor sleet, nor... could keep us from these appointed rounds.*

*In summer, I would leave the house by ten, baseball, glove, bat and basketball hanging off me one place or another, holler outside a friend's house until I could find someone to join me, and we would move on to the next friend's house until we had enough kids for a pick-up game. If we tired of one sport, we started another—sometimes tennis or badminton or archery. And that same evening we would play seven innings of softball.*

*My three sisters reached puberty. And when they did, boys, like flocks of pigeons, began falling out of the sky around our house to settle onto our stoop each summer day in great hormonal bursts of music and bragging and vying for position on the step closest to whichever sister was preferred at the moment. As for me, I was either nose-deep in a book at the library or off finding an empty field with my ball and glove. Adolescent rituals such as the ones my sisters embraced so fully, simply passed me by.*

*My friends were my safety net.*

*Sports had my back.*

*My friends were for me.*

---

*I went to a girls' parochial high school which, in and of itself, offered some protection from the social pressures of dating, or of having the right clothes. It was remarkably free of exclusive cliques, rumors and bullying. The nuns were primarily of Irish descent and gave an excellent education for which I have been profoundly grateful—except perhaps for my enduring tendency to pronounce French words with a slight Irish brogue.*

*One teacher in particular, Sister Mary Daniel, impacted my life in ways that went far beyond the high level of education in literature for which she was renowned.*

*I was at the time an acne-ridden, sports-playing, rotund, insecure young woman, decked out in my school uniform, Mary Janes and all. And when she intercepted me that day, I was in the process of chasing a friend through the lunch room, trying to aim a rotten old tennis ball at her head for some un-remembered thing she had recently done. I recall that the ball had spent far too much time in the slobbering mouth of the pastor's bulldog—which was, of course, a huge part of the fun of throwing it in the first place.*

*I was winding up for the pitch, then literally froze in place when her voice cut into my brain, commanding me to "desist". She was, after all, an English teacher and it would have been beneath her standards to have simply said "stop".*

*Head down, ball tucked quickly under my uniform jacket, I turned to face what I thought would be another lecture on decorum. The school was high on decorum then, and my behavior frequently rated far down on the acceptable-level-scale, as evidenced, perhaps, by my actions at that moment.*

*And then she sighed. Deeply. "Donna, Donna, Donna," she began, and I remember thinking, Uh, oh. This cannot be good.*

*And that is all I remember. Her exact words are lost to me. She spoke for only a brief time, quietly and directly into me, about me, about ending the horsing around and getting serious about my studies, about taking myself seriously. Because, she told me, I was someone unique, someone who could achieve whatever I set my mind to, because I was smart, because I was ca-pable of anything, because I had something she called depth of soul, and because she knew I knew I wanted more.*

*Never in my sixteen years had anyone, anyone at all, spoken into the very heart of me like that.*

*How she knew this about me, I do not know. Why she chose that partic-ular day to speak of it, I do not know.*

*What I do know is that in my very bones, from some preverbal place, or from a star I wished upon as a child, there lived within me a belief, a hope perhaps, of something better beyond the existence I was living within my family. To this day, I do not really know how to describe it or exactly how I knew it, only that I became aware of it early in my life.*

*It was a fragile thing, like an elusive Trillium blossom that quickly dies when removed from the plant. And I kept that hope in an envelope, close to my heart, and only allowed myself the briefest of peeks before falling asleep each night.*

*And so it wasn't what Sister Mary Daniel said, or even how she said it. It was that she said it at all. And when she did, her words tore open the slightest corner of the envelope of hope that I held close to my heart. The tearing let out just a wisp of my fear, and let in just a whisper of possibility, and everything about my future changed with that brief encounter.*

*How she even knew that hope existed within me at all did not matter.*

*That she spoke to me the way she did changed me forever.*

*Sister Mary Daniel was for me.*

---

*I realize that I have spoken of my father and uncles as if they were an identical set of ruthless brutes focused on my destruction. In my fear and shame, in fact, I often felt that way.*

*But I had another uncle, their youngest brother, Raymond. He had been ravaged and changed by war. He found a way to have power even in war, and became the go-to person for drugs and porn. He came home and built an empire for himself, garnering control of the entire east coast pornography industry.*

*I was well into my twenties before I understood what he did for a living. But it was even later before the full implications of how adult pornography directly feeds the market for abuse to younger and younger children and women became real for me. I was then, and continue to be, repulsed by these realities.*

*None of these things are secrets about him. None of these things are unknowns. He, and his operations, have been investigated by every level of jurisdiction from local sheriffs to the FBI. And while what he does is reprehensible to me as well as to most of society, information has never been found to suggest that anything he is doing is illegal.*

*This uncle. This often vilified uncle of mine has always, always, been for me.*

*This uncle with the repugnant lifestyle, who makes his money from porn, has never once acted like his brothers toward me.*

*This uncle who came back from war so much less than when he went, who lost so much of his youth and heart and soul, never zipped his love for me into one of those hundreds of body bags and sent it home to someone else's family.*

*When I was angry, this uncle emptied a trash can and turned it bottoms up. He gave me two sticks and played the Beatle's "Maxwell Silver Hammer"* and "Yellow Submarine" as loud as possible on his boom box while I beat the bejesus out of my pain.

And when fear clung to me like scales on a fish, this uncle sat close to my bed and played "Imagine" so softly it calmed my booming heart rate and let the words caress me into a safe and peaceful sleep.

How he appears to the outside world does not concern me. And while nothing that I can say about him is meant to minimize or excuse the dreadfulness of what he does for a living, I do not judge him.

I cannot.

After my father's death, my family and I benefited from his money. He paid for all of our education beyond what scholarships we obtained. When my sister Maggie required treatments and medications and stem cell replacement and home health care and the myriad of ancillary items and services attached to fighting her rare disease, Raymond took care of all of these without question, without hesitation. And if you ask if in those times I gave any thought to where the money came from, I would tell you simply that I did not. I did not.

I have one uncle who did not hurt me.

I have one uncle who is for me.

And I love this uncle.

———————

Perhaps people can indeed survive just about anything if they have someone who is for them. To my knowledge, none of those who were for me had any idea about the painful reality of my childhood. I know I never told them back then. And yet each of them played a crucial role in my survival, in my ability to move past the day-to-day pain and eventually step into a future that held the promise of something better.

I do not think I could have arrived there on my own. I do not believe I had the strength or the vision had it not been for these small lily pads of hope that I hopped on throughout my childhood and adolescence. They managed to hold me up just long enough for me to negotiate my way out of the labyrinth of fear and shame and onto more solid ground.

Eventually, people walked on the moon.

And eventually, I began to believe in myself.

And to this day I believe, "You no hurt the child."

# TWENTY-SIX

OFF TO HIS PORT SIDE, Cole can see the last few J-boats finishing their race and heading for Rockport harbor. It looks to him as if some have given up entirely due to lack of wind power and are running their engines. Boats with a spinnaker still up are sitting calmly atop the water, sails flopping pitifully, crews sitting along the starboard rail with their feet dangling over the side, patiently awaiting the breeze that Cole thinks highly unlikely at this time of day in these waters.

He is lost in the memory of winning this particular regatta last year in unusually high winds and seas, and the pleasant memory of being sprayed with victory champagne makes him smile for the first time all day. Cole is therefore caught by surprise when the urgent sound of a large engine just alongside his stern cuts into his reverie. He looks around frantically, desperate to see if he is about to be rammed by a drunk in a motor boat.

"What the hell…" he starts, and then sees it's the Coast Guard and he's about to be boarded.

"Lay to," the guardsman calls and pulls up alongside. "We're coming aboard."

Cole quickly checks to see if the life vests are under the cushions in the cockpit. They are, but so are three empty beer bottles and Martone's opened but untouched one, wedged into the cushions. Vincent has moved defensively close to his boss and Cole cannot help but see that the snake tattoo is practically jumping off his arm.

Cole cuts the engine and leaves the wheel to swing protective fenders over the side so the Coast Guard boat can tie up with his, thankful for the calm seas and mild swells. Two officers step cautiously from one boat to the other and one—the badge on his shirt says Mendes—offers his credentials to Cole. Both men cast wary glances at Martone and the two oddly clad crew.

Mendes addresses Cole. "Mr. Alexander, we received word earlier today that you might be having some difficulty on your boat. Sorry it took so long to track you down but one of the regatta boats snapped a mast and the sails were dragging over the side. Had to get it towed in and secure the crew. How are you doing? Are things okay here?"

As he speaks, he moves steadily around the cockpit, opening the storage bins and counting life vests. He empties the full beer into the sea, and sends his fellow officer to check below.

"How much beer have you been consuming today, Mr. Alexander?" he asks.

Before Cole can respond, the second officer shouts from below, "Just one six-pack in the fridge here, sir, with two left in the pack. No sign of any empties, bottles or paper."

"Just the one each, sir," Cole finally manages to find his voice. "We're actually heading in ourselves. Had a bit of a problem with the engine early on, but we're in good shape right about now. Thanks anyway."

What Cole is thinking however, is quite different. *This is Stan's doing. I'll bet my job on it. This is his idea of calling in the cavalry and coming to the rescue without having to do anything himself. In the meantime, he's set me up for things to get much worse with these guys. And I'm not thinking about the Coast Guard. Cripes. Martone's sitting there smiling again, and Mutt and Jeff look like gangsta cartoons with their hairy belly buttons showing and… Oh what the hell. Could this day get any worse for me? Really?*

The guardsman maneuvers Cole up to the bow to inspect the rigging. He whispers to Cole that he is well aware of who the old man is, and that the call to their Boston office made it clear that these men might be giving him trouble.

"So, I'm asking you again, Mr. Alexander. Is everything okay here on your boat?"

Cole grabs the rigging and braces himself to roll with the wake of a passing boat, noticing that more boats are heading their way to check out the Coast Guard action. He takes his time to think about how best to answer the question. Every fiber in his body wants nothing more than to be rescued by these officers, to leap across to the gun on the bow of the Coast Guard boat, aim it at his own beloved boat and blow it and the three men in it all to hell and gone. Either that or leap into this guy's arms and cry like a baby.

He removes his cap, releasing his hair, and nervously runs a hand across his scalp.

"That would have been my boss who called this morning. He was on the phone and my *guest* and I had just had a serious disagreement. Stan was concerned for my safety. But I promise you, things are fine. I know they look like hell," Cole tries humor and a reassuring smile, "but they came up from the city and had nothing suitable for sailing. The worst part is that neither one of the big guys can tell the difference between the bow and their own asshole. Thankfully, it's been an easy day out here."

That last comment gets a laugh out of the officer.

"My house and dock are just over there at three o'clock," Cole continues. "We can make that in about twenty minutes. So thanks for your concern, but we really will be fine. I'll call Stan as soon as we dock and let him know. I really appreciate your help."

Officer Mendes steps across to the bow of his own boat. "We'll just escort you in, Mr. Alexander. We're going that way anyway. And I'll be leaving my second officer on board until you dock."

He calls to his officer. "Cast us off, Max. We'll pick you up on shore."

As Cole turns the motor on and sets a course toward home, he can feel the glares of fury from Martone and Vinny boring into him like light sabers. Tony, on the other hand, is fairly useless. The pitching motion of dip-and-climb, dip-and-climb, created by the wakes of other boats including the rigid Coast Guard zodiac right alongside, coupled with the fact that they had been lying dead in the water at the total mercy of the swells, has left him greener than ever and doubled over, clutching his stomach.

Cole couldn't help but think *Now there's a guy who's a great chef, but a total fuck-up as a sailor.*

Tying up at his dock is much easier with Max's assistance, especially since Cole's crew members remain rooted in their respective seats until the zodiac is well on its way again. Cole is a bit puzzled by this, especially since Tony has been looking at solid land as if it's his only salvation, but he understands as soon as he sees Vinny remove Martone's coat jacket from its hiding place against the gunwale. The jacket is heavy with three guns and Cole's cell phone, and makes a solid thunking sound as it accidently hits the deck.

*Humph. Small wonder they were looking like deer in the headlights when* the Guard was aboard, Cole thinks. *Now how in hell am I going to get rid of them? I'm sick to death of their silent stares and twitching tattoos.*

His musing is interrupted by the ringing of Vinny's cell phone which he answers with a sharp, "What?" He says four more words, "Yeah. When? Got it," then hangs up and speaks privately to Martone.

The old man struggles slowly to his feet and requires the assistance of both his men to negotiate the portable steps that Cole provides for the short climb up to the dock. He heads toward the house, supported by Vinny on one side and Tony on the other, then stops and sends Tony back for the manuscript which he has left on the cockpit bench.

Cole remains on his boat and begins to clean up when Martone calls to him.

"Coleman," he says. "I wish to speak with you. Quickly, if you don't mind."

*Oh, crap. Now, what? Why can't they just leave me be?* "Be right there," he calls and finishes coiling his lines and checking to ensure that the fenders are hanging correctly. He gives his boat a fond pat as he steps off the bow and onto the dock, striding quickly to catch up with Martone.

To Cole's surprise, Martone heads straight for his limo where Vinny helps him into the back seat. Tony is directed to follow the limo in his own car, which Cole now spots tucked alongside the beach roses off the edge of the porch.

Cole is told to get in the back seat with Martone.

"Oh, now, wait just a minute here," he protests, fear once again gripping him around the gut. "I'm not willing to keep this charade going any-"

He is interrupted by Martone. "Please, Coleman. I only wish to speak with you here in the drive. I have a time constraint and am not feeling well. Please get in and let us be finished with this business, which, I assure you is not a charade. I shan't keep you long."

*Shan't? Cole thinks to himself. Shan't? What kind of a pompous asshole says 'shan't' in the middle of all of this crap? I think it's time I told him to take his 'shan't' and shove it.*

But, of course, Cole's spurt of mental energy is cut short when Vinny takes him by the elbow and all but shoves him into the seat next to Martone.

"No need for that, Vincent," chides Martone. The big guy closes the limo door and then rests his ample behind against it.

Martone has the manuscript on his lap. "I will make this brief," he says.

"You will not publish this. Period. I will talk to my niece and she will tell you exactly that. Are we clear?"

Cole studies Martone before answering. He sees age, perhaps illness, definitely sadness and something Cole could only guess was determination, or perhaps, resignation. And with that he gives up his own decision to reargue his case.

"Raymond," he says, shaking his head sadly, "I do not get you at all. You are one stubborn old man. How you could read that chapter and not understand what you will be doing to someone you love and who loves you. You must be some kind of dead dude inside. That's all I can figure."

Cole puts his hand on the door handle. "You do what you have to, and Stan and I will do what we have to. I'm sure we'll meet again."

He gives the door a shove and Vinny steps aside. Cole turns and asks Martone to return the manuscript. "I'll need that copy, Raymond. It's the one with my edits."

"It's my copy now, Coleman. What you do next is up to you. And do let Stan know I was asking for him and Francine won't you?"

Cole is startled. "That's not his wife's name. That's his sec…"

"Exactly," smirks Martone. "Exactly. Vincent, I believe it is time to head to our next appointment. Good bye, Coleman."

Cole exits the car and steps away when he sees the passenger window go down. Martone leans over in his seat, finally offering Cole his cell phone. He says, "Oh, and by the way, Coleman. Your day is not yet over. That car parked just across your causeway there? My guess would be the Feds. Best of luck, my friend. And just remember. You're the one who called me. Fifteen times."

He hears the old man cackle as Vinny gives it the gas and the car skids on the clam shells. Cole slaps his palm against the top of the car as it swerves dangerously close to him. "Shit."

"And it was only *eleven!*"

COLE STANDS AND WATCHES THE LIMO wend its way back toward town. When the black Lincoln Town car starts moving his way, he wonders what more can happen to him in just one day. *Stan having an affair with Francine? I had no idea, and I work for the guy. How in hell does Martone know this stuff? Miserable old prick! And if he thinks for one second that I'll put my ass in a bigger sling by bringing that up with Stan, then the old bat's really toying with dementia.*

*And what in god's name am I going to tell these guys?* He watches two serious looking men in dark suits with American flags on their lapels, crew cuts and shiny black wing tips climb out of their vehicle. The driver approaches, offering his identification.

"Afternoon, sir, I'm Special Agent William Creighton and this is Special Agent Lawton. We're with the FBI and would like a few words with you now that your, ah, guests have left. Can we step inside, please?"

Cole glances at their credentials, satisfied that they are, indeed, with the FBI, but is reluctant to have them in his house. He uses his foot to begin moving shells back into the gouge left by the limo, stalling for time.

He taps down on the shells to even them out with their neighbors.

"Mr. Alexander, we're on a time line here," the one named Lawton complains.

Cole looks up at them. "Well, I suppose we should have a seat on the porch and get ourselves out of the sun, now, shouldn't we?" It had occurred to Cole to say "Shan't we?" but he curbed the urge just in time.

At Cole's direction, each man carries a chair to the shady side of the porch facing the water. Cole turns his rocker just enough to see the *Editoria* rocking slightly with the incoming tide. Both FBI agents bring their chairs way too far into Cole's personal space for his comfort and he feels his heart rate quicken.

"Just what is it I can do for you gentlemen?" he asks, trying to gain some control over his growing anxiety. "I suppose Stan called you earlier to say there was some concern aboard my boat, but I'm sure you saw that the Coast Guard came to our rescue and everything worked out just fine."

Creighton looks at his colleague. "Who's Stan?" he asks, turning back to Cole.

"Stan Whitman, my boss? I'm an editor at Whitman, Westminster and Yarrow. He didn't call you?"

"What specifically was your business with Raymond Martone, Mr. Alexander? Our sources tell us you called his offices eleven times yesterday. Seemed a bit unusual and somewhat frantic, I'd say."

*I cannot lie to the FBI. I cannot lie to the FBI.* The unintended rhyme is charging though Cole's head like a runaway horse, clogging his thoughts and impeding his ability to focus.

"I, er, we... my publishing house, we... we needed to see him about a book." *Okay, good, good. This is actually the truth so far.* "I knew this was going to be a great day to be out on the water and I thought we could mix a little business with pleasure and do some negotiating, you know, before someone else got to him first." *Whew! This is good!*

"Ray 'The Zipper' Martone is writing a book? What, his memoirs? Hell must have frozen over and I didn't get the memo. When did this happen?" Creighton is astounded.

Cole is now on a roll choosing to ignore the fact that they now believe Martone is the author of his own work. *They said it. I didn't.* He tells himself.

"We got the word relatively recently, so we felt we had to act precipitously. Hey, stranger things have happened, right guys?"

Creighton's colleague, Sam Lawton, is harder to sell. "So, where is this book now? I'd like to get a look at it."

"It's not a book yet, fellas. Just a manuscript until it's published. Then it's a book. Right now he has it and we want to publish it. We're still talking it over."

"And that's it?" asks Lawton.

"Yep, at this point, that's all there is." Cole can feel the relief pouring off him like rainwater down a drainpipe.

Both men stand abruptly and Cole rises after them. Creighton hands Cole his card. "You need to call us the minute he gives you that book. *Capisce?*"

*What? Now he thinks I'm Italian because I know Martone?*

"Manuscript." Cole can't stop himself from interjecting.

"Manuscript, then, but we want to see it before you make any moves to print it. Do I make myself clear on this?" Creighton's forehead creases when he's serious. *This guy's head has more wrinkles than my ex-wife's Shar Pei.*

Thumbing the official FBI card, Cole considers this demand. "I'll run that by our lawyers and get back to you asap," he says.

"Figures," murmurs the Shar Pei.

Lawton is suddenly much friendlier. "We appreciate your cooperation, Mr. Alexander. As you must know, Martone has a history of questionable behavior and associations. Any help you can give us in our ongoing investigation would be of great benefit to society as a whole."

"You bet," is all that Cole can say.

He walks the men to their car and watches as Lawton takes the passenger seat. Creighton strides around the front of the car and opens the driver's door. Before he gets in, he looks across the top at Cole, takes his two fingers, points to his own eyes, and then aims them at Cole. The car pulls out with much of the same gusto as Martone's limo, leaving a mess of kicked up clam shells in its wake.

Rather than frighten him, the gesture causes Cole to become somewhat giddy. He does a dance step playing air guitar, sliding shells with his foot to fill the new ruts in his driveway, and fairly floats up the steps. He gives a fleeting thought to going in and cleaning up the mess he knows is waiting for him in his kitchen and dining room then disregards it. Settling once again into his rocker, feet resting on the porch rail, he inhales the cooling salt air, flexes his muscles and thinks, *Way to go Alexander. You did not lie to the FBI and you still have your skin attached to your body. You rock!*

# TWENTY-SEVEN

COLE ENJOYS A FULL SIXTEEN SECONDS of triumph before trouble finds him again. His vibrating left pocket brings him back to earth. *Stan! Shit!*

He punches a key and barely has time to say "Hello" before Stan rolls right over him.

"What the hell is going on up there? I've been trying to reach you all day. I called the police. I called the Coast Guard. Where are you? Damn it, Cole, why haven't you called me back? Is Martone still there? Let me talk to him."

"I'm okay, Stan. They're gone." Cole has his phone in a death grip, struggling to maintain control of both his temper and his tongue.

"And, Stan, while I totally appreciate the gesture of calling in the Coast Guard, you might have given some thought to how Martone and his flunkies would react to being boarded and searched. I don't think it did our cause any good at all."

"Why? What do you mean? What did they do?"

Cole rolls his eyes. "They didn't *do* anything, Stan. It dawned on me pretty quick when we got out on the water that none of them knew their ass from their elbow about sailing and that they needed me in order to run the boat. If anything happened to me they'd have been found some months from now tooling around in the Bermuda Triangle eating each other for lunch. Basically, I think the guy was getting off on watching me sweat, and the boat ride was his idea of sadistic fun."

"So what's the bottom line then? You say they're gone? For good, or are we still being jerked around?"

"I really don't know what to say about that, Stan. He's still threatening us if we publish the book and-"

"Us?" Stan shouts. "What do you mean by us? Our whole company? I thought this was about you."

*Oh, shit. I really don't want to go here.* Cole pulls his feet off the rail and starts the chair rocking.

"Look, Stan. I mean no disrespect here, but this guy somehow believes you're having an affair with Francine and asked me to tell you this. How and why this guy knows what he knows is beyond me, but that's the kind of shit he keeps throwing on the table."

Dead silence on the other end of the phone is enough for Cole to decide Martone hit the nail on the head. Stan and Francine have a thing going and, while it's none of Cole's business what either of them do, suddenly it's in the middle of the decision about DJ's manuscript.

"You okay, there, boss?" Cole asks as gently as he dares.

"Not one word. Not one word to Fran, or to anyone. Can we agree on that, Cole? Not one word."

"Not from me, chief. You have my promise on that."

Cole would have liked to hear Stan thank him, but the most he receives in response to his promise of secrecy is an abruptly uttered, "Good."

Stan then remains quiet for so long that Cole feels compelled to fill the silence.

"Look, I hope I didn't overstep when I was out there with him, but I told Martone that we were definitely going to publish DJ's work. I said that he could threaten us and every other publishing house until pigs shit pumpkins, but that DJ is our author, she's written a powerful piece and we are honored to publish it. That okay with you?"

Stan is slow to respond and sounds somewhat distracted. "Yeah."

"I also asked him six ways to Sunday why he's so hung up on stopping us from publishing but I couldn't get any kind of an answer. Nothing. He finally said he'd talk to DJ himself and that she would agree with him and pull the manuscript. I told him that if she did, we'd respect her decision, but not his threats."

"Frankly, I don't get it," Stan finally engages. "He comes off smelling like a rose in this manuscript. I can't figure what his objection could be other than she makes him look like a pussycat and maybe he's trying to protect his well-deserved reputation as a tough guy. Any ideas after spending all day with him?"

"None at all," Cole answers. "He was pretty quiet and spent most of the time reading. I purposely had him read Chapter Twenty to try and get him to see how much DJ said he means to her, but that sure didn't work."

He thinks for a moment as he paces his porch. "You know, I could be wrong about this, Stan, but he had to take pills a few times, and his bodyguard was pretty solicitous toward him. Could be he's sick. Might be worried some other thug would try to move on his territory if it was known he was both ill and a pushover for his niece. Whoa. Here's a scary thought. Maybe he's worried that the publicity would mean someone would try to use her to get to him."

"Huh." Stan is considering Cole's idea. "Could be what's going on. Although…" he draws the word out slowly, trying to put his thoughts into words, "didn't you say he threatened you even before we ever printed one word she wrote?"

"Yes, but he backed right off when he learned she was writing romance. The threat only pertained to anything about the family. And here we are. She's written an autobiography and it's got his undies in a bundle. There's something here we're not seeing."

Cole settles back into his rocker. "Stan, I think I'll give DJ a call and set up a meeting for Tuesday to let her know what's going on. I won't tell her that Martone is threatening us, but I will ask her if there's anything in the manuscript that might damage any family member. Or that might mean legal trouble for us if we publish it. That might work. What do you think?"

"Hell, why wait 'til Tuesday? See her this weekend."

"She's on the road visiting family from what she told me, and I'm not real comfortable doing this on the phone. I'll ask her to come in Tuesday and sit with us."

"All right, then. But, Cole, this time I mean it. I want to be there. No horsing around on your own like you did with Martone."

"Jesus, Stan," Cole cuts in, exasperated. "I woke up this morning and the guy was in my living room. He had another guy in my kitchen cooking breakfast. Just what was I supposed to do, ask them to go back to Boston and pick you up?" Cole's already frayed nerves are starting to crumble. The rocker is moving faster and faster, propelling itself along the porch floor.

"Okay, okay. I see your point. Let's just try to be more planful here." Stan responds nervously. "I don't want any more, ah, surprises from this guy. Understand?"

Now it's Cole's turn to waiver. "Ah, listen, Stan," he starts, "about surprises. The FBI was here this afternoon when we got in-"

Cole quickly pulls the phone away from his ear, trying to prevent drum damage from Stan's high decibel level.

"What?" Stan shouts. "The FBI? Because of Martone? What the hell are we in the middle of here, Alexander?"

"Give me a chance to expl–" Cole starts, but Stan bulldozes ahead. Cole has heard, and seen, Stan go on rages like this before and is confident his boss will eventually wind down, but he keeps trying to get a word in.

"Let me just tell-" Cole sighs heavily, moves to his porch steps and sits facing the horizon and the gathering fog bank. A trio of sea gulls flies overhead and lands on his roof, squawking energetically, their ruckus competing with Stan's tirade.

Cole tries once again. "Stan. Stan," he sounds forceful, even to himself and decides to keep right on talking.

"Look, they must have had a wiretap going and wondered why I had called Martone a few times on Friday. *No way am I telling him I called the guy eleven times.* That's all. I told them we were talking with him about a book deal. Didn't say it was *his* book but that's what they surmised."

Stan had quieted, so Cole just keeps on going. "They want to see his manuscript. I said we didn't have one, Martone did. They insisted we call them as soon as we have it. I said I'd have to check with our lawyers. They didn't like that part. Then they left."

"That's it?"

"That's it, yes. And, Stan, Martone *did* take my manuscript with him. The one with all my edits. So it was the truth that I did not have *the* manuscript. The one from DJ."

"Good. Good. No problem there, you can have my copy. I made a few edits myself when I read it last night." Stan is still a bit distracted, but has mostly managed to pull himself together. Cole thinks much of Stan's losing it has more to do with his embarrassment about Francine than anything else, but he wisely keeps that to himself.

The question foremost in Cole's mind now has a chance to be asked. "You read the whole thing then. What did you think of it?"

"I'll tell you something, Cole. I think we have a blockbuster best seller on our hands. I don't give two shits what Martone thinks or wants. We're going to sit with DJ and let her know that she has just written the most powerful piece of work WWY will have published in a decade, maybe longer. You hear me, my man? We are not letting this one get away. Certainly not because of a guy like Martone, no matter what he threatens."

Cole hears Stan building up to a good finish.

"You let me deal with the lawyers. They'll help figure how to manage Martone. You get on the horn to Brava and set something up for Tuesday. Call Franc… Call Francine and let her know so she can put it on my calendar." Stan hesitates. "And, Cole, on this other thing, Martone's, um, threat. We're good on that, too, right?"

"Absolutely, Stan. You have my word."

"Okay, look I have to go. Dinner with the in-laws. I'll check in with you sometime tomorrow. Let me know if you hear anything more from him."

"I'm not really expecting to, Stan, but I will stay in touch. I'll be up here for the rest of the weekend if you need me."

Stan asks if Cole thinks he still ought to have some protection nearby, but Cole declines.

"Hell. They turned the one guy you did send, and got into this place even with all my security on. Seems to me they'll find me if they want me. Besides, they know I got the message, loud and clear. I think I'm fine, for now at least. Thanks, anyway, boss. Talk with you soon. Enjoy dinner."

Cole thinks Stan has hung up, and then he hears, "By the way, son. Good job handling those FBI guys. They won't like us much when they find out. But they came to the wrong conclusion. You didn't lie to them. Nice going. Good night."


AFTER RESTORING THE KITCHEN and dining rooms to presentable condition, dumping the offensive ricotta pie, and grabbing a bite to eat, Cole again heads to his porch armed with Scotch and two cigars. No manuscript this evening. The fog is closer in to shore, but still far enough out to allow him to enjoy the harbor fireworks that always end the first day of the regatta.

Cole is dog tired, but he is also feeling a satisfying sense of pride and accomplishment at the way he handled things today. It's an unusual feeling for him but he has no difficulty basking in the newness of it, trying it on for size, liking even the concept of it. He puffs a smoke ring into the night air and watches it be taken on the breeze, then loses it in the mist above the clumps of beach roses that cling to the leeward side of his porch.

He thinks of the days, years ago now, when his children ran themselves to exhaustion on the beach all day then sat with him on this porch in the evenings, he with his cigar and the children with their bubbles—each blowing into the evening breeze and losing them in the same beach roses.

"I think I still have it in me to once again be the man I was then," he says out loud, perhaps to share this renewed sense of himself with someone, if only his slumbering roof tenants.

Cole reaches into the pocket of his shorts, fishes out his cell phone, and calls his daughter before the fireworks start.

# TWENTY-EIGHT

DJ IS LEADING THE PACK out of the plane and down the concourse. She turns to her friends for some kind of consensus.

"We're going to have to grab a cab out front. Should we pick up a car at your place first, or just book it to Raymond's in Newton? It is getting a bit late." She cuts around a slower woman carrying an enormous shopping bag. "We can ask his driver to get us back to your place tonight. What do you think? Kate? Tuck? Anybody?" She looks around.

The Kate/Tuck duo is frantically weaving its way around other passengers and trying to keep close enough to DJ to be heard.

"Jesus, doesn't anybody here have half a brain?" Tuck mutters, mostly to herself. "We need to go in there with a god-damned tank, and she wants to know if we should rely on him for transportation home. This is just nuts."

"Frankly, Deej," Kate shouts, "we don't know what his mood is going to be after you talk with him. How about we grab our own car and plan an exit strategy if things get too tense? Gives us a bit more control."

Kate's pleading look lands on Tuck. "That okay with you?" she asks softly, fully aware she is walking a delicate balance between two opposing factions at the moment.

DJ stops dead in her tracks, causing the others to bump into her and creating a minor traffic jam. As passengers struggle to get around the three women, freeing themselves from the pile-up, DJ practically hisses to her friends,

"Raymond's the one who better have an exit strategy when I get done with him. The longer I thought about this on the plane, the angrier I got. He had no damn right to take matters into his own hands with my uncles. And my father! None."

She resumes her strident walk, an arrow on its way to the target.

Kate looks at Tuck, adjusting her shoulder bag. "Well okay, then," she says, and they take off after DJ.

*Oh, great!* Tuck thinks.

DJ no sooner exits the terminal from the Baggage Claim area, stepping out into the din and exhaust of Logan's pick-up circuits, than someone is calling her name.

"Miss Donna. Miss Donna. Over here."

She spots her uncle's driver, Vincent, to her left, standing next to the limo and waving. DJ turns to wait for her friends to catch up. "This ought to be interesting," she says in response to their questioning looks. "Come on."

"This is quite a surprise, Vincent. How nice to see you. Is my uncle flying in this evening as well?" DJ asks.

"Oh, no, Miss Donna. We received your message that you would be visiting and he sent me to fetch you," Vincent responds seriously.

Kate whispers in Tuck's ear. "He's been sent to fetch us. I think this is the very first time I've ever been fetched, honey, how about you?"

The whispers catch Vincent's attention and he turns to the two women. "Good evening," he says. "Good to see you again, Miss Kate," he reaches to shake hands. "And you too, Miss Tucker."

"Oh, sorry Vincent," DJ stutters. "Where are my manners? And it's just Tuck. Not Tucker."

"My apologies, madam," Vincent addresses Tuck. "I will be taking Miss Donna in the limo and have made arrangements for transportation into Cambridge for both of you. If you'll just come this way, I-"

He is abruptly cut off by DJ. "That won't be necessary at all, Vincent. My friends will be accompanying me this evening. We have our own transportation." She closes the limo door Vincent has opened.

Vincent is frozen in his tracks. "But that is not exactly what your uncle wishes, Miss Donna."

Surprising even herself, DJ stops, looks directly at Vincent, and snaps, "Goodness, Vincent. You're so right. That is not exactly what my uncle wants, but it is what we're going to do." She gathers her purse and bag.

"My friends and I will take a cab to their home and pick up my car. Please inform my uncle that we shall all—all three of us—be at his place in one hour. Thank you."

Vincent tries again. "But Miss Donna, please. Your uncle wishes to speak with you alone."

"That's where you're wrong Vincent. It is I who wish to speak with my uncle. And two more things: First, he'll live through this tiny disappointment, believe me. And, second, it's Donna, or DJ. Not *Miss* Donna. I respectfully request that you call me by my name. Donna."

She steps quickly around him and he reaches out a hand to stop her. Vincent is thoroughly puzzled by her behavior and worried about returning to his boss without her. DJ merely has to glare at his hand on her arm then up at his face before he releases her.

"Thank you," she repeats. Then adds sweetly, "And Vincent, I'd put some salve on that sunburn of yours if I were you. You are certainly going to blister something awful."

Tuck has quietly taken the initiative to commandeer a cab, and the three women hurry to jump in.

Vincent watches them go, unsure of his next move. "Yes, ma'am," he mumbles, "uh, Donna."


"WELL, HELLO, MADAM-TAKE-CHARGE," Kate slaps DJ a high-five in the back seat of the cab. "Poor Vincent is still standing there with his mouth open." She twists to look out the rear window as Tuck gives their address in Cambridge to the driver. "Yep, he's still there," she grins.

"I doubt anyone's ever questioned Uncle Raymond's wishes before, would be my guess," DJ gloats. "I'm not sure I'd want to be in Vincent's shoes when he shows up without me. But I'd just like to say that he ain't seen nothin' yet."

"Okay, folks," Tuck pulls her seat belt across her lap with a grunt. Her voice is grim. "Doesn't anyone else think his being here to meet us is just a tiny bit odd? How did he know when we'd be arriving at Logan, or that we were out of town at all? Seriously, you two, I wouldn't go celebrating anything. This is the kind of thing I'm worried about."

That stops Kate who has been busy checking her cell for messages. She plunks her purse down on her lap and looks at Tuck.

"Oh," says DJ. "You're right." She looks dazed.

"Damned straight, I am. And we need to get smarter if any of this is going to work, DJ."

"Smarter?"

"You know what, DJ?" Kate says. "Tuck's right. We need to be more focused about what we're doing. And we need to question Raymond's motivations and his actions, all of them. We need to be sure you can get the information you need about your father and uncles, but also be safe enough to get out of there. After all, your sisters are saying he killed them. That's scary enough as it is. But now, the fact that he knew where we'd be and when, right down to the correct airline *is* creepy. Maybe we're being watched or something."

DJ sincerely wants to roll her eyes and say 'oh, please', but she stops herself.

"So what do we do about it?" she asks instead.

"We need to be more cautious and less impulsive—think things out before we jump in and act. For right now, let's just get home and do what we agreed to do. What were you doing when I interrupted you?" Tuck says.

"Oh, right. I told Chris and Sarah I'd let them know we got here. Guess I ought to do that now." DJ searches her purse and finds the phone tangled in its own charging cord. "Ugh. What a mess."

When she finally extricates the phone and checks her own messages, she counts four from her mother, all within the last two hours.

"Oh my god, my mother! We're supposed to be at her place right now, and with all this stuff about Raymond, I forgot to call and cancel."

As if on cue the cell rings in her hand, causing DJ to start. She glances at the screen, then answers. "Hi, Mom, I'm so sorry, but my plans changed and I simply forgot to call."

"I got so worried when I couldn't reach you that I called your sisters. They told me you were on the plane back to Boston to see your uncle and that you wouldn't be coming here until tomorrow."

"Oh, they did. Good. So you're okay with tomorrow then?" DJ asks.

"Is tomorrow Sunday? Oh, yes, but I have to go to church first. I'll be going to the ten o'clock mass, but I should be back by noon. I don't suppose *you'll* be going to church tomorrow, will you?"

Her mother's derision, thick as molasses, crawls through the airwaves and drips into DJ's ear.

"No, mother, I won't," DJ says, as patiently as she is able. "How about we go out for lunch?"

"Or would you prefer to eat here in the dining room with me?" suggests her mother.

"Uh-huh. Sure, that would be fine, but are you positive you wouldn't rather go out for lunch if you're up to it? After all, you eat there every day. We could-"

DJ listens, rolling her eyes at Kate and Tuck.

"Well, I don't know what to say, dear. Won't it be hard to get seated on a Sunday? If you had come when you were supposed to, we could have gone to the lovely Italian place you like just up the road. Oh, maybe we could go to that seafood place in Bristol. You remember, the one on the waterfront there. I haven't been for years. Do you suppose they still have that lovely lobster pie? That would be nice."

"Good idea, Mom. I'll try to call and make reservations when we get in, how's that? If you can be ready when I pick you up at noon, we should be able to be seated by one. Does that sound okay to you?"

"Well, I still don't understand why you couldn't have come today. I have some mail I need you to look at. Now I'm not sure we'll have time if we drive all the way to Bristol. And just why would you prefer to go see Raymond today instead of coming to see me? You haven't been here in a long time."

DJ has found an old hair scrunchie in her purse and, with the phone tucked under her chin to keep it from slipping onto the floor she's snapping it hard against the door. Dealing with her mother has always been easier for her sisters than for her. Yet she is now the one living closest, and has sole responsibility for all the tiny details of her mother's life.

"Uh-huh. Look, Mom. It was my mistake not to call you earlier. I'm sorry. And I certainly don't *prefer* Raymond's company to yours. I just didn't think you'd mind whether I came down on Saturday or Sunday. You are kind of a captive audience, after all."

DJ has inadvertently opened an old can of worms.

"There is no need to be so prickly, Lady Jane. I should think the least you can do is give me the respect I deserve as your mother. And after all I've had to put up with from you and your sisters."

DJ sighs and holds the phone away from her head, covering the mouthpiece.

"Aaaarrrrgggghhh…" she complains to her friends.

When she thinks her mother might have finished her rebuke, DJ says,

"Yes, you're right, mother. There was no need for that last comment. I apologize. I-"

Her mother is not done, but she has changed topics and is reciting a list of stops she wants DJ to make with her tomorrow. "I need to pick up a few things at the drug store, and I am totally out of cereal and milk. You know how I hate to get up early and go down to breakfast here. And I want to stop in and see Marilyn at the nursing home. She's not going to be with us much longer you know."

"Listen, Mother. Mom!" DJ cuts in forcefully. She is gripping her forehead and kneading her temples.

"I have to go. I'm in a cab, Mom. We'll be there by noon and we'll go out to lunch. See you then."

"Who's the we you keep mentioning?" insists her mother.

"Kate and Tuck, that's who."

"Oh, Donna, for the love of Pete, can't you go anywhere by yourself yet? You always had to travel with your pack around you and you're still doing it. Don't you think it's time you grow out of that? And must you bring those two everywhere you go, dear? I know they're quite lovely girls, Donna, but you know as well as I do that at some point people will begin to talk."

Now DJ's eyebrows are hiked up so high they threaten to get lost in her hair.

"Talk? What people will talk? About what, mother?"

"Don't pretend you don't know what I mean, young lady. They'll think you're one, too."

"And just who is *they*, mother? And what kind of a *one* might they think I am?" DJ says. "You know what? Never mind. And, yes, they do have to come with me. It's in the contract. We'll be there at noon. Goodbye." She drops the phone into her purse, letting it go as if it were poison ivy.

Tuck and Kate are staring at DJ. "Contract?" they say as one.

DJ clenches her teeth and growls. She throws her head back in the seat and closes her eyes.

"It was all I could think of to say that didn't involve weaponry and threats of personal harm. Besides, it gives her something to think about, doesn't it? That ought to make for an interesting day tomorrow."

———————————

THE THREE WOMEN have managed to drop their bags at Kate and Tuck's. They've left the agreed-upon message with the answering service, and DJ has written a detailed note giving Raymond Martone's address, stating the time they left, and the nature of their visit. At Tuck's insistence, DJ even called her own home and left a similar message on her answering machine.

They take a minute to freshen up and change out of their travel clothes, with Kate and Tuck repacking after a quick decision to spend the night at DJ's house, and thus ensure a shorter ride home later tonight. That, in turn, necessitates dropping Kate's car off at DJ's on the way to Raymond's. Even with all the deviations, they are heading out to the Mass Pike within thirty minutes. There is so much more to accomplish on this already busy Saturday.

Halfway there, DJ remembers to call her sisters. She uses the stationary cell setup in her car.

"What did you two manage to put on my tab today?" she asks in jest when Sarah answers her cell phone.

Sarah laughs, "You lucked out. We spent most of the day out of the hotel and away from that phenomenal spa, but still found ways to spend a bundle of our own money this time."

Chris grabs the cell. "However, we just discovered some great shops right in the hotel itself, and I plan to send Sarah back with lots of presents from you and me for that grandbaby. And, it's pouring blue murder again, so we are dining once more on your dime. Well, on your much-more-than-a-dime. It really is nice to help empty your pockets."

"So how are you doing, Chrissie? You sound better, happier."

"I really needed to unload that on you guys, Donna. Thanks for letting me and putting up with my funk. Sarah and I have been talking quite a lot, and I think I'll take those names from Kate. I really don't want to hurt Garret any more than I already have, even if he doesn't know it."

"Great, Chris. I'll get you those as soon as I can, okay?"

But it's Sarah back on the phone now.

"I'm sure you know by now, but mother called earlier. You're in for it tomorrow, sis. I hope you know that."

"Yes, thanks, Sarah. Just my luck you'll probably be at your friend's house tomorrow after I spend most of the day with her. You know how much it helps to talk while I'm driving home from her place and banging my head on the steering wheel."

"Why do you think I moved to the furthest edge of the continent?"

Sarah asks, laughing. "Hey, what happened with Raymond, or haven't you done that yet? And by the way, we still think you're nuts!"

"We're on the way to his place, now, lucky us!" DJ says. "The plane was delayed twice. We're exhausted. But we're going to do it tonight. As the Blues Brothers have said so eloquently, 'We're on a mission from God.'"

Sarah laughs appreciatively and then gets serious. "I mean it DJ. Good luck from both of us. Given the time, I know you can't call us tonight, but please call us in the morning before you go to mother's. And be careful!"

"I will. This is turning into one killer of a weekend, exhaustion-wise anyway. Oh, hey, before I forget, you did tell Chrissie you didn't mean it when you called her a 'snake' didn't you?"

"Yes, I did." There is a hint of mockery mixed with patronizing in the tone of Sarah's response. "Can't help yourself, can you big sister?"

"Sounds like my cue to stop talking. I'll save it for Raymond. Love you both. Enjoy this evening and tell Chris to buy something gorgeous for the baby."

"Love you right back, and tell the posse I'm glad they're with you," Sarah adds.

"I am, too. Bye." DJ says.

"So…We're off to see the wizard," Kate sings, "the creepy old wizard of odd."

"Stop being a jerk," Tuck says, giving a hefty shove to Kate's seat in front of her, "and pay attention. This is definitely not funny."

# TWENTY-NINE

"SWEET MARY, MOTHER OF JESUS, would you look at this place!" Kate has her hands against the dash as she leans into the windshield to get a better look at the Martone estate. "Did they film *Harry Potter* here? It's bigger than Hogwarts, and creepier, too."

DJ laughs as she slides her card to open the electric gate allowing them access to this virtual palace in the Newton Highlands.

"My uncle has never been one for subtlety when it comes to letting people know he has both power and money, that's for sure. I forgot that I've never brought you out here before. Of course, the place being lit up so it can be seen from the far side of the moon does lend it a bit of drama, doesn't it?"

"I'll stick with Kate's selection of 'creepy' as the operational word here," Tuck says and undoes her seat belt. She pulls herself up so she can see better between the two front seats while DJ drives slowly up to the front portico. "It's kind of like Al Capone meets Alfred Hitchcock—huge enough to let you know who's got the power and spooky enough to scare you into doing whatever the bad guys say. We need to be very careful."

"Please stop freaking me out, honey," Kate begs. "Couldn't we have done this in the daytime, Deej? Seriously, this is way out in nowhere land and it's very, very dark. I'm with Tuck on this one. What's the plan?"

They can see the portico door open and Vincent descending the stairs to await their arrival. DJ stops the car in the middle of the driveway, well short of Vincent.

"Well, Kate, my dear, I do have a plan. I am going in there to confront my uncle and, depending on what he says, I will reach in and rip his heart out—providing he still has one in there somewhere—or I will apologize for ever having thought he could have done what my sisters think he has. Oh, but first I'm going to eat whatever he's serving. I'm famished. Are you both with me on this?"

Tuck puts a hand on DJ's shoulder and gives it a reassuring pat.

"You know, Deej, I'm all for the dinner part of this," she says. "But the rest of it doesn't sound like a plan as much as it does a tantrum, especially the first part. Do you think you could be a bit more specific, here? And kind of hurry, would you please. Old Vincent there seems to be wringing his hands and staring, and his face is awfully red."

"Sorry, pal. It's the best I can do with what I've got left." She lets the car coast under the portico. "Between my sisters last night and my mother an hour ago, any capacity to think or behave rationally has been sucked right out of me. You know that phrase 'on a wing and a prayer'?"

Kate attempts a very weak, "Yeah?"

"Well, just so you know," DJ turns off the ignition, "we're winging this one."

"Hard not to love a girl with such a good plan," Tuck mutters.


VINCENT OPENS THE DRIVER'S SIDE front and back car doors simultaneously, assisting both DJ and Tuck out of their seats. Kate fends for herself and climbs out the passenger side.

"Good evening, again, ladies." Vincent greets them with a slight bow as he hurries to open the door to the house. "Perfect timing, Donna, dinner is just about to be served. Your uncle awaits you in the dining room."

DJ and Vincent exchange the briefest of smiles in acknowledgement of his acquiescing to her earlier request that he call her by her first name only.

"Thank you, Vincent," she says quietly.

"Right this way, ladies," Vincent closes the door behind them. They follow him through the vestibule and down the marble and oak hallway lined with magnificent works of art and statuary, most of it by early Italian artists.

"This could be where that painting is that was stolen from the Gardner Museum," Kate whispers to DJ. "Who would ever know?"

"Well, it's not out of a Crate and Barrel catalogue, that's for sure." Tuck struggles to walk forward, look up and around, all at the same time. "Although maybe it's the Italian version. Jeez, Katie, will you look at this ceiling? There are frescos up there. Did you really get to crawl all over this place when you were a kid, DJ?"

"No such luck," DJ responds. "This is a fairly recent acquisition. Some other mucky-muck politician or criminal died or went to jail or something, and Raymond acquired it. His word, not mine."

Vincent turns into the dining room and announces, "Your guests have arrived, Mr. Martone," at exactly the same moment both Kate and Tuck say, "Whoa!"

"Does the Pope live here, too?" Kate whispers to DJ. The room is huge, and stunning in its opulence. One entire wall is a mural of scenes from St. Peter's Basilica in Rome. Another backs an elegant high-boy displaying a variety of silver and gold chalices.

Raymond rises from his place at the head of the table. "Donna, my dear, I am so pleased to see you." He wraps her in a hug and kisses her on both cheeks, then holds her at arm's length with both hands.

"Hello, Uncle Raymond," DJ says. "Goodness, you have a terrible sunburn on your neck!"

"It's nothing. Just let me look at you," he croons. "Beautiful as ever, with those eyes that sparkle like the stars. And becoming more famous by the day I hear. It's a pleasure to see you. And you, too, ladies," he turns and extends his hands to both women. "Welcome, and come and sit. Dinner is ready and I have a wonderful new chef who has prepared his first formal meal for us this evening."

The table, which could easily sit twelve, is set for four. Vincent moves to assist Raymond back to his seat. DJ studies her uncle's unsteady movement as he sits, and she senses a new frailty, a marked change since she last saw him two months ago. This is the first time she can recall his needing assistance with anything, never mind his allowing anyone to help him. Vincent takes great pains to be discrete, but the action does not escape her notice.

"It's lovely to see you again, Mr. Martone," ventures Kate, as she sits directly across from DJ and next to Raymond and Tuck. "Your new home is positively grand. The art work itself is awe-inspiring. Are you a collector?"

"Please," he responds, "call me Raymond. No sense standing on ceremony when you've been like family to my niece. And, yes, in the past few years I've had the opportunity to acquire quite a few good pieces of Italian art. I've been extremely fortunate to have a place large enough to display them. Are you a student of the Renaissance arts?" he asks.

"No, not at all," Kate chuckles, "I'm just an appreciative observer."

"Well, then, you must allow me to show you around after our meal."

While Raymond is chatting amiably with her friends, DJ watches him closely. As always, he is impeccably dressed and groomed, smelling of some expensive cologne that hints of almonds. But DJ senses his silk dinner jacket has outgrown him, and his pants bag just a bit too much at the shoe.

*Something's changed here,* she thinks, *but I can't quite put my finger on it. Yet.*

They are interrupted by the chef and Vincent, who cooperate in serving a rich butternut squash soup dolloped with crème fraise and sprinkled with chives. A sizeable wedge of rosemary focaccia graces the side. The aroma is intoxicating, and the three hungry women are grateful for their first real meal of the day.

"This is fantastic, Uncle Raymond," DJ takes a hearty spoonful, "and delicious. Thank you so much," she says to the chef.

His face is bright red and he bows just slightly, tells Raymond that he will return shortly with the salad course and returns to the kitchen with Vincent following.

The remainder of their gourmet-style dinner is spent in small talk about travel, book signings, and Kate and Tuck's practice. At one point DJ ventures to ask Raymond about his health, but his response is an abrupt and dismissive, "I'm fine," and she does not question him further.

"Shall we take coffee in the study, then?" he asks after they have finished a magnificent crème brûlée. "Or perhaps you would prefer a cordial? I have a primo Limoncello that I brought back from Milan just a few weeks ago." Raymond presses his fingers to his lips and kisses them. "*Delizioso!*"

"I think we'd better stick with coffee, Uncle Raymond. Decaf, if that's okay. We're pretty much exhausted from our travels today and I still need to talk with you about something serious. Plus, it's getting late and I'm sure you're tired as well."

"Now, don't you go deciding I'm old yet, Donna Jean. I still have a lot of spunk left in me," he rebukes her with a smile. "Tell you what. *I'll* have the Limoncello, and you young ones can have the coffee. If we head out this door to the right, I can show you some of the better paintings on our way."

"That would be nice." Tuck pats her stomach and pushes her chair back from the table. "Oh, and please give our thanks to your wonderful chef. That was an exceptionally fine meal, and I do think we did it justice."

DJ tries to be unobtrusive and tucks her uncle's arm beneath hers, helping him rise from his seat. She is surprised that he allows her to do so, and is equally amazed at the weakness she feels in his frame as she steadies him.

"Will you show my friends the chapel?" she asks as they leave the dining room and turn left down the hall. Kate and Tuck are trailing along, still taking in the sights. Tuck looks back often, trying to make a mental note of where they are in relation to the door they entered.

"Exactly what I had in mind, my dear," Raymond pats DJ's hand and they turn into a small alcove with a floor-to-ceiling wrought iron gate at the end. Behind the gate is an exquisitely carved double oak door with a solid brass handle and lock. All of the panels contain carvings of religious figures, including Moses receiving the Ten Commandments, Jesus multiplying the loaves and fishes, St. Peter in his fishing boat, and a great many more.

Kate is running her fingers across the panels, naming as many as she can.

"Was this place ever owned by the Church?" she asks Raymond. "It was here when you bought the place, right? I mean you didn't, like, buy this somewhere else and have it installed, did you?"

Raymond laughs. "No, it was here. It's actually the major reason I bought the estate in the first place, and it's what got me interested in collecting period pieces which would accentuate the beauty of this room. Now, look in here," he says as he pulls open the doors to reveal a chapel-sized replica of a Roman cathedral, stained glass windows and all.

The drama of his move has the desired effect on Kate and Tuck. Both are speechless. They are captivated by ornate plaques depicting the Stations of the Cross along three sides of the chapel and are making a closer inspection of the stained glass with portrayals of psalm verses on each one.

"Amazing, huh?" DJ asks, smiling at her friends.

"And all along I've been thinking we didn't have any secrets from one another," Kate teases, plopping into the closest pew and trying to take in all she is seeing. "What else have you been hiding?"

"She probably hasn't told you that all of this will be hers one day, has she?" Raymond is having his moment in the sun, glowing with the pure pleasure of their admiration for what he owns.

Both Kate and Tuck turn to look at DJ, mouths agape.

"You could at least have the presence of mind to look the tiniest bit embarrassed for not telling us," Kate says.

DJ laughs. "And just why should I have told you about something that is never going to happen?" she asks. "Just because Raymond says so, doesn't mean it's written in stone. Which reminds me, there's a conversation we need to have before we leave tonight, isn't there? So, if you two are done worshiping at the shrine of opulence or whatever it is, can we please get a move on?"

Raymond has raised his eyebrows at DJ's words, but simply smiles and says, "Of course, my dear." He turns to Kate and Tuck. "Shall we?" he asks, offering his arm to Tuck.


THEY EACH SETTLE INTO A rich brown Italian leather arm chair, the girls with their decaf and Raymond sipping his *delizioso* Limoncello. The small talk has wound down and DJ becomes pensive, staring into her coffee cup as if it was tea and the leaves would tell her how to start. She looks over the lip at Kate, receives an encouraging smile and just the slightest nod of the head.

She sets her cup down and sits forward in her chair looking directly at her uncle, determination propelling her.

"Uncle Raymond, I need to talk with you about something serious," she begins. "I've written another book."

She pauses, but he does not fill the silence. Kate notices the shadow of a grimace cross his face, and perhaps a tensing of the hand holding his cordial. For some reason she wonders if he knows what is coming.

DJ continues. "I've been writing novels for almost sixteen years now, and I've been very successful and pretty happy doing so. But early last year I started to experience what we in the business refer to as writer's block. I was stuck. There was nothing there. I couldn't write a word. I tried, but it just would not work for me. Not for months."

She stands up and moves to a chair closer to her uncle.

"When words finally did come, they came pouring out as if a dam had set the water free. To my surprise, it was all about me—my life and what happened to me as a kid, dad, JJ, Eddie and Joey, and all of that. I've written an autobiography and WWY is looking at it now to publish it."

Raymond has not looked at DJ, but Kate again notices a pause in the way he has been slowly swirling the Limoncello around in the cordial glass as DJ talks. He still makes no comment.

"I'm finding this whole process of putting my life out there into the world for all to see very taxing emotionally, and so my best friends here have been my super support system. I set aside this weekend to tell Sarah and Chris, mom, and you—just so no one would be surprised when the news breaks, which I kind of expect to happen soon."

*There's that look again,* thinks Kate as she continues to observe Raymond. *At first I thought it was a smile but it certainly looks more like a smirk. This guy knows this already. I'd bet on it.*

DJ is nervous, but plows ahead. "I was planning to see you tomorrow and Mom today, but something came up when I spoke with Chrissie and Sarah. I had to talk with you immediately." She takes a deep breath. "This whole process of writing about my past has been excruciating. In many ways it's been like reliving it emotionally."

When DJ pauses again, Raymond finally speaks, but he does so slowly and deliberately, all the while refilling his cordial.

"Then why put yourself through this, my dear? I remember the pain you were in so often as a youngster. Why revisit it?"

DJ thinks about that before she responds. "Because the need to write it down seemed to come from some place so deep inside, forcing itself out and up to the surface and onto the page, that I felt as if I almost didn't have a choice."

Raymond's eyes bore into DJ. "There is always a choice, my dear Donna. One just needs to be open enough to see it and brave enough to choose it."

"That is precisely what I did," she responds, meeting his look and returning it. Her chin goes up a notch or two, and Raymond pulls himself away just the slightest.

"May I ask just how revealing this book is, then?" he questions. This time he does not look at her.

"Honestly, Uncle Raymond, everything is in there. All of it. And, yes, you are, too. It's no secret out there in the universe that we are related. Never has been. And so the role you played in helping me survive is a major piece of this work. Frankly, I think you'll be pleased with what I have to say. But I am also quite graphic about what my father and uncles did. It's not pretty in print. It certainly wasn't pretty when it happened and there aren't words in any language I'm aware of that can make it look different from the ghastly experience it was. And if words like that did exist, I wouldn't choose them anyway."

Raymond tries again. "Do you think it wise to bring all this out now? I mean that you have done so much work over the years to heal from what happened. How can this be good for you?"

DJ smiles at the memory of Sarah asking almost the same question just twenty-four hours earlier.

"Here are a couple of things I've learned about healing, Raymond." DJ leans closer to her uncle. "The first is that it's not an event. It's a process. And it can take all the time it needs to take. It's not a straight line from one point to another—like from despair to joy. You can be all over the map, to hell and deeper, just trying to get anywhere better than where you started."

Raymond fumbles with the buttons to his dinner jacket, concentrating on opening each one and thereby avoiding eye contact with his niece. DJ seems not to notice.

"And the second is that taking the journey is sometimes the only good choice, because it also hurts like hell not to. The thing no one knows, mercifully, in the beginning is that it can hurt like deeper hell to do the work of confronting the past. I used to console myself sometimes with words from an old Lui Collins song where she sang about the only way out being *through*. Turns out she was right on the mark with that one."

Raymond finally looks up from his buttons, shaking his head.

"All I am asking, Donna, is why put yourself through all that again?"

"I'm not. I'm actually feeling very confident about what I have done in writing this book. It's very important to me, Uncle Raymond. I'd like you to understand that. What did happen, however, is that in talking with my sisters, I realized I have not closed the book, so to speak, on what I need to do about my other uncles."

Raymond's startled look is obvious, although DJ herself is not cognizant of the effect her words have had on her uncle. Kate, however, is totally aware that he is feeling some very strong emotion which she cannot quite name. A slight tap on her toe from Tuck's foot signals that her partner has also noticed.

DJ moves ahead, more cautiously this time. "What I really need from you most at the moment, Uncle, is help finding Eddie and Joey. I want to see them and talk with them. It's time I put this to rest. I have tried to find them on my own, but I cannot. The last I heard, they work for you in different cities. I've looked in phone books when I've been on book tours in major east coast cities, even Googled and whatnot, but I've come up with zilch. So! Can you get me their addresses and phone numbers? I'm not sure yet whether I want to call, write, or drop in on each one separately, but it's something I've needed to do for a long time and only just recently realized I could. I'm strong enough now to do it, and I must."

Kate can see Raymond's discomfort growing. He's looking smaller by the second in his Italian leather armchair. *Wow! He didn't see this one coming. And he hasn't seen anything yet,* she thinks. *DJ's just winding up for the bigger pitch!*

Raymond places his glass on a silver tray and clears his throat. "Ahem," he starts then repeats himself. "Ahem. Ah, I don't quite see what purpose that would serve, Donna. They've been gone for some years now, and the agreement we had was that they never return. I did this for you, dear, and I don't understand why now, so very many years later, you would want to bring all that up again."

DJ's response is both brief and cold. "Oh, you don't?"

"No, dear, I don't. I'm sorry, but my answer has to be no. I will not give you any information about their whereabouts." His eyes avoid hers.

DJ pulls herself to the edge of her seat and leans as close to him as she can. "And that, my dear uncle, is because they are dead, isn't it?"

Her voice rises in pitch and strength. "And they are dead because you arranged for them to be dead—all three of them—my father as well as Eddie and Joey. I do not know how you did it, especially making my father's death look like a heart attack even to the medical people. But you did." It's a statement, not a question.

She stares at him.

Tuck and Kate are both surprised. DJ doesn't ask him if he did it. She is confident he did.

At some point during the evening's conversation DJ has resolved the issue for herself.

Moments pass. DJ continues to stare at her uncle, waiting patiently for an answer. Raymond's rapid eye movements show he's engaged in a battle of mental gymnastics and is beginning to wither under her gaze.

*Kind of like a dandelion zapped by Weed-B-Gon,* Kate thinks and allows herself a tiny smile. *I've got a feeling he's gonna cave to her. I'd bet on it. Too bad I can't say anything to Tuck right now. She'd take the bet.*

A grandfather clock somewhere in the mansion strikes, and all four people slowly count out the hours to themselves. Nine. When silence returns it is almost unbearable. And still DJ waits.

When Raymond finally speaks, his voice has lost the air of righteous pomposity that they've been hearing all evening, but it is still surprisingly direct and firm.

"I did what I had to do. I did it to protect you."

Much as DJ expects this answer, she is nevertheless so stunned that her body lurches backwards, and she feels in danger of passing out. She sucks in a huge gulp of air.

"My god, Raymond, you really did do it. You actually killed them. How could you? They were your brothers!" shouts DJ. "You killed them and you use *me* as your excuse?"

"They never hurt you again, did they?" he demands. His hands grip the armrests like talons around prey.

"That's it? The end justifies the means? You think that makes it all okay? Just like what you do for a living? How you make money off of other people's sick needs? That's all okay, too?"

DJ continues to push with her words. "It certainly explains why you have no friends and live up here in your ivory tower acting like you're above everyone else then, doesn't it?" DJ spits out the words like venom from a cobra strike. She has no idea where this depth of anger in her is coming from, or that she had ever thought these very things about him that she is now saying out loud.

"Don't you go judging me, Donna Jean, not after all I've done for you. And don't you dare disparage what I do for a living either. You've certainly benefitted from it."

DJ is shaking her head, trying her hardest to make sense of her uncle's warped reasoning. But it is her friends who are about to explode.

Tuck simply can't contain herself any longer. She stands, having every intention of making herself an imposing presence over him.

"Hard to understand how you could do so much to 'protect' DJ," she fairly shouts, using air quotes to elaborate her point, "and at the same time sell all your porn that contributes to the problem in the first place. Hell of an itty-bitty conscience you've got there, Mr. Martone," she adds.

Raymond turns on her with a vengeance, partially in relief at having a different topic on the table.

"Who do you think you are to comment on what I do or do not do?

Have you ever been in one of my stores? I think not. Well let me tell you, young lady, there is not now nor has there ever been any child pornography in my stores. Ever! I monitor them directly myself. The government keeps coming around. They try, but they find nothing because there *is* nothing. I have fired employees who try to bring it in. I will not tolerate it."

He is furiously stabbing a finger at Tuck but he is clearly winded from his outburst. Taking a deep and wheezy breath, he continues.

"What some adults find entertaining is their own business and I am willing to provide it. I make good money off it, but I have never, and I will never, stoop to the level of selling anything that hurts children. You got that, missy?"

"I got that, Raymond." Tuck's face hardens. "But don't think for a minute that elevates you to the level of sainthood either, because it definitely does not. Not in my book, anyway. Not for anyone ever damaged by what you sell—because what you sell absolutely does feed what happened to DJ and millions of others kids. It feeds prostitution and sexual slavery and more. And how you can pretend you don't know that is beyond human comprehension."

Kate's eyes are popping out of her head. *Holy shit*, she thinks, *Tuck never blows up like this. That's usually my style. She'll give this guy a heart attack!*

Tuck balls her fists in fury, and looks around the room, casting a feverish eye on the artifacts of opulence.

"This place is a sacrilege," she says, weary from the burden of her own anger. "*You* are a sacrilege. You can surround yourself with all the religious trappings on the planet and it doesn't amount to a tinker's damn up against the evil you have done."

And then she simply runs out of steam. She falls back into her chair and turns to DJ. "Oh my god, I'm sorry," she says. "I should know better than to let myself spout off like that."

DJ has been as mesmerized by Tuck's outburst as Kate. She is perhaps not as amused, but she is certainly enchanted. And it has given her a moment to collect her own thoughts as well.

"No, Tuck, I think that was perfectly justified," DJ says, and addresses her uncle once again.

"I still want answers, Raymond. I want to know *how* you killed them, and why? I want to know how you could possibly think this would be okay with me—you who know me, or at least *knew* me better than anyone else.

God, Raymond, don't you see how by doing what you did you also robbed me?"

She shakes her head sadly, staring at her empty hands as if answers could be found in the folds of her palms.

"I don't get it, Raymond. I just don't. And now I also want to know what you plan to do about it? You can't think I'm not going to say something. Or can you?"

Raymond has turned a rather strange shade of gray and his hands are shaking visibly. He reaches across the end table for a silver bell that he rings twice. Vincent comes in almost immediately.

"How can I help you, sir?" he asks, worry causing his bushy uni-brow to meld into a straight line. "It's getting quite late for you."

"My guests are ready to leave, Vincent. Can you please show them out? Donna, my dear, I think we will need to continue our conversation once I've had a bit of a rest and a chance to digest what we have discussed. Monday, perhaps? Yes, that would be acceptable. I'll ask the chef to prepare us a nice luncheon."

The three women seem immobilized, their mouths agape at the sudden change in events.

Vincent helps Raymond stand and he moves to shake hands with both Kate and Tuck. The pair finally begins to realize it is time to go. They busy themselves with their coats and purses long enough for him to drop his hand.

"It was a pleasure to see you both. I trust we'll meet each other again at some point," he says, forcing politeness into his tone.

Tuck moves away from the group, fumbling to answer her cell phone which has just rung for the second time this evening.

DJ still sits, shaken with this abrupt turnabout in her uncle—how quickly she is being dismissed. She watches his attempt to interact with Kate and Tuck. And then he turns to her, expecting her to leave also. Her shoulders slump as she lets out an audible sigh of resignation. When she has gathered her things and stands, Raymond offers his cheek for a kiss. DJ hesitates briefly then gives him a quick peck on the forehead.

"We'll all be here again on Monday, Uncle Raymond, all three of us. For answers next time, not questions."

The three friends allow Vincent to take the lead as he walks them to their car. As they near the portico, DJ puts a hand on his arm and stops him.

"Vincent," she says. "My uncle is not well, is he?"

Surprised, Vincent desperately tries to avoid eye contact.

"You should perhaps talk with him about that, Miss… Excuse me, Donna."

"I have," she responds. "He tells me he's fine."

"Well then, I suppose he is fine," he says. Then he whispers, "But he is not."

"And that's all I'm going to get out of you tonight, isn't it, Vincent?"

His only response this time is a sad smile.

# THIRTY

"SHIT. SHIT. SHIT. SHIT. SHIT." DJ pounds her fist against the dashboard as Tuck drives away from Raymond's estate, the black gate closing slowly behind the car.

"I let him just throw me out," she says. "I knew he'd try and he did. And I went without a fight, too. Nice, little, well-behaved Donna Jean. Stands up to a man with power and then backs right down the minute he's not willing to give me an answer. Damn."

"Uh, Deej, before you beat yourself bloody, do you mind if I just observe that you definitely made your point in there? You had the guy quaking in his white Cordovan Gucci's. You scared the crap out of him, girl. Quite a feat, given who he is, if you ask me. That's all good, don't you think?" Kate says.

"Yeah, but that guy isn't just anybody, Katie. That's my uncle. The good one! What the hell am I doing here, anyway? I barely had to confront him and he as much as said he's a murderer.

"He didn't even have the audacity to deny it, did he? It was as if it meant nothing to him. Nothing! And now all I've done is give him time to try and come up with more excuses. I should have just kept pushing. But, no, the second I saw him reach for that stupid bell, his hands shaking all over the place, I just caved. This is great, just great. I am such a jerk!"

Both Tuck and Kate think it best to let her vent.

*Lots of time later on to get her to see what she did for the kindness it was,* Kate thinks to herself. *Raymond was shaken to his roots by what she said. All of it. And while I still think he already knew that she had written her autobi-*

*ography, and perhaps even knew what it said about him, I sincerely doubt he had any inkling she was going to lay murder on him tonight.*

As if she can hear Kate's thoughts, DJ hisses. "He's a murderer. He murdered my father and my uncles, his own brothers. And what he wants is for me to think that's all fine because he did it for me. This is way too far over the top. I can't even hold it in my head."

She broods silently for more than a mile.

"He's counting on me doing nothing, isn't he?" she asks without expecting or waiting for an answer. "He actually thinks that I will be fine with all this."

She quiets, and gazes at the night sky full of stars dulled only slightly by the sliver of moon traveling with them through the tall pines along the drive. "And you know what?" she asks no one in particular. "Maybe I should be fine with it. Maybe I should just leave it alone. They're dead. He's not. But if what he wants is for me to appreciate what he did for me... Well, I don't and I won't."

"I think I pushed him a bit too far when I lost it, Deej. I'm so sorry," Tuck says. "I usually have better control of my temper. Maybe if I had just shut up, he wouldn't have thrown us out when he did. Truly, I'm sorry."

"No, Tuck. I think all it did was give him the excuse he was looking for to squirm out of the box I put him in. But he was heading in that direction anyway," says DJ.

"Oh, yes," says Kate, "he was definitely looking for an out. And, if I do say so myself Tuck, you really laid into him. Proud of you, I am."

DJ is quiet the rest of the way to her home in Mansfield. Their earlier decision to stay with her tonight proves prescient. Kate reaches forward from her seat in the back and massages DJ's neck. *Feels like iron slabs in here*, she thinks, *which shouldn't surprise me at all.*

THE THREE WOMEN LOUNGE in DJ's living room, wrapped in chenille throws, watching the eleven o'clock news. More precisely, the news is on and the three women who have showered and prepared for sleep, instead, sip chamomile tea and review their day. Channel Four merely provides background noise.

DJ's calico cat, Saffron, drapes herself around DJ's neck and kneads the emerald throw, purring her contentment.

"Well, at least you're happy to see me," she says to the cat. "You must have been a pretty lonesome kitty without Sadie around to torment, huh?" The cat dials her purr up a notch. "Well I miss her too. And I honestly can't ever remember having one other day in my adult life that has left me feeling so positively wretched."

"It was one heck of an undertaking in the first place, my friend," Tuck says, "and probably wouldn't have been any easier if you had seen your mother this evening instead of Raymond. The whole endeavor is fraught with emotion for you."

Kate looks at her partner. "Fraught? Did I just hear you say *fraught?* Hum…" she pauses to think about it. "By George, I think you've got it! Fraught it is."

Kate turns to a very puzzled DJ. "Here's one of many very charming but heretofore unspoken secrets about my lover." She looks at Tuck and bats her eyes, and Tuck pokes her with her toes under the blanket.

"You and me, DJ, we'd just up and say the day sucked a big one. But my love here, she has been struggling all the way home to find the precise, albeit the most obscure, word to describe this shithole of a day. She actually does this at the end of every day. It comes from her childhood addiction to that vocabulary thing in *Reader's Digest.*"

Kate raises her cup in salute. "Here's to you, darlin'," she says with a smile, "once again you have hit the mark. It most certainly has been a day that has been fraught! We are definitely fraught. The sisters were fraught. Raymond was very fraught. And if I may be so bold as to venture a prediction, Deej, tomorrow your mother will also be fraught. Although, Tuck darling, you'll have to find another word for tomorrow, won't you?"

Tuck shrugs. "Can't use the same word two days in a row," she explains. "It's against the rules."

DJ's sudden laugh startles the cat which jumps down to her lap and does a full circle twice before collapsing into a furry ball with one paw covering her nose. When DJ strokes her back, Saffron rolls over for a belly rub and her purr kicks into an even higher gear.

These three have spent a great many evenings together just like this one, either at Kate and Tuck's townhouse or here at DJ's. Long silences are comfortable, and there is no felt need tonight to do more than try to relax and reflect.

DJ continues to sip her tea and rub the cat's belly, thinking. *Fraught, huh? Yep, that certainly describes this day. Wouldn't be the only word I'd use, though. I also feel pummeled—seriously, deeply, unmercifully, unrelentingly*

*pummeled. Don't know how Tuck can work each day down to just one word.*
*Practice, maybe. Hum, Kate said something…"*

She looks worried. "Katie? What was it that you said about Raymond? Exactly when was he quaking in his Gucci's, and why? Was it something I said that made him do that? And didn't he look sick or something? Vincent kind of agreed with that even though he wouldn't be more specific. Maybe it was just that?"

Kate freshens her tea cup from the pot and adds a bit of honey.

"He really started to sweat when you asked about your father and uncles, Deej. He had no idea at all that you were leading up to that bombshell and I think it knocked him on his ass. He couldn't get away from you fast enough. And, I think you're right. He needs time to figure out what to say to you to get you to keep this quiet. But, DJ darlin', I don't think that's all there is to what's going on with him." Kate shakes her head and blows on her hot tea before taking a sip.

"What, exactly, are you thinking, then?" DJ asks.

"Oh, boy," Kate answers and twirls the ends of her still damp red hair. "Look, I'm not sure about this at all. It's just conjecture on my part. However," and she places a strong emphasis on the word, "I do happen to think I can read people pretty well—helps in my line of work—and I'd stake my professional reputation on the fact that everything else you said to him was stuff he already knew."

It's Tuck who responds first. Throwing the covers off and dropping her feet from the couch to the floor, she looks at Kate and shouts "Damn!"

Saffron yowls and vaults off DJ's lap, making a beeline for the upstairs bedroom.

"I knew it!" Tuck continues, addressing Kate. "Did you see his face when DJ told him she had written an autobiography? He was totally ready for whatever she was going to say. Right up to the murder part. That's why I was trying to kick your foot, Katie. Damn, but we're good!" She deposits herself back on the couch and snuggles under Kate's blanket.

DJ is confused. "What about his face? What are you two talking about? And how could he possibly have any clue whatsoever what I wrote? Really, come on now, be serious."

Kate is relieved that Tuck saw what she saw. "We are serious, Deej, my friend. He knew. I don't know how and I don't know why, but he knew. He wasn't just looking at you. He was *gloating*. And there was an air of pomposity about it, too. He was merely listening, and patiently waiting for you to finish, so he could simply tell you, 'no'. Honestly, it was infuriating to watch. I bet he still sees you as a ten-year-old. You know, as if you're someone who's unable to think for herself about what's best for her and needs protection from herself. And here he is, big old Uncle Ray to the rescue once again."

"Shit," DJ mutters. "And that changed only when I mentioned my father?"

"Hell, yes. Couldn't have changed more if you had beaten him upside the head with a two-by-four, right?" She flicks her eyes at Tuck.

"Right as rain," Tuck wraps the throw around her arms and Kate pulls her close, "and wouldn't we have loved to have had our hands on a spare two-by-four, huh?"

"Frankly, I think it might require an Uzi to take him out," Kate jokes, "but I'd settle for getting in a few good whacks to wake him the hell up. Perhaps I'll get my chance on Monday."

During this exchange between Kate and Tuck, DJ has been pensive and the color has slowly been draining from her face.

"Much as I'd enjoy giving him a swift kick in the ass myself right about now, I think something just as worrisome is going on—as in, if both of you are correct, how in hell did he find out I wrote my autobiography and am trying to get it published?"

DJ looks at her friends. "Seriously, how does he know? My sisters sure as hell didn't tell him, and other than Cole, no one else besides you two knows anything about it. Sometimes things leak out when a manuscript gets to the publisher, and I half expect that to happen sometime time in the next week or so, but I only met with Cole yesterday." She looks from one friend to the other hoping for an answer, but they are as mystified as she.

"He got it earlier in the week, though, didn't he? Cole, I mean," Kate says. "Didn't you send it to him by mail a week ago? Someone there could have made a call to Raymond or something."

"Yeah, that's a possibility, but I think it's pretty remote. Maya is Cole's secretary and she'd be the one to open it and make copies, but I can't imagine she'd know enough to call Raymond. I mean, why would anyone? Even if they read it, the manuscript only mentions him in a good way. Honestly, I just don't understand any of this."

"Could Cole have called him?" Tuck asks.

"Well that's the only thing that I can see that makes any sense. But, why would he?" DJ is truly perplexed. "There's not one bit of logic to this."

Kate sits up straight, puts her cup on the table in front of her and looks around conspiratorially.

"Okay, here's another possibility," she whispers, causing the others to bend toward her voice, "what if he has this place, or your phone, bugged? Suppose he's always been afraid that if you wrote about your family, you might implicate him? Suppose he always thought you knew what happened to Ed and Joe and your dad? I mean, Sarah and Chrissie knew—or at least they figured it out. Maybe he thought you always knew and were okay with it because you never mentioned it. That might explain why he got in such a twist when you brought it up tonight, wouldn't it?"

"Yeah, but, really girls, come on now. This is my uncle you're talking about," DJ says.

"Yeah, but, really, DJ, come on now," Kate says right back. "That's precisely the point. It is your uncle Raymond we're talking about. Look what he does for a living and who he associates with. He certainly has the wherewithal to pull something off like co-opting Cole, doesn't he?"

Kate wrestles more of the blanket away from Tuck and wraps it around her feet.

"Look, DJ," she says, "your uncle has a major case of what people in AA call 'stinking thinking'. Ways people like him tell themselves that things they do, no matter how wrong, are just fine and don't hurt anyone. In fact, the stench coming off of him is so bad he might as well be road kill in July! If you ask me, it's a wonder there's not a wake of ugly buzzards circling over his head everywhere he goes. So, yeah, I one hundred percent think he'd do it."

Tuck stifles a laugh with her blanket. "Oh, good one," she says. "Perfect."

"Maybe he could do it. But he wouldn't do it."

"Why not, what's to stop him?" Kate asks. "Or, more to the point, who could stop him? Everybody's afraid of him, including you Deej. Including you."

"What do you mean, Katie? Why would I be afraid of him?"

"Well, first of all, you admitted it in Atlanta just this morning, if you want to get technical about it," Kate says. "But that's not what I mean just this second. I think the issue has more to do with the fact that he's always been such a powerful force in your life. Because when almost every other adult in your family was either absent or hurtful, he was the one to deliver comfort and safety. Makes him a really powerful character, wouldn't you say? And that can make it really hard, even though you're an adult now yourself, to see him as capable of doing something overtly hurtful to you."

DJ looks at Tuck. "And I suppose you also agree with this mumbo jumbo?"

"Yes, I do, Deej. Harsh as it sounds, it's neither mumbo nor jumbo. It's why so many of the kids we work with who have experiences like yours find it so difficult to get angry at the person who hurt them. It's hard to stand up to so much power. Instead, they get angry at whoever's closest, usually someone without any power, someone who didn't or couldn't protect them from the person with all the power."

DJ takes this in quietly, reflecting upon how this makes so much sense in light of her own experience.

Tuck continues when she sees DJ's shoulders slump.

"Look, we're not saying he has the place bugged. There's really no way to be sure about that without having someone come in and find out. But the reality is that he does have the capability. And, as I recall, he's the one that gave you that new Smart Phone you use. Do you know that spyware can be put on cell phones so that a person's whereabouts can be traced, and even their conversations monitored? It can be turned on remotely, even the camera…"

"Okay, now the two of you are just plain paranoid." DJ has to get up to search for the remote that slid somewhere into the couch cushions. She turns off the TV.

Kate wants to comment on the accusation, but DJ holds up a hand to stop her.

"Look, I can see how you could come to the conclusion, or at least the suspicion, that Raymond could bug me or this place or my phone or whatever. I get it. He certainly could. But I am still not willing to believe that he actually would. At least until it's proven otherwise to my satisfaction. So there has to be another explanation, and we have to find out what it is."

DJ sits again, across from her friends. "I am not willing to whisper in my own house, or act like I am somehow being stalked. I've never liked conspiracy theories of any kind, even in novels, and so you can be damned sure I'm not willing to place myself in the middle of one, especially without any real facts. So, let's try to figure this out, rationally. Please?"

"You know what?" Kate considers what DJ has said. "You're right. So far we have no solid evidence whatsoever that Raymond bugged anything.

But we are convinced that he knew about the autobiography. So, the only other explanation is that someone told him."

"And that could only have been Cole," DJ picks up Kate's train of thought and adds to it. "Cole… or someone in his office, I guess, but why? I mean it seriously, girls, why would Cole call Raymond for anything, never mind to tell him I wrote my autobiography?"

Tuck is thoughtful. "Here we go again… I don't think there's any way we can find out without going right to the source. We have to ask Cole. Otherwise all we've got is even more conjecture. Seems to me you're going to have to call and ask or have another meeting and put the question to him then."

"I agree with Tuck. In fact, it would probably make sense for all of us to go see him. There's more power in numbers for one thing, and we'll be able to contribute our mutual and extensive competency at reading people," Kate fairly preens at her own suggestion.

"Alright, I'll call him tomorrow and try to set something up. Providing…" here she pauses and glares at her best friends, "providing you both restrain yourselves from concocting anything that smacks of conspiracy. Anything at all. Agreed?"

Kate and Tuck have the presence of mind to at least look innocent enough when they nod their heads. DJ stands and begins collecting the cups and tea pot.

"Good," she says. "Now I'm going to bed. And we can sleep in a bit in the morning, so long as we're ready to leave here by eleven." She thinks and then corrects herself. "Let's make that ten-thirty. I want to stop at the grocery store and pick up some things for my mother. It will save us from following her up one aisle and down the other because she either can't remember or can't decide what she really wants. I'll make a shopping list in the morning."

Tuck folds the throws and drapes them over the back of the couch while Kate helps DJ feed cups and saucers to the dishwasher.

"So do you think you can manage to get some real sleep tonight, given what your day has been like?" Kate asks as she opens a cabinet door to replace the box of tea.

"God, I hope so. I'm bushed," DJ responds, rubbing her face and yawning.

"I also have to think a bit about the role my uncle's power is playing in all this. I don't want you to think I didn't hear what you were both saying.

It's just that for so long he felt like all I had that was safe. But what he did to my uncles has really shaken me. I mean it's shaken me so much that I can't yet land on what I want to do about it."

DJ punches a few buttons to start the dishwasher. "I get that what he's done fits with how both you and Tuck see him. But, honest to god, Katie, I'm lost somewhere in a weird kind of fog in my head about this. He admitted killing them, and I still can't picture it being the truth about him. What the hell is wrong with me?"

Kate reaches a hand to rest on DJ's arm. "I want to tell you something else I observed tonight," she says gently. "For all of your fury at what Raymond said and did, when you saw his hands shake the way they did when he rang that bell, you backed right off him."

"But-"

"Shush. I know you think that backing off made you feel like you let yourself down, DJ, but what I saw was the depth of your love and concern for him. Yes, even in spite of what he did. That doesn't take anything away from your anger at him. What it does show me is the extent of your capacity to have compassion for someone you love. And I need to tell you my friend, it's a flaming miracle you can have compassion for anyone after what you've been through."

Kate hugs her. "Think about that tonight if you have trouble sleeping, okay?"

Tuck sticks her head into the kitchen. "Good night, DJ. I'm going up, sweetheart, you coming soon?"

"I'm right behind you. Good night, my dear friend." Kate steps away from DJ. "May sleep bring you strength for tomorrow," she smiles. "And, if past experience is any indicator, we're all going to need it."

Alone in her kitchen DJ leans against the sink and looks out her kitchen window into the darkness. Saffron twines her tail around her legs and DJ stoops to pick her up.

"Let's go to bed too, baby," she whispers into her fur. "Sometimes it's the safest place to be."

# Sunday

"*Be patient toward all that is unsolved in your heart and try to love the questions themselves, like locked rooms and like books that are now written in a very foreign tongue. Do not seek the answers, which cannot be given you because you would not be able to live them. And the point is, to live everything. Live the questions now. Perhaps you will then, gradually, without noticing it, live along some distant day into the answer.*"

# THIRTY-ONE

KATE HURRIES DOWN THE STAIRS, hoping she's up early enough to make breakfast for everyone. Sleeping late has never been one of her failings. She's been a morning person since childhood and even living with Tuck, who at one point slept through an entire earthquake in Alaska, has not changed her. She wants to start the coffee and get the zucchini quiche she put together last night into the oven, then grab a few scoops of yogurt and a bite of fruit before heading out for her morning run. She especially loves running out here in the "burbs" as she calls DJ's small town. Better air and more hills than at her and Tuck's place in Cambridge help give her a good workout.

She's surprised to see DJ fully dressed and grinding coffee beans.

"Top of the mornin'," Kate says and gives DJ a quick shoulder hug. "You're up early. Cat fed and orange juice already squeezed. Hum... either you didn't go to bed at all, or you're raring to get this day over with. Which is it?"

"A bit of both, actually. I slept rather fitfully, I'm afraid. Even drove the cat out of the bed with all my thrashing around. Good thing poor Sadie's still at the kennel or she'd have been yowling. And, when I finally did manage to fall into a deeper sleep, Saffron paid me back by dipping her paw into the glass of water on the nightstand and sprinkling my face with it. Gotta love the little beast." They laugh and DJ flips a plastic milk jug tab off the counter for the cat to bat around the kitchen.

The two of them watch Saffron's antics for a minute or two then Kate takes the quiche from the fridge and turns the oven on. She notices an acrid odor and wrinkles her nose.

"Yeah," DJ says, "it's the milk. I was planning to do my walk anyway, so I'll go an extra few blocks to the local grocery store and grab a fresh carton. Should be back about the same time you're done with your run. Then we can pry Tuck out of bed with a crowbar and get the day moving. That sound okay to you?"

"Perfect." Kate places the quiche in the oven and checks the temperature. She looks at her watch. "This should be ready when we get back, but I want to leave a note for Tuck in case a miracle happens and she wakes up before our return. Don't want her to smell this cooking and worry about when she should take it out."

DJ fishes in her junk drawer for a pad and pen. "You'd think a writer would have the necessary tools to write someone a quick note," she mumbles, mostly to herself, "but I am just a computer kind of gal, I guess. Aha!" she finds a pencil that doesn't need sharpening and the clean back of an old donation envelope, and gives them to Kate.

"This'll do fine," Kate says and scribbles a quick message for Tuck, leaving it next to the coffee machine. "Oh! Let's ditch the milk so she doesn't use it. There's not much she can be expected to observe in her newly awakened state before she's mainlined a cup or two."

DJ rinses the jug and places it in the pantry recycle bin. "And how about you, Katie, how did you sleep?"

"I always sleep like the angels at your place," Kate says. "It's so much quieter than Cambridge, of course, but it's mostly that you've made a wonderfully comfortable home for yourself here."

DJ automatically reaches for the dog's leash.

"If that's for me, you're going to have to catch me first," Kate says, grinning.

"Oops, sorry, I usually take Sadie, not you. Poor thing's going to think I deserted her." She hangs the leash back on its peg.

They lock the door behind them as they leave.

"You have a key, right?" DJ asks, as they turn to go their separate ways at the end of the drive. "Just in case?"

Kate pats the back pocket of her running shorts.

"Yep." Her left leg lunges forward into a stretch.

DJ stands watching for so long that Kate notices. "What's wrong?" she asks.

"Nothing's wrong." DJ shrugs and looks beyond Kate to the far hills dappled with pines and with maples already starting their autumnal transformation. She takes in a deep breath of the cool fall air.

"I'm just thinking. How long have we been friends, Katie?"

Kate stops stretching. "Forever. Why?"

"I don't know," DJ says quietly, needing to say this, but embarrassed all the same. "You and Tuck... I'm just grateful is all. Unconditional friendship, I don't know what I ever did to deserve it, but I'm pretty lucky to have it—to have you and Tuck on my side. So, just, thank you. That's all."

Kate struggles not to say something half-assed and silly right now to try and lighten the moment—something she has been notorious for throughout her life. Instead, she looks directly at her friend and shakes her head.

"DJ, no one should ever have to *do* something to deserve friendship." She lunges with her right leg. "Okay, this has to do with seeing your mother today, doesn't it?"

Kate stands erect and kicks an errant stone across the driveway.

"That woman can drive you round the bend faster than Danica Patrick in her Indy car. Are you sure you want to take her on right now? Don't you have enough on your plate already, dealing with your uncle?"

"I don't know." DJ waves as a neighbor rides by and beeps. "It just makes me crazy. All of it."

"Girl, you are not crazy. For god's sake, this is how your mother *is*. Remember when Maggie was dying of that immune-deficiency disease? What was it? I can never remember what it's called."

"Amyloidosis." DJ stares off into the hills, reflecting on how everything the medical world did to try to help Mags simply had not worked.

"That's it. Remember when we kept flying out to St. Louis to relieve your sisters and help Todd care for her?" she asks, not waiting for an answer. "The times when we took your mother? That poor woman didn't have a clue about how to deal with the fact that her own daughter was dying, did she?"

DJ just shakes her head. "No."

"No, she didn't. She just kept pressuring Maggie to get married in the Catholic church, as if the Episcopal church didn't count, and yammering about praying for a miracle, going to confession, and whatever the hell else was banging around that strange brain of hers."

DJ manages a smile and says, "Hard to forget all of that. You had to stay at a hotel instead of at the house when she came with us because Todd was just about ready to ban her altogether."

"Well, who could blame him, the way she just wouldn't shut up about the church stuff," Kate says.

"She's a bit of a religious fanatic. Always has been."

"Yeah, well, that's not all she's a nut case about. She'd manage to score a perfect zero on virtually anybody's emotional contact scale."

Kate resumes stretching while she talks.

"Remember? I asked her if she'd said goodbye to Maggie."

"And you got nothing, right?" asks DJ.

"She literally shrank a couple of inches when I suggested holding Maggie's hand and saying she loves her." Kate says. "She said she didn't think she knew how to do that, and I'm thinking to myself, 'No shit, Sherlock, you really don't know how to do that, but I'm going to teach you how'."

DJ nervously tears at a fallen leaf.

"I know all this Katie," she says. "What good does it do…?"

"I know you know it, Deej. But I don't think you *get* it. *She's* the one who's crazy. Not you. Just listen. Please."

"All right, go on."

"And I did try to teach her," Kate says. "We practiced all morning. 'I'll be Maggie. You, be you. Walk into the room. Sit by my bed. No, relax. Don't stop breathing. Smile. Take my hand. Look at me. No, don't look out the window, look into my eyes. OK, just at my face. Breathe. Ask me how I'm feeling. Say you're worried about me. Say you love me. Say you're so sorry. Tell me you're sorry, not the ceiling'."

DJ cracks her knuckles. "I remember."

"Jesus, Deej. We must have done that ten times and she stayed stiff as a stick the whole time."

"Yeah," DJ says, "and in the end, when she finally got to the house, the most she could do was to stand in the bedroom doorway, and whisper to Maggie that she loved her. I remember thinking it was a miracle she could even do that."

"Well, I actually think she thought it would kill *her* to have a feeling or show an emotion. That is, if she even thought at all. And, I'll tell you, my friend, if that's all she could do when faced with her daughter's imminent death, I'm not sure you'll fare much better today when it comes to telling her about the book."

"And asking her about what Raymond did will probably send her right over the edge, too, I guess," DJ says.

"Knowing her, she'll take it out on you somehow," Kate says. "But, listen to me. That's her. It's who she is, and it's also who she isn't. Both. She is not capable of being one bit more than who she is. You are not like her. And you are not her. Period."

DJ surveys the flowered landscape of her redesigned farmhouse and barn set against the backdrop of drying corn stalks on one side and grazing cows on the other. *God, I love this place,* she thinks, and inhales the mixed scent of hay and cow. She watches vapor clouds disperse above the animals as they breathe out into the chill morning air.

"Got to do it anyway," DJ says thoughtfully, finally turning her gaze on her friend. "It's weird, you know. There's just such a huge disconnect between the way I view myself—the way my friends and even the public see me, as well—and the way my mother sees me and treats me. I never come away from there feeling as if she knows even one single thing about who I really am."

"That's because who you really are scares the shit out of her. Nothing new there, my friend," Kate says. "So it's either quit her altogether or gird your proverbial loins and deal with it. And besides, Tuck and I, we have your back girl, always. See? Simple, right?"

Kate plants her hands on her hips and cracks a cockeyed grin. "Now can I run? If we stay out here all morning jawing like this we'll ruin the quiche, Tuck will drink spoiled milk, and we will both wither and die from lack of exercise. And, frankly, I am not willing to take on that mother of yours without at the very least three good miles under my shorts. Otherwise I cannot be held responsible for what I might say or do. It's your call."

DJ throws up her hands, but she is smiling and shaking her head.

"Personally, I still think it's pretty complicated, but right now I'll settle for simple. So, go. Run." She makes pushing motions with her hands. "And I love you right back, Katherine Eleanor Brennan."

"See?" Kate shouts as she sprints across the road to run facing traffic. "Simple."

# THIRTY-TWO

DJ'S CELL PHONE VIBRATES a jitterbug along the kitchen counter. Unfortunately, DJ is unable to take the call, busy as she is at this very moment power-walking her way down Cushing Lane, hell-bent on remembering the shopping list for her mother that she has been working on in her head for the past ten minutes.

The call has not gone unnoticed, however. Saffron vaults her calico frame from floor to counter, tail twitching and ears tipped forward. She reaches out a tentative paw and gives the phone a push, then another. A slap. She pulls her paw back, crouching low in the pounce position. The phone stops vibrating. Saffron sits up, licks the paw and congratulates herself on having tamed the beast.

She hunches and jumps as the phone vibrates again. The game is on! Saffron pushes it closer to the edge of the counter. Another push. One more. Pounce! Swat! The cell sails across the kitchen, hits the pantry door and falls to the floor. Saffron follows the phone, hits it again, sits up and bats it between her two front paws. One powerful slap sends it skidding out of her reach and under the refrigerator. She crouches, eyes and nose as far under the fridge as she can reach, paw flailing about trying to reach the still vibrating cell. Then silence. Saffron pulls her head back, sits up, and for the next twenty minutes simply stares at the bottom of the fridge, waiting—her tail twitching excitedly at each new vibration.

TUCK IS IN THE KITCHEN when DJ returns.

"I was hoping to get back before you woke up," DJ says, pretty much out of breath from walking fast. She takes a few deep breaths and fills a glass of water.

"Got milk for you," she pulls a quart of skim milk out of the bag, "but can't talk until I write down the list of things for my mother. I made a mnemonic in my head of what she needs and I'll forget it if I don't write it down immediately."

Hoping to avoid the problem she encountered earlier trying to find pencil and paper for Kate, she sits at her computer and types the eight-item list. She drinks as it prints, then turns to Tuck and asks how she slept.

"I did quite well once I finally got to sleep. The quiet here always un-nerves me a bit at first. I'm such a city girl. Always will be, I guess."

"I'm surprised you're up already. I tried to hurry with the milk." DJ looks at the note from Kate, then up at the clock. The quiche still needs a few more minutes. She pulls the shopping list from the printer and tucks it into her purse on the counter.

"I appreciate the milk. Thanks," Tuck says as she pours some into her cup. She looks around. "Where's Kate?"

"Still running, why?"

"Didn't you go together?" Tuck cinches her bathrobe tightly around her waist and places a hand on her hip.

"No. Why?" DJ asks. "She wanted to do three miles or so, and I walked into town to get milk."

"You two are unbelievable," she says when DJ looks at her, perplexed. "Let me paint you a picture. Maybe that will help."

Tuck plunks herself down at the table.

"Sit," she says to DJ.

With a sigh of resignation, DJ pulls up a chair and sits across from Tuck.

"Your uncle has people killed when he doesn't like what they're doing. That, we established last night, correct?"

DJ nods her head.

"And you... you are trying to get a book published that he definitely does not want published, correct again?"

DJ's response this time is a barely audible, "Yes."

"So..." Tuck draws out the word, "what part of this don't you under-stand, DJ? Or, let me change the question. Why is it you refuse to see just how dangerous he is and how much danger you're in? And us right along with you, I might add."

This last comment has the effect that Tuck was hoping for. DJ sits up straight and looks at Tuck.

"Oh, my god, Tuck, I never thought… Oh, I should never have involved you two in the first place."

"Well, we are involved and we're not going to get uninvolved just because it might be dangerous. The work we do every day is dangerous in its own way. It's just one of the downsides of our profession. We're used to being suspicious, wary. You, however, are not."

Tuck shakes her head and looks at DJ.

"You don't seem to have a bone in your body that makes you worried about what Raymond might do, and I just don't get it. Especially after all that happened to you…" Tuck's voice trails off.

The second-hand on the kitchen clock ticks half-way around its face, and the cat's tail twitches in time with the clock.

"I'm sorry, Tuck," DJ finally says. "I should have given this a lot more thought than I have. It's just that I know Raymond so well that I still can't imagine he'd hurt me in any way, or you either. I mean, look at the headline: 'Famed romance novelist, DJ Brava, accompanied by her two closest friends, visits her notorious porn king uncle and disappears!' God, Tuck, of all the things Raymond is, stupid is not one of them, you know that."

"Look, DJ. I really do understand how hard this is for you. But the impression I got last night was that your uncle does not take a gun and shoot people. He doesn't get his own hands dirty. He has other people do it for him. And that could mean anything. Anything at all. Like a car accident when the brakes fail, or a hit and run while running. Anything, DJ. Do you see what I mean?"

Clearly she does. DJ walks to the window and looks down the road, hoping to catch sight of Kate on her way back from her run.

"I hear you, Tuck. I do," DJ says. "I'm not sure what to do about it, but I do hear you."

"Well," Tuck sighs, "as I said yesterday at least six times we—all of us—have to take this seriously, like not going off on our own. Frankly, I don't think going back to Raymond's is a good idea at all, but I know I'll be outvoted on that one, won't I?" She gets up and heads for the coffee pot. "We need to talk more when Kate gets back."

She pours a cup for DJ as well and leans against the counter.

"Oh, by the way, when I woke up, I thought I heard a noise down here like something fell. I didn't see anything or anyone, but the darned cat has been staring at the refrigerator for the past fifteen minutes and I can't figure out why."

They both look at Saffron, her glare focused on the bottom of the fridge, head cocked to the right, tail marking time like a metronome against the floor.

"Damn," says DJ, who scans the kitchen counter, then the table and floor.

"She's done it again, the beast." DJ grabs a yardstick from her pantry, gets down on the floor in front of the fridge, elbows Saffron out of the way and looks underneath.

Tuck is perplexed. "What?" she asks.

"My phone..." DJ struggles to get the right angle for the yardstick to nudge the phone in the correct direction, "is under here." She takes a stab at moving it, but only succeeds in wedging it further into the far corner.

"Because..." she grits her teeth and tries to wiggle the stick between the phone and the wall, "...my pain in the ass cat just loves to mess with my stuff."

"Can I help?" Tuck asks, somewhat amused by her view of the cat audibly purring away, waiting expectantly for DJ to release her plaything.

DJ is frustrated. She sits up and glares at Saffron.

"How many times do we have to do this before I send you to the naughty kitty farm? Huh? We have a long talk every time you do this. Do you learn? No, you don't." She gives Saffron a rub behind the ears.

"Usually she does this with my keys when I'm late for a meeting. Brat! And yes, Tuck, it might help if you grab a long umbrella from the front hall closet and come at this from the other side. The two of us working together should be able to move it enough to knock it out. It's really jammed in there good this time."

Working in tandem, the two women manage to dislodge the phone and maneuver it slowly into a position where DJ can grasp it before Saffron swats at it again.

"Got it. Whew!"

The back door opens and Kate walks in on her partner and best friend kneeling on the floor, talking to the refrigerator.

"Faith!" she cries, "can't leave you two for an hour without you both going weird on me. Anything interesting under there I should be concerned about?"

Both women sit up laughing.

"Cat," says DJ, glaring sharply at Saffron, "verses phone." She wiggles the cell in one hand as Kate pulls her to her feet with the other.

Kate helps Tuck up. "And it took two women, a yardstick and, what's that, an umbrella, to reclaim the phone from a defenseless cat?"

"You have no idea just what this *defenseless* cat can accomplish when she puts her mind to it," DJ responds as she works at checking voice mail.

"And I'll second that," affirms Tuck. "We've been fishing for that damn thing for ten minutes. And I think its past time to take your quiche out of the oven. Sorry. We got carried away under there."

Kate turns to the oven, intending to check the quiche.

"Wait just one second, Kate," she says. "I gave an earful to DJ about the two of you not staying together out there, and now you're going to hear it, too. I thought we discussed all this last night in bed."

"Oh, yeah, we did," Kate says. "I forgot."

"You guys discussed what?" DJ asks, distracted, and trying to get into her phone's message system.

Tuck folds her arms across her chest and looks at her partner, waiting for Kate to answer the question.

"We both think Raymond's a total nut job and that he's frantic about this book of yours," Kate says.

"And..." Tuck taps her foot.

"God, sometimes you make me crazy," Kate unzips her running jacket. "And, we all need to stick together in order to be safe."

"Because..." Tuck's slippered foot is now attracting attention from the cat.

Kate grits her teeth and says, "Because, we do not at this point have enough information to know what he might actually do, but we now do know what he has done in the past, and that's always a good indicator of what someone like him might do next. Okay, she-who-has-to-have-every-thing-spelled-out? Did I get it right this time?"

"Yes, you did fine," Tuck says, still finding the whole situation quite frustrating. "Thank you. Your memory seems to be intact. But what's really annoying, Kate dear, is why you couldn't have recalled all that, and acted accordingly just an hour or so ago."

She turns to DJ, hoping the conversation is having the desired effect, only to discover that DJ is still absorbed in her messages.

"Oh, damn," DJ says, "the phone must have rung. There are two messages from Cole. I was going to call *him* this morning. Let me see what he wants from me."

"He must have heard us talking about him earlier, the creep." Kate says as she finds an oven mitt in the drawer and takes the quiche from the oven. Tuck sets the table and takes orange juice and a cut up mixture of cantaloupe and honeydew melon from the fridge.

"Don't pour my coffee yet, please," Kate says. "This needs to set a few minutes before we slice into it. I'm going to run up and take a quick shower just to rinse the sweat off."

"Wait!" DJ says, her voice full of alarm. "Cole wants to see me in his office first thing Tuesday morning, along with his boss. Says he has some questions about the manuscript. It's pretty unusual for him to have Stan there, too. I wonder what the hell is going on." She looks at her friends.

"Can't help you there, girl," Kate answers. "You're the writer in this crowd. You're better at figuring out what they're up to than either of us. Besides, you've got questions of your own for him, don't you? It might be an interesting meeting. If you'd like, I'll change my morning schedule and join you."

DJ's answer is a rather distracted, "Sure. Thanks."

Kate waits for more, but not receiving it, heads for the stairs.

"Be right back," she calls over her shoulder. "Don't start without me."

"Hey," Kate hollers down, leaning over the bannister. "The entertainment value in this weekend adventure is really starting to gear up, wouldn't you say, girls?"

"You ain't seen nothin' yet, my friend," DJ shouts after her, bounding up the stairs to shower and change as well. "We're due in Providence in two hours. That's when the party gets rockin'."

"Entertainment, my ass," Tuck mutters, frustrated with both of them. She grabs DJ's cell phone from the kitchen table just as Saffron catapults herself off the window ledge and onto the chair nearest the phone.

"Hah! Not this time." Tuck glares at the cat and stuffs the phone in DJ's purse.

"Rooaawwl." Saffron complains. But no one listens.

# THIRTY-THREE

COLE'S PLANS FOR THE DAY don't include much time for home-work, but he can't get started until the air warms up just a bit more. Frustrated when he was unable to speak with DJ directly, he left two curt messages about Tuesday's meeting and decided he just had to believe she would receive them and be in his office at the appointed time.

Nothing more I can do about that today, anyway, he tells himself. As a result, he has been left with an extra few minutes of free time. He decides to fill it with a third cup of coffee and another chapter of the manuscript.

There's a definite chill to the air this morning, so he settles onto the brown wicker couch of his enclosed sun porch. The room this morning is brilliant with sun reflecting off the water, and mirroring ripples of light dancing across the walls. Cole has to wear sunglasses to offset the light's glare on the white pages.

Pen in hand, Cole opens the manuscript to a new chapter, very near the end of the tome.

## 22 • Peeling the Onion

*There are some people who survive horrendous abuse and the very fact that they have survived is enough to carry them forward into a happy and ful-filling life.*

*I believed myself to be one of those people.*

*I believed that I could be safe once I realized my uncles were gone.*

*I believed that I would be fine because my father no longer walked the face of the planet.*

*I believed these things with the same rigid convictions people used to have when they thought the world was flat and that the earth was the center of the universe.*

*I believed that the myriad ways my life was pebbled with moments of terror, that the multiple yokes of shame and guilt and self-loathing I carried, that the shrink-wrap of protection against hurt I was enshrouded within—that all of these had nothing to do with anything that had happened to me. I needed the past to be past. And so I tried valiantly to put it there. And over time I doggedly wore myself out attempting to keep it there.*

*There comes a time, however, when every castle built of sand by the most optimistic of children is inevitably swamped by the one wave no one sees coming. That its coming is entirely predictable, or that its passing holds the dual possibility of change for better as well as worse, is inconsequential to the degree of pain felt in its wake.*

*For the moment, it is enough to say that I was totally unprepared for the tsunami-driven turn my life was about to take.*

---

*My father had been dead a good number of years. I was working as a newspaper reporter in New Hampshire. My youngest sister still lived at home with my mother, grandmother and great-aunt.*

*I had returned home late from covering a town council meeting when my sister called in a panic. My father's paranoid-schizophrenic girlfriend had been calling the house all evening threatening to kill my mother. Fortunately, my mother was at work and my sister had answered the calls. My sister and I had both had previous experience with this woman and considered her quite capable of harm, so we decided that she would follow up our conversation with a call to the police.*

*The incident shook me so severely, however, that I could not replace the receiver when the call ended. He had been dead for years, and yet I still felt that my father could reach out from his grave with a long muscled hand and trap me in his embrace to hurt me again and again—any time he wished, forever and ever. The things he and my uncles had done to me suddenly became so vividly real that my body reacted as if they were happening all over again. And I could not bear it.*

*I sat for hours in my cold and dark apartment, holding onto that phone and shaking, believing—knowing—that if I let go of it my next move would be to commit suicide. I remember screaming "but he's dead, he's dead!"*

*As absurd as this may sound now, it was frighteningly real to me that night. And in that moment of desperation, I could not envision any other way out except to end my own life.*

*That I did not is perhaps obvious. What I did instead, in choosing life, was to set into motion a journey of true recovery. I chose, purposely, to walk directly into and through my painful past in much the same way fire tempers steel. It was patently clear to me, even in the state I was in, that merely surviving my abuse was no longer enough. I needed to do the work required to heal from it. I wanted even more than healing. I wanted to thrive—to be the one in control of my own life, no longer brought to my knees each time the past lurched out to try to suck me in and down.*

*When I was finally able to think clearly, I called my closest friend— thankfully a therapist herself—who responded exactly as I needed her to, tracking down the best therapist in my area, making the appointment and driving me to the first of what would be many sessions, and with more than this one therapist.*

*I had survived the abuse itself. I now set out to survive healing from it.*

---

*He was a man—his features soft, his smile wide and welcoming. That he was both young and Boston Irish was not easy to discern, facts well-hidden behind dark eyebrows and hair that had already started to thin and take leave of his forehead. Comfortable in khakis, knit sweaters, loafers, and argyle socks, he was not at all what I had pictured when the word 'psychiatrist' entered my life as a reality. No pomp, no ceremony, no tweed jacket with suede at the elbows, no pipe and stiff British accent. Just a real mensch who offered hot herbal tea on cold mornings and often had evidence of baby spit-up over his left shoulder.*

*He was a brilliant man of deep compassion and an unerring ability to both cut through and wait out all the crap I initially dealt him. His patient eyes watched over my barely disguised attempts to test his tolerance of my behavior and feed my errant belief that he, too, would be someone who would eventually hurt me one way or another.*

*I threw things around his office. I spent entire sessions in bitter silence if a question of his had the slightest shred of anything I could consider a challenge to my pitiful self-esteem. By virtue of my behavior I was, in truth, acting like an angry five-year-old pain in the ass. To his phenomenal credit, however, he was able to see into my profoundly wounded and tortured soul. I both needed him and the security and promise working with him offered, but right down and through our very last session I resisted stepping fully into the abyss that telling him everything about my past would require.*

*Our work together had not been about my sexual abuse. It had focused almost exclusively on the betrayal of trust I had suffered in the commission of that abuse and the physical and psychological abuses that also ran through my early history, twisting around and through the sexual abuse in much the same way chain link fences are formed and made virtually impenetrable.*

*With a few well-chosen words—or as was often the case, with stories—he managed to reach gently into the heart of my most serious issues. He was, in many ways, a bibliotherapist. I read more, and more widely, under his influence than I had during all the years of my education, and in so doing learned more about the workings of the mind and spirit than I thought possible to know. And, in the doing, I was learning more about my own innermost self—my needs and wants and longings, as well as, of course, the depth of my own pain.*

*He had an affinity for the poems of A. A. Milne, and would quietly pick up the book during sessions that had ground to a halt when I had planted my feet in resistance to one issue or another. Gently, in a manner so non-threatening that it took me a while to realize what was happening, his reading could shake me loose of my own resistance and open me to understanding something important about myself.*

*He read Milne's poem of the boy (was it Christopher Robin?) who sat on the stairs, halfway between the top and the bottom, and was thereby "neither up nor down". Even in my pain, I could not avoid the obviousness of the image—or the message to, literally, pick a lane and keep moving ahead.*

*Another frequent read was "James, James, Morrison, Morrison, Weatherby George Dupree". He's the little guy who "took good care of his mother, tho' he was only three". At that stage in therapy I remained fairly defensive of my mother, in spite of her lack of protection, her inability to believe me, her emotional distance from my siblings and me, as well as her all too frequent verbal attacks. This particular poem was his way of reminding me that adults were meant to carry responsibility for caring for children—not the reverse. Granted, it lacked subtlety, but the fact is that it often made me smile, and I always got the point. It was much more effective at lowering my defenses than any direct statement or question about why I was protecting my mother would ever have been.*

*He also used Sufi stories to demonstrate a point relevant to a behavior or issue of mine. The stories often became like small guides on the path I was trying to travel, much like using a compass to orient in the daylight, or a sextant in the dark. There was a goal, perhaps far ahead, and I was determined to reach it, but there were hurdles in the way that I had to navigate through or around. Things I had to recognize or accomplish first. His Sufi stories felt like coded messages of hope for the journey.*

*One, in particular, still resonates. He read of a man being crucified for a crime he has committed and of his stoicism as the village people pass by him all day, flogging him or spitting at him. He shows no emotion as he sears in the sun, lips parched, and limbs being pulled from their sockets. It is only late in the day when a small child approaches him and holds a fragrant flower under his nose that the man weeps.*

*The story's message was about the effect of tenderness and compassion shown to someone unused to compassion. The meaning for me, I came to see, was not only about believing that I was deserving of compassion and tenderness from others—but that healing from my own pain would also require me to begin treating myself with tenderness and compassion as well.*

*It would be years before I could understand that his leaving to do volunteer work in an underdeveloped country was in fact a gift that freed me to do the much deeper and painful work I still had left to do.*

*The testing and pushing I was doing with him eventually helped me to allow my own sense of trust to emerge. What I did not realize until after he had left was that while I was learning to trust him, I was also blossoming in my ability to trust myself.*

*This was to prove vital to the next stage of my healing.*

---

COLE HAS LOST TRACK OF TIME, but the chiming of the stately grandfather clock in the hall brings him out of DJ's struggle and back to the reality of his day. He closes the pen into his place in the manuscript and lays it gently on the hassock.

"Duty calls," he says, talking to the manuscript as if it could both hear him and take solace in his words, "but I will return. I promise you that."

# THIRTY FOUR

"THANKS, GANG," DJ SAYS to her friends as she folds her reusable shopping bags. She's grateful for the extra hands helping to restock her mother's food cabinet with the heavy items like water and soda. Ordinarily she would have to make quite a few trips back to the car and up to her mother's third floor apartment to bring in this many groceries.

"I just need a few minutes to clear the old stuff out of the fridge. Sometimes I find things covered in mold, all green and blue and brown. With her macular degeneration, I'm afraid she'll just eat some of this stuff." DJ's head is well inside the small refrigerator, and she backs out holding something long, black and slimy.

"Like this," she says, displaying her find. "Any guesses?"

"Gross." Tuck moves out of DJ's reach. "I'd say banana gone bad. And it stinks, too."

"It's a wonder she hasn't died of ptomaine," adds Kate, wrinkling her nose at the odor. DJ deposits the relic in the trash.

"Good thing her memory is as bad as her eyesight. She usually forgets this stuff is in here," says DJ as she grabs wet paper towels to swipe the goop left on the shelf of the fridge.

When they arrived, her mother was waiting for them on the sunny front porch, sitting in a rocker, still dressed in her church-going best, all set for a Sunday drive to lunch. She had wanted to leave immediately, was actually quite insistent about beating the crowds, but DJ reassured her that not only did they have reservations, but that the food she had just bought would spoil if they didn't get it into the fridge quickly.

"What can we do to help," asks Tuck, "anything?"

DJ pulls her head out of the fridge again and drops several stale sandwich halves wrapped in paper napkins into the trash.

"Yeah, can you feel around her chair and the couch for old wrappers or dropped food, please? Thanks. And, Kate, can you give her kitchen table and even the chairs a quick wash? She can't see what she spills. I'm almost finished with this, but I have to check the bedroom and bath, too. It's much easier to do all this when she isn't here, frankly."

The phone rings and DJ answers, listens, says "We'll be right down," and hangs up.

"That," she says emphatically, "was the front desk. My mother wants to know what in God's name we're doing up here and why all three of us have to be doing it. She wants us to come down immediately and bring that white envelope that's there on the hope chest. I need to check her mail. She's in high gear today, ladies. We're in for a ride."

"And did you hear what she said when we got out of the car?" Kate asks. "She had a big hello for me, and one for Tuck. For you, just 'what took you so long'? and 'do you really think your hair looks good like that'?"

"No surprise there, girls. You've both experienced life on my mother's planet before. You know, where negativity grows like the fungus in her fridge. That's just par for the course."

"All too true," Tuck says, "but I still loved it when she said, 'I don't suppose any of you have been to church this morning', and, Katie, you just put your arm around her, hugged her, and said 'Now, Mrs. M., how many times do we have to ask you not to go making assumptions about our spiritual lives'? You took the wind right out of her sails for a minute or two."

DJ is heading for the bedroom, but turns and looks at her friends.

"You were expecting anything different? Kate, you've known her for almost thirty years now. I gave up hoping for something different many years ago. It was killing me to keep being disappointed over and over again. I don't like it, not one bit, but I am resigned to it. It makes it easier to bear."

"Yeah, might be easier to ask a zebra to change its stripes than expect her to show some kindness," Kate responds, wiping milk stains off the kitchen table.

"Might be easier to turn the pope gay," Tuck laughs as she pokes her hands under the couch and brings out a magnifying glass and four wrapped caramels. "Ooh, booty!"

"Might be easier to turn me straight," counters Kate, rinsing the sponge.

"And that's absolutely never going to happen, if I have anything to do with it," Tuck responds, moving over to give Kate a kiss.

DJ comes out of the bedroom with a handful of used tissues for the trash.

"Aha!" she says, "can't leave you two for a minute, can I? Save that for later and do it in front of my mother. Might solve some of my problems rather quickly," she laughs.

DJ picks up the envelope full of a week's worth of mail.

"Let's get this show on the road, shall we?"


THEY FIND MRS. MARTONE sitting in the lobby across from the receptionist, tapping her nails on the edge of the overstuffed armchair.

"What's taken you so long, and what on earth were you doing up there anyway?" she demands of DJ as soon as she recognizes her daughter.

Before DJ can respond, Kate takes over. She sits on the arm of the chair.

"Just doing some interior decorating, Mrs. M," she says brightly. "The bedroom walls looked dull, so we painted them a soothing pink. We added floor-to-ceiling drapes in the living room and installed a wide-screen TV above the Jacuzzi in the bath. It's part of our friendly service. No charge, of course."

The look of puzzlement on her mother's face, along with the hearty laughter from the receptionist, is enough to ease the tension in the room.

Her mother finally gets the humor, or at least she pretends to do so. "Oh, you," she says to Kate.

"Come on, Mother, let's go to lunch," says DJ, helping her mother to her feet, and giving Kate a nudge in the ribs at the same time.

It's a slow walk to the car with her mother on her arm.

"Would one of you be willing to drive?" DJ asks. "It will give me a chance to go through the mail with my mother and save some time later in the day."

Kate volunteers and DJ climbs into the back seat next to her mother, clicks both of them into their seat belts and begins pulling mail out of the larger envelope. She looks up.

"Thanks, Kate," she says, "and just take 95 to 195 East over the bridge until the Bristol exit. I'll let you know what to do then." She focuses on her mother and the mail.

"I'm going to put the bills aside, Mom. There are about four of them in this pile and I'll pay those tomorrow at home. They're for the cable, phone, your meds and rent. Oh, and offering envelopes from the church. Then you have six or seven charities here, looking for a handout."

She notices her mother leaning into her.

"What's wrong?" she asks. "Are you slipping on the seat?"

"Shush," her mother whispers. "I want to know what they were doing in my room. You didn't let them see any of my investment information did you? Did you leave them alone in the front closet where my papers are? Why did you have to bring them in the first place? Now you expect me to pay for everyone's dinner, is that it?"

DJ can see Kate's questioning look in the rear-view mirror and rolls her eyes at her. This paranoia is nothing new to DJ. Her mother is legally blind, but won't allow DJ to hire a reader for her because she thinks they'll pry into her personal belongings and steal them. She whispers back to her mother.

"Nobody saw your things, Mother, except me. They helped me carry your groceries upstairs and put them in the fridge and the kitchen cabinet. That's all. Honestly, you exasperate me when you do this. And you're not paying for anyone's lunch. I am, okay?"

She takes more mail out of the envelope.

"Oh look," she says, "Sarah sent pictures of Jennie and the new baby. Your first great grandson! He is just adorable. Looks like Jennie when she was a baby. Can you see this? Do you have a magnifying glass with you?"

Tuck interrupts and asks for directions as Kate turns off 195 toward Bristol. DJ attends to the road for a brief time to get her bearings and focus on where they are headed. Her mother searches her purse for a magnifier but is unable to find one.

"That's okay," DJ says as she shifts her attention back to her mother. "It's probably too bumpy for you to see the pictures well in the car anyway. We can try when we get back to the apartment. Besides, we're almost to the restaurant." DJ shuffles through the rest of the mail.

"Most of these are catalogs, Mother, and your monthly newsletter from the diocese. I'll put that aside to read to you later."

"What's this, a bill?" Her mother takes a long white envelope from the stack on DJ's lap.

"No. Just a statement from Blue Cross telling you what they paid for your eye doctor visit." DJ looks up.

"Oh, Kate, take a left at the light and the restaurant is just there on the right along the water. See?"

"Got it, thanks," Kate pulls in and parks in a handicap spot. Tuck hangs the necessary sign from the rear-view mirror.

Between the slow movements of her mother and the business of The Lobster Tale, it's a full ten minutes before they are seated and looking at menus. DJ reads the specials aloud to her mother who interrupts to ask how much the steamers cost today.

DJ tells her.

"How much?" she asks loudly, "twenty-five cents! Apiece? They're charging for them individually, now? I'm not paying that price. You used to be able to get a whole pint of steamed clams for twenty-five cents."

"Calm down, Mother. You're not paying for anything. If you want steamers, get steamers. How many would you like?" DJ tries to maintain her composure.

"This is how you show off to your friends? Paying big money for something that's way overpriced, is that it? That's what you do with your money?" Her mother is off and running. DJ looks at Kate and Tuck for some help.

Kate comes to the rescue once again.

"Oh, look, Mrs. Martone. They have both lobster stew and lobster pie today. Which one is it that you like so much?" Kate looks over the top of her menu and gets DJ's mother's attention.

"It's the pie that I want, dear," she answers sweetly. "The stew has too little lobster and too many vegetables. You get more for your money with the pie. And it's delicious here, too. Why don't you try it?"

"Hum. I just might," she responds, "although the baked stuffed shrimp seems to be calling my name. I'm just not sure."

Kate is doing her best to keep Mrs. Martone engaged in order to give DJ a break.

"Do you remember all those fall Sundays you used to come up north when DJ and I were in college? You'd take us over to Portsmouth and we'd go to that place right on the docks where we'd have the best seafood ever. What was the name of that place, do you recall?"

"Oh, goodness, that was so long ago. My memory's not what it used to be. You two were just girls then, so young."

"Why, Mrs. Martone, are you implying that we are no longer sweet young things? I find that hard to believe."

DJ's mother laughs.

"Well, you'll never be as old as I am, that's for sure. And you may still be as sweet as you always were, but I can't say the same for my daughter. It has never been in her nature to be sweet, in spite of all that sugar she eats."

DJ can sense the conversation going south, and she certainly hasn't missed the coldness that fills Kate's eyes at her mother's last remark, so she is relieved when the waiter asks what they would like.

Kate orders first and Tuck says she'll have the same. DJ requests steamers and lobster pie for her mother and then salad and baked stuffed shrimp for herself.

"Are you really going to order the stuffed shrimp, Donna?" her mother says. "All that butter can't be good for you, you know." She turns to the waiter and puts her hand on his arm as he is about to leave the table.

"She'll have the grilled shrimp instead of the baked stuffed," she advises him and he, in turn, looks helplessly at DJ.

"The order is fine as is, thank you," DJ states firmly, trying to hold on to her quickly fading good nature.

"Still making poor choices, I see," says her mother, tucking her napkin into the collar of her suit jacket.

"You know, don't you, how much better you'd look on the back of all those so-called books you write, if you'd clean yourself up a bit and lose a few pounds. Pictures, just like the television, always make people look bigger. And if you must write that, that, material that you write, you might as well look good on the book. That's all I have to say."

*That's never all you have to say, Mother. And that's only part of your problem,* DJ thinks. *Tuck and Kate are looking exactly like Saffron when she's about to pounce on prey. This could be funny if it weren't so stinking pathetic.*

DJ smiles to herself at the thought, but is interrupted by her mother asking for rolls and butter. Tuck passes the rolls, opening the napkin they are covered in to make it easier for Mrs. Martone to find one. Kate peels the cover off a pat of butter and places it on a plate, while DJ removes the paper from a straw and inserts it in her mother's drinking glass. She crumples the paper and drops it next to her plate.

*Now or never* DJ says to herself, and shifts slightly in her seat.

"Mom," she starts, "I wanted to get together today because I need to tell you I've written another book."

"That's nice, dear," her mother responds absentmindedly as she struggles to butter her roll. DJ notices that the paper from her straw is clinging to her mother's knife and she is trying to spread this across her roll.

Kate and Tuck are watching, trying valiantly not to laugh out loud, and DJ has to suppress her own urge to chuckle. With anyone else suffering from macular degeneration, they would have nothing but empathy. With her mother it feels like payback for the insensitive things she has just said. And if history repeats, as it is wont to do, she will continue to say throughout this meal.

DJ moves to shake the paper loose from the knife. She takes the knife from her mother and butters the roll for her.

"Try this now, Mom. Better?" She waits until her mother bites into the bread.

"This new book is different, Mother. It's my autobiography, and it's quite explicitly graphic about our family and the things that have happened in it over the years, especially in my childhood. And I definitely write about what dad and his brothers did to me. I want you to be prepared in case there's any publicity that might be upsetting to you. Understand?"

"That shouldn't be a problem, dear. Why would you think it might? You and your sisters had a pretty happy childhood as far as I could tell. I mean, we had problems, yes, but everyone does, don't they? And what makes you think anyone is interested in what went on in our family anyway? Can't you just keep writing those other silly books you've been writing for years? I know your sisters like them, but for the life of me I can't see what makes them so special."

She turns to Tuck.

"Do you read the drivel she writes?"

Tuck's answer has to wait. Their salads and the steamers have arrived. There is prep work to do so that DJ's mother can remove the clams from their shells, dip them into the broth to clear them of any sand, dip them in butter, and get them to her mouth without mishap.

Kate and Tuck have been uncharacteristically silent throughout this ordeal, although they have been kicking each other under the table and making eyes at one another each time Mrs. Martone takes another stab at her daughter. They now find themselves inhaling their salads and remarking on their ingredients simply for something to say.

DJ tries again to get her mother's attention back on the issue at hand.

"I have a few questions that I'd like to ask you, Mom. There are some things I don't quite understand about what happened with dad and with Joey and Eddie."

Her mother's hand pauses between the broth and butter bowls.

"What do you mean, Donna? What about Ed and Joe?"

"I want to know what happened to them, Mother. Where did they go and where are they now?"

"You know as well as I do," says her mother. "They went to work for your uncle Raymond down south someplace." She slides another clam out of its shell, grabbing it by the neck and starting the dipping sequence.

"And you've never wondered in all the years that have passed, why they never came home again? Never saw Nana again? Why no one ever even heard from them again?" DJ notices her own tone becoming more strident and struggles to control herself.

"No, I haven't," her mother responds. "They're men. They work, and they probably have their own lives and families now and don't want to be bothered with all of us. That's all."

"Well, they're no longer working for anyone, Mother. Raymond had them killed. That's what happened to them."

Apparently appalled at DJ's comment, Mrs. Martone sucks in a sharp breath and covers her heart with her palm. After a moment, she pulls herself upright in her seat and points a finger slick with melted butter at her daughter.

"Now you stop that right now, young lady. I will not tolerate you telling lies about your uncle. He's a wonderful man who took care of all of us after your father died."

She turns to Kate and Tuck.

"This is what she always manages to do. She can ruin your day with her questions and lies. How do you girls put up with this?" Her mother reaches for another steamer, but this one slides out of the shell and into her water glass. She tries fishing it out with a fork. DJ puts the glass out of her mother's reach.

Kate has tried her best to stay out of the conversation thus far, but her resolve to do so fails at this point.

"But you must have known this years ago, Mrs. Martone, didn't you?" she says.

DJ's mother turns on Kate as fast as a cobra strikes its prey.

"How dare you, young lady? Why Donna brought both of you to stick your nose into our family business is beyond me."

DJ holds her hand up to stop Kate from answering.

"Mother, listen to me. For once, just listen." DJ is determined to have this conversation.

"This is not a lie. Raymond admitted it himself yesterday. I am going to see him again tomorrow and I plan to find out exactly why he did what he did. But he did do it. Now, I have just one more question for you. What happened to my father?"

"Oh, for the love of Pete, Donna Jean, all this happened so long ago. Why do you keep bringing these things up again? Aren't you over all that yet? That business with your father and his brothers was years ago. You just continue to make my life difficult, don't you?"

"I know he died of a heart attack at work. Who else was there, any-one?"

"Raymond was with him. Is that what you need to know? I'm just so grateful he didn't die all alone. I'm glad Ray was there, even if you are not." Her mother is fairly hissing at her at this point. "You are impossible, Donna Jean. You always have been. It always has to be your way, doesn't it? You want to write your autobiography? You go right ahead. But you'd better be clear about one thing. You're the one responsible for most of the problems in our family. You and that mouth of yours that you don't know when to keep closed. And if anybody ever asks me, you'd better be prepared for me to say that to them, Lady Jane. We'll see what all your fans think of you then, won't we?"

While Tuck and Kate hold their eyes wide in wonder at the outburst, they know that DJ is neither embarrassed nor defensive that they are pres-ent to witness. This is not the first mother-on-daughter hurricane they have seen and heard. Nor is it likely to be the last. It's the sadness in DJ's eyes and the slumping of her shoulders that they are having trouble with, and they fight their mutual desire to pull her in and offer shelter from the invective raining down on her.

*God, now I know why DJ called her latest character Serpentine! She's lived with one all her life! Perhaps if there is a God, one of those clams her mother's eating will be tainted,* Kate thinks, trying to give herself some dis-tance from the anger and sadness she feels at the scene in front of her. *It might just put her out of her own misery. And everyone else's, too!*

Mrs. Martone finishes the steamers she can see, leaving a few on the plate. DJ struggles with her impulse to tell her mother where they are or move them closer to her fork. Not today.

"Like it or not, Mother, I'm pursuing this. I met with Sarah and Christine yesterday in Atlanta and with Raymond last evening. I'm seeing him again tomorrow. I take it he's not well these days, but I am going to get the information from him that I need, one way or the other. I am merely trying to take you into consideration by letting you know. That's all. You don't have to like it. You don't have to like me. I don't really care. I just needed you to know."

Her mother looks at her, obviously confused.

"Not like you? Of course I like you. I'm your mother. I have to love you. What kind of a mother would I be if I didn't try to help you? I've only been trying to help you all your life, but you are just so stubborn and arrogant. You just don't listen. I wouldn't speak to you this way if I didn't love you. No one else will tell you the truth about yourself. Even your friends here don't have the courage to tell you to your face, do they?"

"Tell me what, Mother? Just what is it you think they are afraid to tell me, huh?"

"Oh, honey, you tell stories. You always have. You make things up. Don't you see that yet? It's probably what makes you such a good writer, but I think it's also why you're unable to have someone in your life who will love you." She looks quickly at Kate and Tuck, then back to DJ. "A man, I mean, a husband to take care of you and give you children. That's what God intends for us women. And you'll be much happier and stop all this nonsense if you would only go back to the church where you belong."

"Are you finished with your clams, ma'am?" the waiter asks over her shoulder. When she turns to tell him yes, the three friends open their mouths wide. Kate and Tuck mimic guns against their foreheads. DJ bangs her own forehead with her fist.

The waiter serves the entrees and the three friends attend to their food—anything to avoid the way the conversation is heading.

Mrs. Martone, however, is not satisfied.

"And just what did your sisters have to say to you about this new book of yours?" she asks, stabbing a fork through the crust of her pie as if she were spearing a shark. "Didn't they have the sense to tell you they don't want their family secrets spread across the front pages of the *Providence Journal?*"

DJ puts her fork down and prepares to give her mother a thoughtful answer. But there is no need as her mother powers on.

"Because that's exactly what they should have told you if they had any sense whatsoever. However, usually they do not, especially when you've been able to work them up about something. Oh! You girls are all such a disappointment." She pauses and looks hard at DJ.

"I'm only going to ask you for one thing, Donna Jean, just one." She points her fork almost directly under DJ's nose.

"If you must do this, then at least show me the courtesy of waiting until I'm dead." Then, without skipping a beat, she resumes her attack upon her lobster pie.

This time, however, DJ, Kate, and Tuck are all aware of the way that the hand holding the fork is trembling.

DJ stares at her mother, shakes her head, opens her mouth to respond, then closes it and looks down at her plate, pushing the shrimp to one side, then the other.

Both Tuck and Kate wiggle around a bit in their seats. Kate purposely drops her napkin and the two bump heads reaching to retrieve it.

Kate gets the worst of the bump, grabbing her head and saying "ouch!"

"Sorry, honey," Tuck says, then whispers quickly, "if DJ has to wait for the old girl to kick the bucket, her book will never get published. Remember, only the good die young. This one's got lots of miles left on her yet."

Kate covers her mouth with the napkin and makes a coughing sound in an attempt to stifle a laugh.

Mrs. Martone hasn't heard the exchange but doesn't miss the collision.

"Are you okay, dear?" she asks sweetly.

"I'm fine, Mrs. M. Thanks. Just bumping heads a bit."

DJ, who does overhear the stage whisper, crosses her eyes and puffs her cheeks at her two friends. She looks at her watch and sighs.

The rest of the meal passes uneventfully, marred only briefly by Mrs. Martone's outburst over the cost of her dessert, which, in the end, does not stop her from ordering it and devouring every bite.

Her mother makes a feeble gesture about picking up the tab, but is visibly relieved when DJ insists it's her treat.

*All three of us get freaking ulcers from eating with this woman and I get to pay for it to boot! My lucky day,* DJ tells herself as she helps her mother on with her coat.

DJ opts to drive and thus avoids the back seat again with her mother, letting Kate do the honors instead.

*If my friends were anything but social workers,* she thinks, *my mother would be toast right about now. Perhaps I do need to cultivate different relationships. Maybe I'll take a paid assassin with me next time.*

# THIRTY-FIVE

WHEN THEY PULL INTO THE assisted living facility parking lot, Mrs. Martone breaks the silence.

"That was a lovely dinner, girls. Thank you so much. Why don't you all come up and we'll have a nice cup of tea?"

*Oh my God, DJ. Do not say yes to her or I may have to strangle you,* thinks Kate. *I overdosed on her shit about two hours ago.*

"No, thanks anyway, Mother. We have a couple of other stops to make on the way back home. None of us have done our own grocery shopping yet and tomorrow's a holiday."

"But you haven't read me the newspaper today," her mother whines, fully expecting DJ to give in.

"I'll have to do that during the week, Mother. I have a meeting with my publisher on Tuesday and there are a number of things I need to clear up before then, including seeing Raymond again tomorrow." DJ's voice is firm, clearly indicating resolve.

Her mother's bottom lip slips into a pout.

DJ spots the move. *Ah, so that's where that mouth thing comes from. Remind me never to do that again.*

"It would appear that you are going ahead with this book in spite of my wishes then, doesn't it? Honestly, Donna Jean, I don't know why I even bother with you. You manage to disregard everything I ask of you. You're lucky I don't disown you."

Something inside DJ snaps. She has had more than enough of her mother's criticism. She turns in the driver's seat and looks directly into her mother's face.

*"I'm* lucky you don't disown *me?* That's a joke, right? You listen to me and you listen good. *You're* lucky I haven't disowned *you!* And if you want to know why, here's the list…"

DJ starts with her pointer finger and ticks off a list one at a time.

"One, I tell you the guy next door tries to rape me. You do nothing.

"Two, you call me a liar every chance you get, to anyone who'll listen.

"Three, you ridicule my weight, my choices, my friends, my education, my career, my writing. Everything. Incessantly.

"Four, I told you my uncles abused me and you asked me what I was doing to make them do that to me."

DJ pauses a beat to give her racing heart a chance to recover, and then charges ahead, this time punctuating each of her words by stabbing additional fingers into the air.

"Five, I told you my father abused me and you told me you hoped that wasn't why I hadn't found a man to love me.

"Six, any time anyone says anything nice about me you counter it with a negative remark intended to diminish me.

"Seven, any time I receive an award for my writing, you assert that if people only knew what I was really like they wouldn't be so quick to award me anything."

She stops for another deep breath, and feels Kate place a supportive hand against her back.

"Is that enough, or would you like me to continue? And you want to disown me? You go right ahead. I have truly had it with your rude and callous behavior toward me. Got it? Do you? I could have and should have disowned you years ago. God knows I've had enough reason and enough opportunity."

DJ is drained and turns in her seat intending to get out of the car, but she catches sight of her mother in the rear-view mirror as she does so.

"Shit," she mutters under her breath and slaps the steering wheel.

The look of shock on her mother's face, the tears in her eyes, and the rigid quiver of panic in the hand she holds against her head brings DJ off her high horse and down to earth again with a *thud.*

Kate and Tuck see it also.

DJ scrambles out of the car, opens the rear door and offers a hand to her mother. Mrs. Martone's teeth are clutching her bottom lip so tightly that she has broken the skin and a small trickle of blood is visible on her chin. Her eyes flicker wildly as she grasps DJ's arm and struggles out of the back seat.

"I'm sorry. I'm sorry. Mommy, I'm so sorry." Her mother clings to DJ's arm, pleading with her, her body shaking in palsied tremors.

DJ holds on to her mother.

"It's okay, Mom. It's okay." She walks her mother into the facility.

DJ understands that this is not remorse. It is not fear of hurting her daughter's feelings. This is the dread of being left—of staring into the void of being abandoned.

Of being left and sightless, with only her memories.

And, in spite of everything, in spite of all the years of pain, it still matters to DJ.


THE RIDE HOME IS QUIET, but the air within the car is filled with nervous apprehension, the aftermath of DJ's spent fury still pulsating with the hum of the tires on the road. Tuck drives and DJ is slumped in the back seat, as close to utter physical collapse as she has been in a long, long time.

They are halfway to DJ's house before Kate has the courage to speak, and she wants to say something before the opportunity passes and the memory of DJ's mother's trembling statement fades.

"Deej, hon, are you awake enough for me to tell you something?" she asks quietly.

"What is it?" DJ mumbles from the rear.

"I want you to know I get it. We both do, Tuck and I. I used to wonder why it is that you keep going back for more, when she just keeps on being so abusive to you like she was at lunch. I mean, my God, Deej, nobody should have to take that." She shivers.

"It's all about terror, isn't it?" Kate continues. "Your mother knows what happened. She knows perfectly well what it's done to you. She knows what she didn't do for you—perhaps was incapable of doing, driven by fear as she was and still is. And she's petrified to admit it. But equally petrified of losing you and having to face what it would mean for her not to have you in her life."

"Yep, that about sums it up," DJ says softly.

Then Kate adds, "Going blind doesn't help, because she needs someone to do just about everything for her. But the bigger issue for her that

I see is that aging brings her closer to facing the very God she spends her life worshiping and who she now thinks might ultimately condemn her for what she didn't do, rather than what she did."

DJ sits up a bit. "I think," she says, "that my mother lives with incredible shame. And it keeps her isolated and in a constant state of dread."

"And the religion she's always depended on for solace and direction is now scaring her half to death," Kate offers.

"Amazing. Totally freaking amazing," Tuck says.

Kate smiles ruefully. "And hence the PPT diagnosis, my friends. She is definitely the Poor, Pathetic Thing poster child."

"Then there's the way she wants to silence you. Again. Wait until she's dead! Really?" Tuck says.

"Okay you two, but you do know there's another whole side to this, don't you?" DJ says. "I mean, I hardly feel like defending her at this point, but she's not the first or the only person to want to silence me. It's what's done to anyone who tries to speak about the unspeakable. Says the things no one wants to hear. Hell, just look at the times she was brought up in, for one thing."

"Point taken, DJ, and you're right. Wasn't so long ago that Freud had all those female clients reporting sexual abuse as a child. He believed them, and he wrote about it," Kate says.

"Yeah," Tuck grabs the conversation and runs with it. "He believed them right up to the point his cronies had a huge hissy fit and it threatened his credibility. Scared the big guy right back to the Stone Age, and he ended up calling all his clients 'hysterical'. All the women, that is!"

"And that…was that. Slammed the door shut on women's reality even before it was fully opened." Kate slaps her palms together to emphasize her point, and the hollow sound resonates within the small car.

"Women's experience, women's pain, women's right to free expression have all been stigmatized, vilified, silenced for centuries," Tuck says. "Women have suffered alone, each one's experience privatized: no one to tell, no one to listen, no one to believe. It left each woman believing that child sexual abuse, rape, domestic violence, only happened to her and that it must be her own fault. At least that's how it was until the Women's Movement began the conversation."

"Well…" Kate's response is deliberate, indicating previous thought given to the subject. "The Women's Movement may have begun the conversation, but it's certainly revved up the people with the power to shut us up. We must have scared the crap out of them." She pauses. "I don't know if either of you noticed, but when we had the TV on last night, one of the reports was about the growing national effort to turn the page back about four decades. Taking away pretty much all the territory women have gained."

"And the beat goes on," says Tuck. "So no matter how old we get, we also get to keep on fighting for our voices to be heard. The same fight we've been at since we came of age. How nice for us."

DJ has been listening closely.

"So, it's not just that my mother's a stubborn old coot with her feet firmly planted in the nineteen fifties, but that everything around her conspired to silence her from the very beginning. People, and agents with power, do it all the time. Men, churches, governments. She was as affected by them as anyone else. Still is, sadly."

Kate adds, "And then here you come along, making waves, saying the things girls and women aren't supposed to say…"

DJ finishes the thought. "You were right on target this morning, Katie. She truly doesn't know what to do with me. Never did."

None of them has a second to process DJ's comment. A deer runs across the darkening highway in front of them, caught momentarily in the glow of the car's high beams. Tuck brakes sharply and pulls hard on the steering wheel to avoid hitting it.

"Holy shit!" she says, "can't see a damn thing out here in the sticks."

The jolt of adrenalin has affected all of them.

"God, but I'm weary," Tuck says, shaking. "And I'm driving—not a wise thing, girls. It's good we're almost there."

"Just one more quick question, Deej," Kate says. "Did she really call you 'Mommy'? Did we hear correctly?"

"Yeah…you did." DJ's response is measured. "It's only happened a couple of times before, when she's either been very upset or ill. I don't quite know what to make of it, but it's certainly odd, isn't it?"

"I think it is, yeah," Kate says after giving it some thought. "I'm not that familiar with the aging process. Maybe it's just a function of old age and stress."

DJ mulls that possibility over in her head.

"Both of those are probably contributing to her state of mind, I'd think," she finally says. "But I also think it's mostly because she sees herself as having failed as a mother. Not because of the abuse that happened, necessarily, but mostly because none of her children are like her. None of us practice her religion, and she sees that as her biggest failure. And I also think she's petrified that other people will see her that way too. That's one of the many reasons she's so afraid of what I say, and now what my book might say. Frankly, I can't think of anything more horrendous for a mother than to have that kind of abject fear."

Kate considers DJ's comment.

"You really don't hate her, do you, Deej?"

"No, I don't, surprisingly. I used to when I was young, though. You know, when I thought that anger might change things."

"I guess she's more to be pitied, than hated, huh?" Tuck says.

"Actually, I think it would be more accurate to say that I have come to have a great deal of compassion for her. No expectations. Not any longer. Just compassion."

"Hum," is all that Kate can say in response.

After a mile or so of silence, DJ adds, "There's one more thing, too, that pulls me in. It's a decision I made when we were all dealing with Maggie's death."

Her voice gains strength as she talks.

"I don't want to spend the rest of my life regretting something I could have done and didn't do. Hard as it is to deal with her shit, I don't ever want to feel I knew the right thing to do and didn't do it. That's why I see my mother."

"Because it's the right thing to do?" Kate asks.

"Because it's the *only* thing I can do," DJ responds.

Three heads nod in agreement.

"And sometimes... sometimes it truly sucks," utters DJ into the night air.

TOO TIRED TO DO MUCH ELSE this evening, the women decide against shopping and instead opt to relax at DJ's and rent a movie.

Once home, DJ feeds the cat, puts out the trash for morning pick-up and closes herself into her bathroom for a long, hot shower. Within minutes her cell starts chiming and Kate picks it up.

No sooner is "Hello" half way out of her mouth, when shouting starts at the other end.

"What did you do to mother? She's a full blown mess. And not only that, she now wants-"

"Christine," Kate has to yell to be heard, and even then, she has to repeat herself four times.

"Sweet Mary, Mother of God, Christine, will you put a cork in it for once and just shut up," she says with her Irish taking over. "You sound like a flock of magpies. Stop and listen for a minute, will you please?"

"Kate? Kate? What are you doing on DJ's phone? Where is she? Put her on. I just got home to Ann Arbor and Garret tells me this phone has been ringing off the hook for the past two hours. It's my mother. He even tried talking with her, but she's just far too upset, and now she's saying she wants to move in with us. Where's my sister and what did she do?"

*Oh, my Lord. Now we have two lunatics on the loose,* Kate sighs.

"She's in the shower. I'll have her call you as soon as she's out."

"Oh no, you won't," Chris insists. "You march right in there and give her this phone right now. I'm not waiting another minute."

"Okie, dokie, then," Kate says. "Have it your way. Hold on."

Kate knocks on the bathroom door and, hearing a muffled response, enters to find a dripping DJ stepping out of the shower. Startled, she grabs for a towel to cover herself.

"Kate," DJ says in surprise, "I'm naked!"

"Nothing I haven't seen before, toots, so relax," Kate responds and presents the cell phone. "Your sister is having a hissy fit. Her knickers are all in a twist over something to do with your mother."

"My sister? Which one?" DJ asks as she reaches for the phone with one hand and struggles to hold the towel with the other.

"Which sister?" Kate says, rolling her eyes. "You really need to ask? The one whose picture is next to the words 'hissy fit' on Wikipedia. That one." Playfully, but unsuccessfully, she grabs at DJ's towel and leaves the room, singing, "She's all yours."

Evidently Christine has been talking the whole time. DJ listens for a minute, sits on the edge of the tub and dries herself off, waiting.

"I'm here, Christine," she finally says, "whenever you're ready to listen."

"No, you listen, DJ," Chris says, "I don't know what you did, but mother is packing her bags as we speak and she fully intends to move in here with us. That is not going to happen. It's just not. I will not have it. Didn't you listen to me yesterday? I have enough going on right now…"

DJ sighs heavily and interrupts. "Christine, mother isn't going anywhere and you know it. Calm down for just a minute. She can hardly see, for goodness sake. How on earth can you even think she can just pack up and move anyplace without one of us moving her? She's upset, and she's embarrassed, and she'll get over it. Let her have the time she needs to get used to this, would you?"

It's quiet at the other end. Then just the faint sound of "oh, okay… maybe…"

DJ shakes her head. *Oh, Christine, you are such a mess.*

"But she said that if I wouldn't take her, she'd go to California with Sarah. In fact, I think she tried to get to Sarah first, I know she likes her more than me, but Sarah's with those friends of hers and they went to some vineyard today. Did you know they had vineyards in Georgia? I didn't. Anyway, they've all been drinking since about two o'clock. No way Sarah would even talk with mother when she's under that much influence."

DJ lets her run on again for a few more minutes, and then cuts in once more. "Mother is not going with either one of you. She's staying right where she is. I'm sure that by Tuesday afternoon the social worker will be calling me wondering why she's so upset, and the nurse will call about her blood pressure, and I'll go down there again on Wednesday and spend the day with her and things will be back to our family's strange idea of normal by next weekend. So, please, can I just go to bed now? I'm exhausted. And you must be, too."

"Well, yes, now that you mention it. It's been a long weekend," Chris sighs.

DJ seizes the moment. "Look. I'm going to call you tomorrow with those names I promised anyway. How about we talk more then?"

"Okay… well… goodnight. Love you," Christine says, sounding not all that sure she's truly ready to stop ranting.

"You, too." DJ ends the call quickly before Chris can think of something else to complain about. She dons her nightgown, wraps her head in a fresh towel and walks into the kitchen.

Kate gives her a long look.

"Well, you look like hell," she says.

"Screw you, too," DJ responds with a smile.

"I was just putting tea on for Tuck and me. Want some?"

"Oh no, before the phone call, maybe tea would have been enough. Not anymore," DJ says. "Now I need the good stuff. I am going to stretch out on the couch. What I would like, if you're willing to pour, is about three fingers of Amarula over two cubes of ice. I think I deserve it tonight."

"Ah, ha!" says Kate, turning off the tea kettle, "the Kenyan cure. That's a great idea. Mind if we join you?"

"Be my guest. Well, actually, it's my house so I guess you are," DJ chuckles at her own wit. "Just deliver the drink, turn on the movie, and let's observe an evening of well-deserved silence. How's that?"

Kate opens her mouth to comment, but DJ quickly reaches across to her, places a finger on Kate's lips, and whispers, "Shush."

# Monday

*"Tell them about how you're never really a whole person if you remain silent, because there's always that one little piece inside you that wants to be spoken out, and if you keep ignoring it, it gets madder and madder and hotter and hotter, and if you don't speak it out one day it will just up and punch you in the mouth from inside."*

# THIRTY-SIX

B REAKFAST THE NEXT MORNING is interrupted by both Kate and Tuck's cell phones. Their answering service asks them to respond to an emergency call from child protective services.

"Sounds like they're going to want an evaluation on a kid done today," Katie says to Tuck. "How should we handle this?"

Tuck looks at the number Kate has written on her napkin.

"Let me call the social worker and see if that's really it," she suggests. "If it is, how about you stick with DJ, and I'll do the eval?" She stops. "But only if you two are extra careful today, seriously careful. Raymond's a train wreck, and now that he knows that you know what he did, he could be even more desperate. Do I have your word, both of you?"

DJ and Kate look at each other.

"You two have to stay together. Nothing's changed, DJ. Except that maybe he can tell how strong-minded you are. And if he's talked to your mother since yesterday…" Tuck doesn't finish.

"Okay, okay," Kate says. "We hang together."

"Good." Tuck says, purposely ignoring Kate's choice of words. "I know how to reach you if I have questions. And I'll keep my cell on in case you need help. Besides, I've just about had my fill of Raymond, thank you very much."

She quickly looks at DJ. "No offense, but…"

DJ holds up her hands. "None taken, I'm in complete agreement."

Tuck heads for the den and some privacy to make the call. DJ begins to clear the table, then stops and turns to Kate.

"You know, it's okay if you can't do this and need to be with Tuck today, too. I can deal with Raymond by myself."

"Nope, that's totally out of the question. Tuck will kill me. And, besides, it really is too dangerous. And if I let you go alone, then what? Miss the climax of this psycho-drama he's set in motion?" Kate says. She puts the remains of their bagel breakfast on the counter. "I'm sticking with you. Can't put the book down just when the plot starts to thicken. This is getting too good."

DJ laughs as she fills the dishwasher.

"I make no promises about today. The best I can predict is a good lunch. Whatever he's got going with that new chef, he certainly can put on a good feed. Beyond that, I anticipate more of what we got before, perhaps with one exception. This time I am not leaving without an answer." DJ reinforces this last statement by slamming the dishwasher door so firmly that the dishes inside rattle. The cat gives a yelp and runs under the table.

"And therein rests my desire to accompany you on your journey, Deej." Kate tucks a hand under Saffron and lifts her onto her lap, soothing her with long strokes from head to tail. The cat settles in and throaty purrs fill the kitchen. "You miss your puppy, don't you kitty?" she croons.

"You're coming for the food or the fight?" DJ teases.

"Well…" Kate draws out her answer, pretending to be giving it deep thought. "Perhaps a wee bit of both."

DJ laughs and reaches to tickle Saffron's ears.

They are interrupted by Tuck's return. With a worried look she seats herself across from Kate.

"They've got a six-year-old whose step-father beat the living daylights out of him last night. He's in Boston Children's with a spiral fracture of one arm, a torn ear and a concussion. They want one of us to sit with him and see what we can find out. Evidently he told a teacher on Friday that someone's been touching his private parts."

The words have an immediate effect on DJ, who quickly pulls her legs off the floor and tucks them under herself on the chair. She folds both arms across her chest and, when doing so, flashes to an image of herself as a child—squeezing her behind into a hole in the wall near her home, valiantly attempting to escape the reality of her abuse. She understands this to be a flashback, a reaction to what Tuck is saying. With considerable emotional effort, she wills herself back into the kitchen and the conversation.

The others do not notice DJ's momentary dissociation.

Kate is considering Tuck's information and says, "Sounds like a good case for the Children's Advocacy Center, Tuck. Why are they calling us in?"

"That was my first question, too. But the boy is too damaged to be moved, the step-father has a bail hearing tomorrow morning on the physical assault charge, and the police want to make a run at getting enough information to hold him longer by charging him with sexual abuse. However, it's hard to know if the step-father is also the sexual perpetrator at this point or whether it's someone else. Understandably, the boy is not talking. Probably can't at this point." Tuck sighs and looks at her friends.

"Feels like it never stops, doesn't it?" DJ sighs. "The only thing different these days is that people like the two of you are there to listen and to help. Could have used the likes of you way back when."

"I hear you, DJ. And no, it hasn't stopped yet," Kate says, "but we're working on it." She is all business now as she turns to Tuck. "I gather you'll take this one then, right?" she says. "You're just aces with boys this age."

"Yeah, I'm on it," Tuck responds, leaning on the table and pushing herself slowly to her feet, already looking weary. "I need to take a shower and gather my things, but I'll also need to take our car. Are we staying here again tonight or going into the city to our place?"

"I'm for coming back here, if it's all the same to you two," DJ says. "Staying close to home feels like something I need to do right about now, okay?"

"That's just fine with us," Kate answers for both of them, "right, Tuck?"

Whatever response Tuck makes is swallowed by the ringing of DJ's cell phone. She screens the call before answering.

"Ugh, my uncle," she says.

Tuck sits herself back down in the kitchen chair, not willing to miss this.

DJ answers, and listens.

"Oh, Vincent, hello, I was expecting this to be Raymond. Are we still on for noon?"

"Your uncle asked me to call to confirm lunch at one, if that meets with your approval, Miss, ah, Donna?"

DJ smiles as she answers. "Why, yes, that will be fine Vincent, please let him know we will be there for one."

"Well, that's the other thing, Donna." Vincent pauses and DJ can just about predict what comes next, so she slips the phone onto speaker mode. Vincent clears his throat.

"Your uncle has asked if you would be so gracious as to meet with him alone today so that you can finish your conversation and keep it within the privacy of the family."

Trying her best not to laugh as both Kate and Tuck pantomime gagging, DJ waves her hand at them to stop, upsetting the sugar bowl and letting loose an avalanche of crystals. She points at the sugar and then at her friends and mouths, *that's your fault, not mine.* Then she turns her attention back to the phone.

"Tell you what, Vincent. I'll meet my uncle half way and only bring one friend today. How's that?" offers DJ.

Vincent clears his throat again.

"Um… That's not quite what he had in mind," he begins, but DJ cuts him off.

"I'm well aware that it's not what he had in mind, Vincent, but it is definitely how it is going to be."

"Yes, ma'am, but I think you need to take into consideration the fact that he is not a well man, and…"

DJ jumps in again.

"Define 'not a well man' for me, will you please, Vincent? This is the second time you have alluded to his health, but given me nothing substantial to go by. So just what do you mean?"

Vincent is silent so long that both Kate and Tuck look up at DJ, mouthing what?

"Vincent?" DJ says into the phone then listens intently. She hears a door click closed, and Vincent's hurried whisper.

"He has cancer of the pancreas. And he does not want you to know. He has very little time left to get his affairs in order. He wishes to see you alone and I think you should respect his wishes. I believe you owe him that much at least."

DJ feels like she's been slammed in the chest, but she struggles not to let herself be sidetracked by either the information or Vincent's cutting remark.

"What I do, or do not, owe my uncle is between him and me, Vincent. Let's leave it at that, can we?" DJ answers as evenly as she can, although her face has turned crimson and her fingernails are tattooing the sugared tabletop to some unheard staccato beat.

She continues in a softer tone. "I appreciate your telling me, and I can well imagine how difficult it must be for you, Vincent. You've been with

Raymond for as long as I can remember. I will not tell him you told me, but I must also assure you that I will still be bringing Kate with me today. He'll just have to deal with that."

Vincent's only response is a barely audible, "Yes, Ma'am."

"And I don't think either he, or you, should expect that this will be a comfortable visit."

"No, Ma'am."

"And please stop calling me Ma'am, Vincent. I'll see you at one. Good-bye."

DJ presses the End button, and collapses into the nearest chair. She looks at her friends.

"Well!" she says. "This gets more interesting by the day, doesn't it?"

Kate vocalizes the Dragnet sound track, then deepens her voice and adds, "And the plot continues to thicken, ladies and… ladies."

"Now I'm *really* sorry I have to miss this one," Tuck proclaims, "especially since I obviously can't trust either one of you to take it seriously." She takes a quick peek at the wall clock. "Speaking of which, I'd better get a move on. They're expecting me at Children's at noon. Be right back down. Oh, and Katie, I'll stop home after that and bring us a change of clothes. We're running out of undies." Tuck takes the stairs two at a time, and they can hear her rummaging around the bedroom above them, gathering her things for the shower.

DJ runs her fingers through the spilled sugar on the tabletop, creating little swirls of white crystals. Sunlight streams through a maze of blue bottles arranged along the window sill and the tiny crystals catch and hold the cobalt light, turning the sugar a soothing shade of blue. She finds the colored crystals mesmerizing, and scrolls her initials in blue along the tabletop.

"You know, Katie," DJ finally says, "I should be upset with the news that my uncle has cancer. And on one level I am. But to tell the truth, on another whole level I'm feeling relieved, and just a tiny bit suspicious that he may have told Vincent to tell me about it as a last resort in order to get me to come alone. I wouldn't put it past him at all."

"He's hurt a lot of people, Deej, and I don't just mean your father and uncles," Kate says. "This whole world will be better off without him. I know how much he means to you, but-"

"Meant," DJ says, holding up the wastebasket and guiding the spilled sugar into it, "meant. Past tense."

"Well, okay, but I'm not so sure you can turn it off so fast. You've spent years caring about him in a big, big way. He was kind of your only salvation on some level and that's hard to move past. Quickly anyway."

"So, what are you saying, Katie, 'cause I'm not really following you here?" DJ's arms are now crossed and she looks ready for an argument.

"I'm saying give yourself some time girl, time for all this to sink in. Let the anger fade a bit and then grieve if you have to. Everything you've learned this past weekend adds up to a huge loss, and like it or not, his death will matter to you."

DJ's still not convinced, and she simply shrugs in response.

"Of course," Kate continues, "the rest of us will be dancing a jig, but we're not connected to him the way you are."

Kate talks on, but DJ tunes out, preferring to let her thoughts take her where she has so far been unable to go.

*All of this is absolutely nuts! I'm such a mess. How can I be so glad my father and uncles are dead and so thoroughly pissed off that they are? All at the same time! And why the hell do I even care that Raymond killed them?*

*I guess he* did *do me a favor! They never abused me again, did they?*

*And even though all of that is one hundred percent true, it still makes me feel so infuriatingly helpless that I can't stand it—especially the way he uses me as the excuse for what he did!*

*Christ, no wonder I'm having trouble agreeing with Kate. Miss Raymond? Ha! Right now I'd like to kick his sorry ass from here to Timbuktu.*

DJ becomes aware that Kate has stopped talking and is staring at her.

"Hello in there," Kate says. "This is earth, trying to make contact with DJ Brava. Any chance you encountered her in your travels around the galaxy?"

"Okay, Katie, enough. I hear you. I'll have fallout. I'll be sad. Whatever. But right now, I have things to do that won't wait. And I can't afford to let myself stop and feel bad about anything at all. I promise to deal with all of that stuff later." *Much, much later.* She lets the last thought go unsaid and simply looks at Kate.

Kate feels no option but to concede. "I'm done," she says.

"Good," DJ says, "because I really am ready for him today. I'm armed, I'm dangerous, and I've got back-up. I want answers and I'm not leaving without them."

Kate nods and says, "Okay, then, game on," just as DJ spots the cat poised to swat her cell phone off the table.

"Don't even think about it, beast," she shouts, and nabs the phone out of reach just milliseconds before Saffron swipes the empty space with her paw.

The cat looks at DJ and gives a "raaoowwll," of protest. She humps her back and stretches before jumping off the table.

"Raaoowwll, yourself," DJ says, laughing. She addresses Kate.

"Tuck's out of the shower. I'm going to grab a quick one and throw some things in the wash. I need to figure out what to wear into the city to see Cole tomorrow as well."

Kate stands up and stares at a sweater's worth of cat hairs clinging to her navy jogging suit. "Uh, Deej…" she says.

"Oh, sorry, I haven't brushed her in a few days. There's one of those sticky rollers for that in the left-hand drawer under the counter," DJ says as she starts up the stairs.

Kate reaches for the roller.

"Let me know when you're out of the shower, Deej, and I'll take one, too. Got to be as fresh as possible for what lies ahead." She starts humming the theme from Jaws.

"And just who are we?" DJ stops and asks from half-way up the stairs. "Are we the shark or the guys in the boat?"

Kate looks thoughtful, pulls her sweatshirt over her head, but stops with her arms caught in the sleeves.

"Now that," she says, "remains to be seen, doesn't it?"

# THIRTY-SEVEN

THE RIDE TO RAYMOND'S is relatively short, and on the way Kate and DJ talk some more about what his death will mean to DJ.

"Sounds like he intends to leave you that monument he's built to himself," Kate says. "Do you plan to tell him what you're going to do with it after he's dead?"

"Not a chance, Katie. No matter how angry I am with him, and no matter what he says this afternoon, I'm not going to risk having him change his mind. The day after he told me his decision to leave that mansion to me in his will, I went to the domestic violence coalition and we set up a plan with a lawyer to transfer the whole property to them as soon as possible after he's gone."

They near the turn onto his estate and can see the house through the trees.

"I mean, damn, just look at the size of this place. What better use for it than a shelter, apartments and educational training center for battered women and their children? I'm hoping he also throws some money into the package so I can help with funding to get this going. Providing he doesn't give it all to the church to try and save his sorry ass by buying his way into paradise, of course."

"It's a fantastic idea, Deej," Kate says, "but he kind of has to die first."

"I'm so furious at him for what he's done that right now I can only hope it's soon," is DJ's dour response.

Kate spots Vincent waiting under the portico once again.

"Well, let's see if we can help push him closer to the edge, then, shall we?" she asks as DJ stops the car and pulls the hand brake up with a vengeance.

"Did I ever tell you how much I love your evil side?" DJ remarks, and they both slide out of the car chuckling.

Kate spots the foreboding look on Vincent's face. Her body gives an involuntary jolt, and she quietly says, "Uh, oh. Let's stay sharp, DJ. We're about to reenter the lion's den."

# THIRTY-EIGHT

VINCENT GREETS THEM as cordially as if their conversation earlier today had never occurred.

"Good afternoon, Donna, Katherine. Right this way, please. Anthony has prepared an excellent luncheon. I expect you will be quite impressed."

He leads them down the long corridor and past the elegant dining hall they were in the evening before. They turn right, walk the entire length of another corridor, and then Vincent opens two large French doors, covered on the inside by exquisitely articulated lacework.

"Your guests have arrived, Mr. Martone," he announces and leaves the room, closing the doors quietly behind him.

Raymond turns from where he has been gazing out the window at two young colts chasing each other across the far meadow.

He, too, is gracious.

"Welcome, my dears," he says, pulling DJ into a hug and giving her a kiss on each cheek.

"How are you today, Uncle Raymond?" DJ asks, holding his arm, but he merely shrugs and turns away.

Kate has her mouth open and, quite unlike her, is unable to find words. With the exception of the floor, the entire room is glass, vaulted ceiling included. It juts out from the back of the main house by a good thirty feet, affording a magnificent view of meadow, stables, and, of course, acres of autumn woods. Kate finds herself wanting to reach out and run her hand over the quilt of colors in front of her.

Raymond puts an arm around Kate's shoulder and her muscles tense in response.

"It's quite something, isn't it?" he asks. "This time of year it's all I can do to make myself leave this porch. See over there on the edge of the meadow? That tall dead pine tree? You can see a ball of white way out on a limb to the left."

Kate scans the panorama in front of her. She nods her head.

"That," he says, with obvious delight, "is an eagle, one of a family of four."

And, as if on cue, the great bird spreads its wings and swoops down and across the meadow, turning out of sight along a small stream. The horses, too, have stopped their frolicking to watch the eagle's glide.

Kate realizes she has been holding her breath and lets out a whoosh of air.

"Raymond," she says, her eyes taking in both the room and the view, "this is truly amazing."

DJ watches and smiles as Raymond charms her friend.

*I don't know how he does it,* she wonders. *You'd never guess he didn't want her here. And old Katie is just letting herself be pulled right into it, too.*

She almost laughs out loud when Kate turns her head away from Raymond and gives DJ a wink.

*Oh, she is definitely one wicked woman. So glad she's on my side.*

The sounds of a metal serving cart startle DJ.

"Ah, luncheon is served," Raymond says, and seats Kate and then Donna before sitting between them at the glass-topped table.

"Oh, my," Kate whispers when Anthony sets a plate in front of her. "This looks delicious."

DJ is equally amazed. "When did you start eating like this, Uncle?" she asks. "This is gourmet dining, to say the least."

"Anthony has prepared a warm salad of roasted vegetables and fresh mozzarella with a balsamic reduction dressing," Raymond says with a smile. "I hope this meets with your approval, ladies." Two wooden skewers of perfectly grilled shrimp are crossed on the plate alongside the salad. There is a citrus-dill dipping sauce on a side plate and a crusty chunk of garlic bread. Raymond pours white wine for each of them.

"You'll especially love the mozzarella, I think. Anthony makes his own and it's the best I've ever tasted. It's soft and creamy, with just the right tanginess to it."

He lifts his glass.

"*Ciao, bella*," he says, and bows slightly toward the women as they raise theirs "now mangia. Enjoy."

"Seriously, Uncle Raymond, where did you find this chef? No offense, but he could be master chef in any number of five-star places in Boston. Both the preparation and presentation are exceptional."

Raymond leans toward DJ.

"I know," he confides, his eyes taking on a bit of a sparkle, "and I stole him right out from under someone else's nose. He only wants to work part-time, and this is just the right setting for him. It was such a lucky move on my part." He chuckles.

He seems to be patting himself on the back more than the situation warrants, leaving both DJ and Kate slightly baffled.

"Would either of you care for dessert?" he asks when they are just about finished with the salads. "There is a lovely white chocolate mousse, or gelato, if you would prefer that?"

DJ has the sense that he is trying to delay the inevitable talk she came to have. When she sees Kate's head perk up at the mention of mousse, she responds quickly.

"No thanks, Uncle, perhaps later. We really do need to talk."

Kate's expression literally deflates and she looks fondly at the long-stemmed silver spoon she is holding in anticipation of the creamy dessert. She looks across at DJ with the eyes of a ten-week-old puppy watching a kid eat ice cream. DJ stifles both a laugh and the urge to give in. She mouths a quick *sorry* to Kate.

Raymond's expression, on the other hand, has turned sour.

"If we must," he says, pouring the last of the wine into his glass and drinking it quickly.

DJ pushes back from the table and moves behind Raymond to help with his chair.

"We must," she says. "Please."

Raymond guides them to a small sitting area in the far left corner of the room. Two plush-cushioned, wooden framed couches with matching chairs, a glass coffee table and four end tables are arranged to maximize the view. One of the end tables has a pitcher of water, drinking glasses and three bottles of medicine next to a book of early Roman art. There is a cashmere throw along the arm of the closest chair, and Raymond seats himself, pulling the blanket across his lap.

Kate settles into the couch furthest from Raymond, allowing DJ to choose the chair or couch closer to her uncle. DJ sits next to him and grips both armrests, much like she did the previous evening in the den. Determined. She looks at Kate and then turns to Raymond.

Before she can speak, however, Raymond starts, placing a feeble looking hand on her knee.

"Let me get right to the point, my dear," he says with an intensity which surprises her, given his apparent physically frailty. "I would much prefer you just drop this whole thing, Donna Jean, especially the book. It's not in anyone's self-interest and it will just make life more difficult."

"Difficult?" DJ responds with an exaggerated look of surprise. "For whom?"

Raymond pulls his hand from DJ's knee and slides it under the blanket.

"All right," he concedes, "for me. I admit it. But I'm also thinking about your mother and sisters. What do you think this will do to them? There's no need for you to air your family history this way. You're very popular. Why do you have to write *this?* Why can't you just write more of what has made you so famous? I don't understand any of this."

"*Why* I need to write my autobiography is not the issue right now, Raymond. Why *you* did what you did is what I want to hear from you." DJ is sitting up straight, her voice firm and focused.

"You killed my uncles and you as much as killed my father. You took something from me when you did that," she continues, every word spit out with the burn of acid.

Raymond explodes.

"Took something? I gave you something. I gave you your life back. I saved you from them." He is shaking his finger at her in rage, but the effort to express himself and still be in control fades. The hand collapses into his lap and he struggles for breath.

"I should think you'd understand that. I should think you'd be grateful." His voice thins to a whimper as his eyes plead with DJ.

"It's *you* who doesn't understand, Raymond. When you made the decision to kill them you took away any chance I will ever have of dealing with them myself—of confronting them, hearing them deny, or, better yet *admit* what they did and take responsibility for it. You took *my* power to help myself."

"What do you mean?" he asks. "What possible good would it do to have them admit something we all know they did, especially after all these years?"

"Validation," DJ responds. Her determination and intensity grow more vibrant with every word. "Validation of my reality, my suffering, my pain, my lost childhood. For god's sake, this stuff has haunted me for years. And you, of all people, ought to have known better than to have done what you did, Raymond. You were the only one with a *soul*. Only you were capable of seeing through to my pain."

Kate sees both fury and sadness roiling around inside DJ, each struggling for control. Her fists are tight, the muscles of her face are taut with anger, yet Kate can see DJ's shoulders sag from the weight of her own words.

DJ gathers her resolve and stares right into her uncle, daring him to look away.

"I hate you right now," she spits at him. "And I also love you, you son of a bitch. I wish my sisters never told me this. I wish it weren't the truth. I'm losing you, and it's killing me."

DJ resists the urge to scream right into his face. "And, yes, dammit," she cries. "Yes. I am glad they are dead. Okay, does that make you happy? I'm glad. But I am also furious that they are dead. Both. Both." She runs out of steam and simply stops.

"Clearly this is all still upsetting to you, Donna, dear. Why go through all that again?" Raymond twists his fingers around an edge of the cashmere throw.

"My abuse is no longer *upsetting* to me, Raymond," DJ responds, deliberately enunciating each syllable. "It is simply a fact. It's a fact about me, a fact about my life, a fact about my family. The book is not upsetting to me. It's a relief, a release for me."

Raymond turns away.

"Look at me," she insists, slapping her chest sharply with her hand. "Look at me and hear me. What is upsetting to me is what you did. It's not in my book. I didn't even know it until Friday night. But you did it. You killed my uncles. You were there when my father had his heart attack. And it is time, right now, to tell me the truth of what you did and why. You owe me nothing less, and I will not leave here today without it."

Raymond has shrunk into his armchair. Whether he is more fearful than chilled is not easy to guess as he wraps the throw up under his armpits and tucks it beneath his thighs. He looks at his watch and reaches for the largest bottle of pills, shaking out two and taking them with water from the pitcher.

*Good stall*, Kate thinks, *but there's no way it's going to work on DJ. Not today.*

When Raymond has finished, he turns slightly in Kate's direction. Before he can say anything, DJ intervenes.

"She stays. She stays for all of it."

Impressed, Kate gives an exaggerated look at the sky above and across the front of the windows, coming to rest again on Raymond who has withered even further into his armchair.

DJ is in hot pursuit of the information she is desperate to have.

"Tell me what happened with my father. I know you were there when he had his heart attack. What happened?"

Raymond drinks more water and rests his head back on the cushion.

DJ waits patiently, only the swinging movement of her crossed leg giving away her nervousness.

"Your father had been trying to reach Edward and Joseph for weeks. I didn't know he had kept contact with them. That was one of the conditions I set with those two idiots—no contact with anyone in RI, especially you or your father. But they didn't listen. Not to that or anything else I ever said either, as it turned out."

Raymond's breathing becomes labored and a slight wheezing sound can be heard at the end of each sentence.

"Your father asked me to stop by his office that day, and I had no idea it was to confront me about our brothers. He accused me of hurting them and I admitted it. He then accused me of killing them. I didn't, of course, but things got heated when I let slip that perhaps someone else had put them out of my misery."

"Semantics," DJ mutters with an abrupt flick of her hand.

"I'm not sure he quite believed until that moment that I knew what our brothers had done to you. Then he said something that made me understand that he, himself, was also molesting you. I lost it. I threatened him, pushing him again and again against the wall. He fell down and went into cardiac arrest. I worked on him. In those days I was good at that kind of thing. I kept at it until the paramedics got there, but it was too late."

Raymond looks as if a great weight has been placed upon his shoulders. He sinks deeper into his chair and looks directly at DJ.

"I'm sorrier about your father's death than you can ever know," he says. "I know that I caused him to have that heart attack, but it was never my intention that he would die. Never. I threatened him. I was furious with him. I wanted to beat him senseless and rip his gonads to shreds."

He starts, aware of what he has just said. "Oh, pardon me," he says, flushing.

DJ just stares, waiting.

"All right, I did want to kill him," he continues. "But I never wanted your mother to be alone, or for you kids to lose your father, especially that way. What he did was so very wrong that I have no way, not even this late in my life, to understand how he could possibly do what he did. And, still, I miss him, Donna Jean. I really do. All of them."

He stops, looking out the window and over the trees, perhaps to some faraway time before life turned sour.

It is very quiet in this room. No clock ticks the moments away. No sound from outside penetrates. Even Raymond's wheezing has slowed. Only the movement of the mid-autumn sun throwing longer and longer shadows around the edge of the meadow indicates that time is moving forward.

"And my uncles?" DJ pushes. She is not willing to respond to Raymond's pain, not trusting he isn't using it to distract her from her mission. "What happened with them?"

Raymond's eyes glass over, and he continues to look as if he is seeing far into a past he would rather not recall.

"You were ten, then, and they had recently abused you," he says, shaking his head sadly. "They would not shut up. They were proud of themselves, thrilled with what they had gotten away with. They wanted more but your father repeatedly refused. You must also remember that at this point I didn't know he was also abusing you."

Hands shaking, Raymond refills his water glass and then struggles with both hands to hold it still.

"One Sunday afternoon the three of us were together watching football. You know how much I hate that game, Donna, and I fell asleep during that silly half-time business. When I woke up sometime during the fourth quarter, both of them were drunk and talking ugly. I kept my eyes closed, listening. And that's when I realized they were making plans to sexually abuse both Margaret and Christine. That's when. . ."

"Say that again," DJ cuts in, needing to be sure of what she has just heard. "Did you say they were going after my sisters?"

"Yes. They thought the idea of having the twins would be fun. One for each of them, they said. And they planned to make a film and sell it."

"Jesus, Raymond," DJ is in shock. "Jesus." She punctures the air with her words, gets up, and walks to the nearest window panel, both hands tangled in her hair and clasped behind her head.

This time, the silence in the room is so palpable it becomes alive, so wild and dangerous it has taken on a will of its own. No one is brave enough to risk speaking first. DJ, Kate, and even Raymond, seem turned to stone, each carved into the shape this latest level of reality—of anguish– has created.

Raymond is visibly in distress, throwing off the blanket, and reaching desperately for the pills next to him. With the blanket removed, Kate spots the rosary beads he has been fingering as they slide off his lap and disappear into the space between his leg and the cushion. She starts praying he'll overdose right in front of her and controls an urgent need to force-feed him all three bottles of pills.

As Raymond reaches for the errant beads, he turns slightly in his chair. The movement has been just enough for Kate to spot the handle of a silver revolver tucked deeply into the cushion on his right side. Her heart skips a few beats. Fear and anger compete for her attention. She freezes in her chair, watching Raymond's every move, mesmerized by the very idea of a gun.

*"Holy shit,"* she thinks. *"He wouldn't use that on us, would he? Me, maybe, but DJ? Okay, calm down girl. He's a mobster; of course he has a gun."*

DJ remains at the window, occasionally shaking her head, but totally oblivious to the fact that she is surrounded by beauty outside herself even as she comes to grips with the evil of what she has just heard.

It is almost a relief when Kate's cell phone ring cuts through the silence. She struggles to remove it quickly from her vest pocket.

"It's Tuck," she says, addressing DJ and getting up from her chair. "I'll need to take this privately. Let me just step into the hall. I'll only be a minute. Will you be okay?" Kate has every intention of keeping her eye on Raymond through the glass of the porch door if she has to, but she will not let DJ out of her sight.

DJ nods and gestures for Kate to go ahead. She takes the seat on the couch that Kate has vacated, just a bit further from Raymond than where she sat earlier. She watches as he swallows eight pills, selecting two at a time from the pile he has assembled on his lap.

DJ again resists the urge to be sympathetic, to find out more about his illness. But she has not yet learned all she wants to know.

"Was that the reason you sent them away? Because you found out what they were planning?" DJ's voice is as strong as before.

"Yes," he responds, wearily.

"But that doesn't explain why you had them killed, Raymond. I want to know why you did that."

"I was in the process of expanding my... my enterprise, beyond New England, and had recently begun operations in Baltimore and in Philly. I set them up, gave them what they needed to run the business, a more than decent salary to live comfortably. The only condition was that they stay away and not be in contact with anyone here."

"Nana included?"

"Nobody at all, except me, of course. And I was keeping an eye on them. They did fine for about a year or so..." He breaks off and shakes his head, sighing.

"Donna," he tries, "you have no idea how much I wanted them to do well, to put what they did behind them and have a good life. They were my brothers and I-"

DJ has no patience for this.

"What did you do?" She enunciates each word, glaring at him, not allowing him an inch of room to wriggle his way out of answering her.

He draws himself up into a self-righteous pose and claps his hands together.

"I found out they started to bring that disgusting child pornography into my places of business. I'm lots of things I shouldn't be, Donna, but I draw the line at that. None of my establishments has ever dealt in that kind of product and never will." He pulls himself close to the edge of his chair and punctuates the next words with some of his old fire.

"That's how I've been able to stay in business so long. I told that friend of yours on Saturday, the FBI is always in my places, trying to find some. But it's not there, and I simply will not have it." Raymond is becoming animated. His breathing sounds labored yet again.

"But they brought it in. My own brothers brought it in. And I found out and I took it out, and then I read them the riot act. They managed all right for a few more months. But then it all went wrong. I discovered they were trying to set up their own shops exclusively for that product. I sometimes think I could have dealt with that somehow, but then I got word they had found some kids and were prostituting and filming them." He was shaking visibly now.

"That was it. I couldn't bear it. I saw how much pain you were in from what they had done to you. How much it had changed you from a happy, confident, trusting little girl. And I just couldn't let them get away with this any longer, letting more children be in that kind of pain."

"Oh, no you don't, you self-righteous piece of crap. Don't you dare lay this one on DJ. You tried that Saturday and Tuck reamed you for it, and here you are doing it again. What the hell is wrong with you?"

No one is aware that Kate has re-entered the room, standing near the door and behind Raymond. She has overheard his last statement and is furious—not trusting herself to move closer to him without twisting him into a human pretzel. Gun or no gun, this is all just too much to listen to!

"How dare you?" she has a full head of steam going at this point and only an avalanche can stop her. "How dare you try to make DJ think you did this for her? How dare you try to leave her thinking she's responsible?"

Raymond attempts to answer, "I'm not-"

"Oh, yes you are." Kate mimics his voice as she paraphrases what she has heard him say. "Oh, my sweet Donna, I would never have killed your uncles if I hadn't seen what pain you were in. You should have been a good little girl and kept all that pain to yourself. But, since you didn't, I just had to kill them to save all the other little children from pain like yours."

She pauses for a breath, her eyes daring him to interrupt her.

"And just what is this sanctimonious bullshit you're trying to sell about not dealing in child pornography? You think that and your precious rosary can get you into heaven? You're the world's most self-deluded man."

Kate throws her arms wide in a gesture of inclusion.

"You live out here in some kind of shrine to yourself, thinking all of this is going to make up for the damage you've done for decades to women and children. You think adult porn doesn't hurt anyone? A thirteen billion dollar industry that air-brushes women to make them look like girls so that men want to have sex with younger and younger girls, an industry that puts women at risk of violence at the hands of people who use that trash to get aroused, that drugs women, turns them to prostitution, and sometimes kills them in order to make movies for people who have no idea how to have a healthy sexual relationship with a real person? Thirteen thousand new videos a year! You think teenagers who access your porn websites aren't permanently damaged by the images of sexual violence that you put out there? You think that hasn't hurt anyone in all the years you've been making your dirty millions doing this? And then you hide out here in your monument to all things religious as if all is forgiven, as if none of that shit belongs to you?"

Shaking with rage, Kate pauses to inhale. *Oh, boy,* she thinks quickly, *wait'll Tuck hears about this. She'll draw and quarter this asshole!*

"You have no idea what I-" Raymond tries again.

"The only idea I have is that you are a totally useless bag of shit, Raymond Martone, and if you think for a minute you're going to get away with passing responsibility off of yourself and onto DJ for any of your delusional thinking, you're dead wrong." She looks at him fiercely, daring him to fight back.

DJ has moved close to Kate and places a hand on her arm.

"Katie," she says, in a calm and reassuring tone, trying to deescalate some of Kate's venom.

Kate whips her arm away from DJ's touch, still too enraged to endure it.

"You think that's how you show someone you love them or help them deal with their anguish? You think killing people is the answer? You-"

"Kate!" DJ's voice is sharp and impossible for Kate to ignore.

"What?" she shouts, although DJ is right next to her.

"Stop."

Kate is genuinely confused. "Stop? But he's-"

"I know full well what he's doing, but just stop now, Katie. Please? I can handle this myself. Honestly, I can. It's what I came here to do, remember?"

Kate looks at DJ and then at Raymond. *If he could shrivel up any smaller, he'd be the size of a pea,* she thinks, suddenly aware of what she has been doing.

"Oh, shit. I'm sorry, DJ," she whispers. "My mouth ran away with me just a wee bit, didn't it?"

DJ nods and gives Kate the smallest flicker of a smile. "Again. And quite a bit more than a wee bit this time, my friend." *And you are absolutely the best friend a human being could have,* she thinks. *But you have to shut up now and let me do what I came to do. Myself.*

As Kate starts to sit down, her cell phone rings for the second time that day.

"Damn," she says. "Tuck again. I'm so sorry."

But the phone call itself refuels Kate's ire. She addresses Raymond again, but with somewhat less bile.

"You think your shit doesn't stink, Raymond Martone? But I've worked on a hundred cases with your stench all over them. All those abusers with their computers and closets full of porn, all of it the crap you push." She shakes the phone at him as she heads to the door. "Hundreds and hundreds of girls and boys, Raymond. Look at your hands, old man. That's your own smut you see, and every craggy wrinkle is the mark of a child's torment you're responsible for. You may have stopped the abuse to DJ and her sisters, Raymond, and I can even understand why you deserve some credit for that. As her best friend I'd even be willing to go so far as to thank you. But what you do, every single day… what you do just makes things worse."

When they are alone again, Raymond gives a quick glance in the direction of the closed door.

"Now you see why I wanted you to come alone, Donna Jean? This has gotten completely out of hand."

DJ is still on her feet and starting to pace. She stops suddenly and puts a hand up to him. The hand becomes a fist.

"Don't even think about getting on her case. Everything she said is the absolute truth, Raymond, and you know it. Everything Tuck said on Saturday was also true, so let's not waste time any more time here." DJ can see Kate watching from the hallway, phone to her ear.

"Tell me this, instead, why don't you? For all your intelligence, for all your street smarts, for all of your capabilities that were far and away greater than all your brothers put together, including my father—for all that, you couldn't think of another way to make a living than through this disgusting pornography? You couldn't, for the life of you, figure out some other way to handle what happened than to freaking *kill* them? Just what the hell is the matter with you, Raymond? You're better than that. You sure as hell are smarter than that. What in God's name were you thinking?"

Raymond winces at her strong choice of words.

"I couldn't think straight, Donna. That's the point. I had just gotten back from Vietnam. I fell back on what I was trained to do. I-"

DJ snaps her head around sharply, fixing him with a cold and threatening look. Her lips harden into a thin, firm line.

"Do not. Do not pull the PTSD card on me, Raymond. Do not. You want to play the post-traumatic-stress symptoms one-upmanship game with me, uncle dear, you're going to lose. Big time. This is about choices. Your choices. Killing was a choice. A choice you made."

DJ looks around in frustration, wishing Kate was with her.

"It's a choice you haven't paid for yet, isn't it? You're frightened to death you'll have to pay the consequences if people find out. It's why you don't want my book published. You already know, somehow, that there's nothing about killing in the book, but you're scared the authorities will start investigating you once someone brings their attention to the fact that you gave two sexual predators jobs running your porn places."

She pauses.

"This is all starting to make some sick kind of sense to me now."

Raymond's coloring has left his face altogether. He is unable to respond.

"What still puzzles me, however, is how you already know what I've written." DJ is almost talking to herself as she thinks out loud. Her pace quickens and she strides alongside the wall-to-ceiling windows, once again oblivious to the view.

"There are only two copies," she muses, just loud enough to be heard. "I have one and Cole has one. So, you're either spying on me or you've somehow gotten to Cole."

She stops her pacing, suddenly struck by something her uncle said.

"What the hell did you mean a minute ago? What did you mean when you said you 'told that friend of mine Saturday'? Told who? Who are you talking about?"

"My money's on Cole." Unbeknownst to DJ who is still stalking the other end of the room, Kate has returned and inserted herself once again into the conversation. She goes directly to the dining table, sits, and begins picking at leftover garlic bread, a look of pure guiltlessness on her face.

Raymond is now so shaken that DJ has to sit next to him in order to hear what he is saying. Once again she dismisses the worry growing in her about how hard she is pushing him and the way this is affecting his health.

"I told Cole long ago." Raymond says, looking at his hands. "No, the truth is that I *threatened* Cole long ago. I told him that I would hurt him if he ever published anything you wrote about your family. He took me seriously. As well he should have, I suppose."

"You *subbose?*" This comment of incredulity comes from Kate, her mouth half full of garlic bread, crumbs now sputtering out and skittering across the floor.

DJ shoots her a piercing look, and Kate stoops to avoid the glare by retrieving the errant crumbs. When she does so, she glimpses Vincent's shadow just behind the lace curtain, the door opened just enough so he can hear.

"You interfering son of a bitch," DJ leaves off staring at Kate and swings around to address Raymond. "Nothing is beneath you, is it? And you're doing all this to me, DJ. You know, the one you 'saved', the one you 'love'? Everything they say about you is true, isn't it? I don't really know you at all, do I?"

DJ is unable to keep still. The tension in her body needs release, and she is moving again, pacing. She stops behind him, leaning close to his right ear, hands gripping the chair to stop them from trembling. Raymond winces at her closeness.

"Well, this is something you need to know about me. I clawed my way up and out of the hell of my abuse once after it happened, and again when I had to face it in therapy. I am not, repeat, not, going to do that again. Not over this. Not over anything. Not even over you."

She sucks in a huge breath.

"I have a meeting with Cole tomorrow. This book will be published, no matter what you threatened him with."

She turns and points a menacing finger in his direction.

"And you will not...you will not do anything to stop it. Not to Cole, not to my friends, not to me. And whether or not I change my book to include any of this, this..." Her mind races for the correct word to describe her feelings. "These utterly *despicable* acts of yours, I do not know."

DJ swipes hard at the air, her hand landing with a loud slap against the back of the couch.

"I can't imagine how you've gotten away with this for so long. You're a fraud, Raymond, a liar. And you need to pay for what you've done."

She grabs at her temples and holds her head as if to prevent it from exploding.

"God," she screams, "I can't even *think!*"

Raymond cowers in the face of her anger. His hands are quivering beneath the blanket.

"And I will not collude with you in covering this up." DJ spits. "I will not. I have had my fill of secrets and collusion, and I will not tolerate it or be part of it in any way. Got that?"

His head nod is barely perceptible.

"Just what is it you really want from me, Uncle Raymond? Do you even know? You want that I should simply accept this new information and move on? Have some sympathy for you? Well the answer is no and hell no! You don't have a prayer of me feeling much of anything except pity for you again. Understand?"

He looks down and away from DJ.

She pushes on.

"Forgiveness? Is that it? If it is, you can be assured that it will never happen, either. What you did is unforgiveable—positively unnecessary and unwarranted and so unspeakably unforgiveable as to be insane."

And then DJ stops, suddenly gripped by a new thought.

"It's absolution you want, isn't it? The removal of all guilt and all responsibility for the acts you have committed. Well, here's a newsflash for you, Raymond. Absolution is not mine to give. You know where you have to go to receive that, and this close to death, the idea of having to do it is scaring you even closer to the brink. No, I'm sorry, but absolution is definitely not mine to give. And even if it were, I still would not give it."

At the table, Kate begins humming the words to an old Helen Reddy song in her head. *I am woman, hear me roar…*

The eeriest kind of silence now fills the room. Late afternoon shadows have thrown much of it into darkness and allowed a chill to enter. No one moves to turn on lights or punch up the thermostat. All three sit wrapped in thought and seem unwilling to take this conversation any further down the road to hell, where it is clearly headed. Ten minutes pass and each person's breathing can be heard by the others.

Finally, Raymond makes a weak attempt at clearing his throat.

"I have just one request of you, then, Donna Jean."

He waits for her to acknowledge him, but she remains impassive. He continues.

"Please wait until I'm dead to publish your book," he pleads with his eyes as well as his faltering voice. "I only have a few months. I'm very ill, and I'm begging you to wait, Donna Jean. Please?"

DJ merely looks at him, maintaining her silence. Kate, however, is having a major reaction to his request. Her ears perk up like the ears of a Doberman hearing a dog whistle.

*What the hell is it with this family and waiting 'til they're all dead? Didn't they ever hear the expression that the truth will set you free? Hum. Okay, actually, the truth won't set this guy free, will it? Oh shut up, Katie girl. Just stay cool. DJ has all this under control.*

DJ merely gives Raymond a dispassionate look.

"I wouldn't count on that if I were you, Raymond. Kate, come on. We're leaving."

DJ gathers both of their handbags and tosses one to Kate.

Raymond manages to raise a hand in Kate's direction. In a feeble attempt to regain some sense of control he speaks directly to her.

"One moment, please. As for you, young lady," he starts, voice quavering, "I believe an apology is in order."

Kate has crossed in front of him on the way to the door and she now turns her full attention to him.

"Why, yes, it is," Raymond, "so pleased you mentioned it. And your apology is graciously accepted. Thank you. In fact, I accept on behalf of all the women and children in the world who have been hurt, dehumanized, degraded, objectified, and otherwise damaged by any means whatsoever related to the materials and practices you so blithely and without conscience create, sell, and support."

She bends over and gives a sweeping bow before him, trying not that hard at all to hide the smug smile on her face.

Raymond bristles, resenting her strong rebuke, "That is not quite what I had in mind, young lady. You-"

DJ cuts him off.

"That's all you're going to get from her, Uncle Raymond. And that was a mild one, believe me. I'd give it up if I were you," DJ warns. "Besides, you deserve every last word of it."

She continues.

"I'm leaving now, and it is highly unlikely that I will be returning. Too much has happened here. I have always loved you, deeply and sincerely. I love you, and will be eternally grateful for the things you have actually done for me, and my sisters. But these things that you are trying to tell yourself that you have done *because* of me? These things, I abhor. You have never hurt my body, and I will forever be indebted to you for that as well. But with these despicable acts, you have irreparably hurt my heart, Raymond. You have damaged my heart forever. I cannot bear that you did this. I simply cannot. And I can no longer be a part of this." She sweeps her hand across the expanse of the room, landing on his shoulder.

She bends and kisses him on the forehead, startled to see that he is gripping his rosary for dear life. It is hard not to know that he has wet himself.

Her hand lingers on his brow. "I do love you. Goodbye."

DJ turns to the door, putting her arm in Kate's as she goes. She does not see the tears Raymond is shedding nor hear his whispered words of anguish over this loss.

"I love you, too, angel. But, please, please understand I had no choice. I had to do what I did. I had no way of knowing it would hurt you so much."

# THIRTY-NINE

HEN VINCENT OPENS the porch door for them, he gives DJ a look that smacks of disdain. "I trust you can find your own way out, Miss Brava," he says, pointedly emphasizing her title. "I must attend to your uncle."

And under his breath, close to her left ear, he whispers, "You should be ashamed of yourself after all he's done for you. I always thought you were better than what you just did in there."

DJ's body freezes for an instant in response to his closeness. She lifts her chin and rejects the admonition contained in his words. She is determined not to falter at this point, shaky though she feels.

"Why, yes, we'll be just fine, thank you, Vincent," DJ rejoins in the kindest voice she can muster, and she and Kate take a sharp left turn and enter the long corridor toward the portico.

"Deej, my friend," Kate starts," did I ever tell you that sometimes spending a weekend with you feels like it takes a month of Sundays to get through? No? Well, let me just assure you that it is never, ever dull. That's all."

"Do you believe the gall of that man?" DJ hardly hears Kate, her mind reeling from the afternoon's confrontation. She is surprised to find that she is sweating, whether from anger or liberation is something she is totally unsure of at the moment.

"He is the most infuriating, pathetic, misguided, power hungry, narcissistic, ass on the face of the planet," she hisses. Fists clenched, arms pumping, she stomps her way down the hallway with Kate struggling to keep up.

And just as quickly, she stops and pivots toward her friend.

Kate's comment finally penetrates and, as she has hoped, works like a life vest thrown to someone in need of flotation. DJ gratefully grabs on.

"How totally unbelievable has this day been, Kate? Honestly, it does feel like we've been locked up in here with him forever. There was one point when I wasn't sure which one of us would go into cardiac arrest first, him or me."

DJ grabs Kate by the shoulders and looks at her head-on. "And, you, you were terrific. He certainly gave you a great chance to strut your stuff in there, Katie my dear," DJ says, loosening up just a bit, "and you went way over the top. You were right on target as usual, but seriously over the top."

"Hey, I was holding back. I didn't get to say half of what I wanted to."

"Well, your apology acceptance was worthy of an Academy Award, if I do say so myself. You are, as always, my dear Kate, absolutely splendid! Thank you."

Never one to dismiss either attention or praise, Kate agrees. "I am, indeed, aren't I?"

And, with that, Kate begins to dance an Irish jig to the tune of "We Are the Champions"—thoroughly impossible for even the most talented of dancers, but somehow she makes it work. And it has its desired effect of making DJ smile. Clearly this is not the time, Kate decides, to tell DJ about the gun.

They are suddenly interrupted by someone calling their names and running toward them from behind. Alarmed, they turn to see Anthony trying to catch up with them, carrying a big white box and huffing just a bit.

"So glad I caught you ladies," he pants. "I thought you might like the desserts you never tried. I spent all morning fixing them and they'll just go to waste here. Be careful with the box, though."

He hands it to Kate.

"It's heavy. I put the white chocolate mousse in there with some fresh crème brûlée ramekins. I heard you loved the ones you had Saturday night. I also made a raspberry soufflé for you this morning, if that's okay? Although I hope it didn't fall when I was chasing you. I almost missed you, too. You be careful with that box in the car, won't you? Don't want all my hard work to just end up a lump in a dish."

"And if it did we'd eat it anyway, Anthony," Kate laughs. "You are a marvelous chef and your baking is heavenly. Thank you so much for this. We'll get the dishware back to you at some point, too."

"No need," he says. "You can't possibly imagine how well this place is stocked. I could send you a box each week for a year and still have what I need." He laughs as he turns away. "You girls enjoy that, now, you hear?"

When he is out of ear-shot, Kate looks at DJ and practically collapses to the floor. "Oh, my, God," she says. "How lucky are we? I wonder if he put forks in this box, because if he did, I am going to devour half of everything before we get home. I really am. I am starving, and I really, really, really love white chocolate mousse. And raspberry soufflé! O-M-G, DJ, I am in piggy heaven."

DJ is standing still, staring at the box.

"What?" says Kate, just a bit baffled, "you're not thinking of leaving this here are you?"

"I don't know, Katie. This is the kind of thing that makes Tuck crazy. I can just hear her saying the box is probably rigged with explosives, not mousse, and that we are about to be blown to smithereens."

"Really DJ? Really? I have within my grasp the best desserts this side of Paris and you choose this moment to listen to Tuck! Three days of Tuck's voice in your head and now you listen! There is something deeply, seriously wrong with you!"

"Well, he could have poisoned it..."

"Oh, for God's sake, DJ, just smell the damn box, why don't you! Raspberries! White chocolate!" Kate places her ear against the box. "Besides, it's not ticking. Wouldn't it tick if there was a bomb in here? And when could Anthony have possibly poisoned it? He wasn't even in the room. Come on, Deej... dessert! I'm willing to chance it! Please don't make me leave it here. Please."

When DJ rolls her eyes and shakes her head, Kate knows she has won. She's had years of experience cajoling DJ into going along with her ideas in just this fashion. The fact that, all too often, trouble has resulted is not a thought she's willing to entertain at the moment.

"Get the door for me, then, will you?" Kate asks, beaming. "This thing really is heavy. Thanks."

They reach the car and DJ offers to place the box on the flat surface of the trunk. Kate reacts as if someone has suggested removing her spleen, hugging the box tightly to her chest.

"No way," she insists, "besides, the trunk is full. There's no flat surface there anyway. I just need a fork or something. Just hold it a sec while I get in and then hand it to me really gently. I'm going to peek inside this corner of the box and check for forks as soon as I can, though. Or spoons? Spoons would be much better. But you don't have any in the car do you, Miss Compulsively Clean? I really am starving."

DJ climbs in the driver's side and fumbles to get the key in the ignition.

"God, Katie," she says with obvious irritation, "it's not that long a drive, given that we're early enough to beat the traffic. You'll live, so give it a rest, will you? Besides, that's for all of us. And Tuck gets to have some, too, don't you think?"

Kate gets the message that DJ needs a bit of space at the moment. She settles back in the passenger seat, embracing her box and waiting.

DJ has some trouble with the starter, but after two failed attempts, the engine finally engages and the tires turn up a spray of pebbles as she rushes to leave.

Halfway down the drive, however, she takes her foot off the gas pedal and the car slowly coasts to a stop just before the gate.

DJ wraps her arms across the top of the steering wheel and rests her head against her arms. Her eyes are closed but her heart is about to burst out of her chest, and she sits patiently, waiting to find out if she is going to shatter.

A good five minutes pass. One huge black crow swoops close to the hood of the car, startling the two women. It perches on a naked limb of the ancient red maple that gracefully drapes the entrance gate just in front of them, setting off a fury of cawing.

DJ raises her head and attempts a smile.

"Okay, okay, we're going," she says to the crow. "Just give me another second."

As if hearing every word, the crow gives one last call and flies out over the meadow. DJ watches and then turns to Kate.

"I need to tell you, Katie," she says, "this has been one of the hardest weekends of my life. But today has been just the absolute worst!"

She looks in the rear-view mirror at Raymond's home, sadly shaking her head.

"Of all the things that have happened in my life—of all the horrors, real or feared—it never occurred to me that I would have to be doing *this*."

"This?" asks Kate.

"I never even entertained the remotest possibility that I would have to walk away from the one person who has been there for me since the beginning the way Raymond has. Had. The way he *had* been. The way I *thought* he had been."

She pauses.

"And yet…"

This time DJ is quiet so long that Kate finally utters, "and yet?" just above a whisper.

When DJ looks up this time, Kate can see that her eyes are tearless and glow with a fierce resolve to move forward.

With one last flick of her eyes to the image still filling the rear-view mirror, DJ steps on the gas and drives away.

"And yet I *did* it!" She looks at Kate. "I know, I know. It's not over. I still have stuff to deal with. But for right now, I feel freer than I ever have before," she announces, her heart filling for the first time in days with something other than dread. She throws her left hand out the open window and beats it against the side of the door, imitating a drum roll, leaning into it with gusto.

"I did it!" she shouts at the small group of wild turkeys foraging too close to the road. She beeps and waves back at the enthusiastic kids in the rear of a school bus, and calls hello to a man frantically trying to rake leaves against the gusty wind.

"Oh, and by the way, Kate dear," she says with a sly smile, once they turn off a series of country roads and head for the interstate.

"You'll find some spoons in the pocket next to your seat. Knock yourself out!"

# FORTY

COLES TAKES A LAST LOOK around the dock area and back up toward the house, grimacing once again at the row of seagulls along the rooftop. *Jesus, those things are multiplying like rabbits. And look at all that guano! Damn seagulls!* He removes his baseball cap and runs toward the house, flailing his arms and whooping at the birds, trying to frighten them off. As for the gulls, a good half of them raise their necks skyward and squawk loudly toward the clouds in what Cole can't help thinking sounds like humans laughing. A few others crane their necks downward, staring curiously at the strange creature and his antics. Two gulls rock from side to side in almost surreal imitation of Cole's behavior.

When he catches a brief glimpse of his own reflection in the dining room window, Cole pulls up short. *Christ, I look like a Looney Tunes character doing the chicken dance.*

He slaps his cap against his leg and shouts up at the birds.

"Yeah? Well just you wait until I can get someone up on that roof to give you the boot. We'll see who has the last laugh then." He climbs the porch steps and, just in case, gives a surreptitious look around to ensure that no one has observed him threatening seagulls with murder. Damned birds!

Cole sits in his rocking chair for a moment, reflecting on all he has accomplished in the past twenty-four hours, and in less than a minute, judges himself worthy to finally relax once again with a cigar and highball.

He had spent all day yesterday cleaning up the *Editoria* and preparing her to be taken out of the water for the winter. Unlike other years, he had no plans this season to race in any of the Florida regattas out of Miami or Key West, so he had dried and stored the sails, emptied the head, coiled the ropes, polished the stainless, hosed her down, and otherwise made her ready for indoor storage. No white plastic shrink-wrap for his baby!

Once the local regatta boats left port this morning, Cole had motored *Editoria* into the marina where she was travel-lifted out of the water. Her mast had been removed before she was trailered to the warehouse. He had watched her be put to bed for the winter with all the love and tenderness some men save for their wives and children. At noon he had treated himself to a full lobster dinner at his favorite tavern, traded racing yarns with some old sailing buddies of his, and was now glad to be back on his porch watching the last of the racers returning to harbor.

Procuring the requisite Scotch and cigar for the next endeavor, Cole returns to his favorite outside work area with DJ's manuscript sitting precariously on his lap. Armed also with his red signature Cross pen, Cole is ready to finish the editing job he started yesterday morning on his sun porch—the same job he has been redoing most evenings since Martone walked off with his original copy. He will be meeting with DJ first thing when he returns to Boston in the morning and plans to be well prepared.

He releases the clamp holding the next-to-last chapter that has yet to be edited, and picks up where he left off.

## 23 · Peeling the Onion

*My healing happened in stages. Much like the monthly phases of the moon, I moved in and out of needing and rejecting, wanting and refusing, to re-involve myself in the task of finding a new therapist.*

*Abuse or no abuse, I find I am much like everyone else on the planet who often has to learn her lessons the hard way—refusing to see the warnings that things are going wrong, and only facing facts when I have been kicked in the teeth and knocked to the ground of reality.*

*After I have dusted myself off, I wonder why someone couldn't have simply tapped me on the shoulder and told me I was headed for trouble and that right now would be a good time to stop and take evasive action. I'm pretty sure most folks have had similar experiences. And sent similar desperate pleadings out to the universe.*

*So, there I was, after my therapist had left for Africa, swimming alone against the current, and pretty much going nowhere.*

*And then…*

*And then I received a tap on the shoulder, and the heavens sent me a message I couldn't ignore.*

————————

*I had been assigned to attend an evening lecture on mental health issues of women, given by a local psychologist with whom I was not at all familiar. At that point in my career I was primarily covering human interest events. As the sole female reporter, all the 'girly stuff' was tossed my way and often treated as having very little importance up against the more 'masculine' news such as sports, or politics and law enforcement.*

*As a result, I was less than enthusiastic about wasting my precious early spring evening on something very few people would care to read about in the morning. In addition, the weather was pulling at me to play hooky. New Hampshire winters are long and dark and cold, and when spring tosses you a gift of daytime sun warm enough to pop open the pussy willows, evening light lasting until well past dinner time, and you can walk the still-frozen woodland paths before mud season sucks at your boots, most folks would rather give up directions to their secret maple sugar grove than sit for two hours in a lecture hall listening to someone talk about 'women's problems'.*

*But sit I did. And listen I did. The information was interesting of course, and as the evening wore on, it became increasingly clear to me that the lecturer not only cared very much about her topic, but also about the women she worked with on a daily basis who thereby informed her talk. I looked around the room, frankly surprised at the number of people in attendance—mostly women, of course, but a good number of men as well. Some folks were, like myself, taking copious notes; some nodded visibly as certain issues were presented; a few dabbed at their eyes with tissues and, in my row, one man reached to cradle the hand of his wife as the topic turned to the effects of early trauma.*

*As the evening progressed, I became less attuned to the people around me and more and more aware of something going on within me. And it was frightening. For the first time ever in my adult life, I both felt and heard a very small child's wail coming from deep inside my chest. I sat cemented to my chair, silent on the outside, but increasingly possessed by the insistence* of this inner being begging to be acknowledged, listened to. There was such a franticness attached to this experience that at first I felt as if I were going crazy. I kept trying to shake it off, dismissing the voice and the urgency of this clearly felt need in me to make contact with the speaker and ask her if she'd be willing to see me.

I tried to use my journalistic objectivity to make sense of what was happening. The psychologist was clearly younger than I was, and certainly more sure of herself as she stood before this large group and spoke with conviction. I liked that. She was taller, broader in the shoulders, stronger looking than I would ever be. I liked that, too, and thought she would be someone able to handle what I would be bringing.

I did not want a 'panty hose' therapist—which had nothing to do with wearing panty hose, but everything to do with acting as if what one wore, or had, or looked like on the outside, mattered more than anything else. And I did not want a silent witness, someone who would respond "uh huh" to whatever I would say. I did not have this in my first therapist, and I would not have it in my second. I had been lied to, betrayed, and not believed long enough in my childhood, and I was not about to abide that now from someone I would be paying to help me. I wanted open, I wanted honest, I required acceptance. Objectively, I liked what I was seeing and hearing. And most certainly my inner world was agreeing with me.

This struggle within me continued for more than half an hour and only ended when I realized that the internal crying dropped off each time I thoughtfully considered actually calling her and making an appointment.

This was, I now know, a very primitive part of my inner self that had the good sense to recognize and insist upon something that I needed in order to heal. The hurt and violated child within me was begging me to do the work needed to release it from the grip of the past. This woman at the podium was the one we could trust to hear all of what happened. This woman, my inner child insisted, this woman. Right now!

———————

How lovely it would be if I could say that after writing an excellent article the following day, I managed to gather the courage to call her and we set up an appointment. That I worked hard in therapy for a few weeks, resolved my issues, and then lived happily ever after.

Ah, but nothing could be further from the truth.

When I called, she had no openings. She offered to give me a referral to another therapist. I declined and chose to wait the few months she said it might take for space to open up. In the meantime, the noise within me grew louder and more insistent. Waiting was taking its toll.

Little did I know, however, that the relief I felt when I finally got an appointment would quickly fade as the realization of the work I still needed to do slowly sunk in.

At that point in my life, I lived frozen in fear, drop dead certain that if I allowed my true feelings to be exposed, my anger would implode the universe. My tears would drown the world. Both my father's overt and covert messages to literally keep my mouth shut had their intended effect. And the fact that he was long dead did nothing to release me from the threats of harm and the fear of his power. Each session in which I was capable of uttering even the smallest new piece of memory filled me with terror. I had flashbacks and nightmares, awakening some nights believing he was actually in my room, not sleeping at all other nights for fear the dark would swallow me whole.

I spent much of my time in therapy sessions dissociated, unable to describe my feelings or make even the simplest connections between events that happened long ago and how I was acting or feeling in the present.

The wish to collapse into my pain was enormous. There were long periods when I was so depressed or, more accurately, so riddled with anxiety, that I required psychiatric consults for medication. I felt so damaged, so wounded, that I often had to call my therapist in the evening or on weekends just to hear a stabilizing voice.

It might be difficult to understand how I could be so damaged internally and yet continue to work, to function in the world, but I was proving to be one stubborn woman. I was utterly unwilling to lose more than I already had.

I cut myself. I scratched myself. To this day I cannot cut up an old credit card and not pause to consider the need I used to have to pull the pointed shards across my wrists and watch the blood trickle down my arm. My journals hold evidence of the many suicide notes I wrote, excruciating layers of pain I endured, the patience and level-headedness of the therapist who walked this walk with me.

There is a saying about trauma therapy that if one truly knew ahead of time the pain one would have to endure to get to the other side, one would have to be crazy to agree to start. I originally believed therapy would be a short-term process. I was wrong. In the words of the old song, The Circle

Game, I easily went "ten times 'round the seasons" before the collective pieces of my fractured psyche became integrated enough for me to begin seeing myself as a whole and worthwhile human being capable of loving and being loved.

Until that time, retrieving each memory, reliving each betrayal, was as painful as playing a real-world game of Operation. In the children's game, one hears a loud buzz and feels a slight vibration when using tweezers to pluck a miniature wishbone out of the heart on the body-shaped game board. In my therapy, the fear and the shame of exposing one indignity after another to my child's body and heart would shake my adult body with enough pain to leave me in a state of near collapse.

There were times when I left therapy exhausted from the effort of recalling and facing my abuse. At other times I fought so hard against my early life, crying and pounding the armrests of the sofa, that I wished was actually my father, and that I was beating him to death. I did not want these memories, but more precisely, I did not want this to be my history. My past. It hurt too much.

I cannot begin to describe how much like a lost child I felt.

The only mercy was this: this time, I was struggling with the memory of abuse—difficult as it was to bear. I was not a child this time, unable to control my universe, unable to speak up for myself, unable to be heard. This time I was safe enough to say it all, feel it all, be seen and heard for the strong and capable person I was slowly, gruesomely slowly, allowing myself to become. And this time I was not alone, crying into the night for someone to help me. My therapist became my lifeline.

My hold on life often felt tenuous, a thread of web, capable of cracking, shredding, dissolving—attaching me to my therapist, but at times to little else.

Of the many things one can say about good therapy, the best perhaps is that it is re-parenting. I had an abusive father and an emotionally absent mother—a black hole of parenting if there ever was one. In my therapy I was able to regress enough to grab the hand of that hurting, crying, left-behind child within myself and, with the careful guidance of an adult NOT my biological parent who was willing and able to be with me through the fires of hell, I literally grew up again through childhood and adolescence and into adulthood. Only this time, the parent with me was kind, and patient, and emotionally present and did not let me squeak through pretending I was fine. This time, I was finally able to experience the type of stability essential to normal growth and development.

*We worked and worked on my family issues. Not just my father and uncles with their abusiveness, but my mother and her emotional absence, her control. We worked and worked on issues of loss, and loss, and more loss. We searched for strengths and found them and built upon them until I could once again believe in my own capacity to be strong.*

*Learning to trust myself, to care for and be tender with myself, to be honest with myself, to have courage and believe in myself when all these things had been denied me for so long—these were proving to be the hard work of therapy. They required active doing, rather than passive telling, and it was as difficult and time-consuming as the earlier stages of treatment had been.*

*But I am a whole and healthy grateful adult today because of it.*

# FORTY-ONE

COLE CAN NO LONGER sit still. The Scotch has warmed him, but his bones still ache from the physical labor of bedding the boat for winter. He puts his work aside and stretches, first in the chair and then on his feet where he bends to touch his toes. Muscles, tendons, and bones respond with creaks and pops of resistance. His arms flop to his sides and he sighs—one long, deep sigh of resignation.

*I am so not the man I used to be.*

That simple thought startles him. He cannot remember the last time he was honest with himself about his age, his physical condition, or his future. And he's not quite sure he wants to do it now, if at all.

*This book is doing a number on me, he thinks, and this has never happened before, ever.*

He looks out to sea and across to the lighthouse, as if an answer would be broadcast in code from the light itself.

*I feel so… so disconnected, or something. I just don't know.*

"Oh, hell," he says out loud, and twists his body a few times at the shoulders, trying to shake the feelings off. He turns back to his work.

"Let me just finish this last chapter before I go opening up my own can of worms."

## 24 • Peeling the Onion

*The phases of my healing continued.*

*Until…*

*There came a point in my recovery when it was clear that, in order to* continue making progress, I needed an adult survivor group. It was no longer enough that my therapist believed me, told me the abuse was not my fault, and that I was strong and capable. I needed to take my work to another level, to hear these things from the mouths of other women who had experienced similar trauma.

It's hard not to smile now as I recall sitting in the waiting area the evening of that first group meeting. Each of the eight women rang the bell and then shyly entered the room, choosing to sit as far from another person as humanly possible in the small space, some hugging the far ends of the couches, almost leaning over the armrests.

One woman wrote furiously in her journal, another focused on her knitting, three hid behind outrageously dated magazines, all of them occasionally sneaking a furtive peek at the others. I found a fairly recent newspaper and tried doing the crossword puzzle, but startled so much each time the doorbell rang that I left pencil gouges in the page. Two women, and I include myself in this pair, seemed overwrought with fearful indecision, clutching the seats of their chairs to keep themselves from bolting from the room as the clock ticked down to the start of group.

The first lesson of group occurred right there in the waiting room before the initial session had even begun: there is no one type of victim. Sexual abuse can happen to anyone. We were all women, but we were tall and thin, short and thin, short and round, just plain average and stunningly gorgeous. We were natural blonds, bottle-blonds, brunettes, gray-hairs, and redheads. We were crunchy granola (that would be me), high-heeled in business suits and diamond-knit stockings, casually dressed in slacks and sweaters, wrapped in shawls and knee-high boots. We were academics, secretaries, journalists, social workers, business mavens, and mothers. Married, single, straight, lesbian.

We were the only child, the oldest child, the youngest child, the one smack dab in the middle of a pack of children. We were daughters of lawyers, doctors, government officials, bus drivers, business men, fishermen, factory workers. We were victims of fathers, grandfathers, step-fathers, mothers, uncles, brothers.

We would come to learn that some of us sought refuge in alcohol or drugs to numb the pain, some overate, some ate and purged, and of those, a few became dangerously anorexic. Some of us self-mutilated or were hospitalized, and many of us could dissociate in a heartbeat when flashbacks, memories, or everyday levels of stress threatened to overwhelm our already fragile sense of safety.

*There was no one, or two, or three things peculiar to each of us that we could point to and say "Ah, now I see why it happened". Only one thing was true: we had all been children. Children without a voice, without power, without the safety net of an adult who was able to prevent, stop, or believe us. We were all survivors of child sexual abuse, and we all walked in that door carrying an overwhelming burden of sadness that we were each desperate to be able to put down. That each of us was a living, breathing miracle was something we had yet to discover.*

*We spent ten weeks with each other taking turns recounting our history of abuse, resonating with each other's account of betrayal, making connections and gaining solidarity as a group of survivors. By week six it had begun to dawn on me that none of these women deserved what had happened to them, none of them were responsible for their own abuse, yet each carried a burden of guilt and shame similar to my own. With that realization came another— perhaps the one reason that group therapy is so important for survivors: If none of them had done anything wrong to make abuse happen to them, then perhaps neither had I. It sounds so very simple, yet it is so very hard to permit one's self to accept. But once I was able to do so, I was freer to move ahead one more step as well.*

*By the ninth week of group, each person had made her statement and we were being asked to think if there were any other related issues we wanted to raise before the final session. I took a deep breath and, with a leap of faith that this group could bear what I was about to say, I was finally able to reveal the one last truth about my abuse that clung to me and left me feeling that I was truly a sick and vile person, undeserving of love or respect. This same fear had also kept me from admitting this to my individual therapist.*

*Terrified that I might never again have such a safe place to let go of this shame, and knowing that I must be shed of it if I was to ever be able to let go of the stranglehold of my past, I literally had to close my eyes and not look at anyone as I spoke.*

*Once my father's abuse ended, I confessed, I became unable to sleep unless I fantasized abuse to myself, including torture, beatings, sometimes savage cruelty of being stoned to death or buried alive. I was still doing this in my adult life and it filled me with humiliation. Even the telling was agonizing, and by the end I was sobbing and shaking, petrified I would be rejected by these women who now meant so much to me, and that I would be shunned by the therapists who had devoted their lives to survivor healing.*

*I had convinced myself that no one else had ever done what I was doing.*

*Never lived through the hell of the abuse itself and then engaged in self-abuse, using much of the same behavior once used against me. Never said out loud to anyone that some parts of the abuse were sexually stimulating, and that the images and memories of those touches often became what I used for sexual stimulation.*

*The room was silent. None of the other women looked at me. Some were crying. And then, in the gentlest way possible without alarming me, one of the therapists took my hand and covered it with both of hers. She explained that this was a creative, perfectly understandable, and all-too-frequent response to being abused.*

*My saying this released other women to talk more openly about things that caused them shame. One had only recently stopped using drugs to numb her pain. Another had managed to pull herself out of a life of prostitution. A third woman said that as part of her abuse, her father photographed her and shared these pictures with other men. One could only feel relief that this happened before there was such a thing as an internet, where her child body would have been seen and misused by perverted minds for decades on end.*

*Each of us had, in one way or another, been treated as objects—sexual objects—by family members whose roles were supposed to be ones of love, protection, and nurturance.*

*From that, we had learned that we could not trust—that we were essentially helpless against power and authority. And that there must be something inherently wrong inside us for this to have happened.*

*And yet...*

*And yet, here we each were, scratching to find even the smallest vestiges of courage and hope that we could gather deep within our fractured hearts and souls and bodies and finally, finally, allowing trust and that illusive spark of hope to begin to bloom.*

*It felt as if even the walls of the meeting room were holding their breath as the need to say these most secret things poured forth. And when silence fell, when we were spent from the release of these things, those walls exhaled with relief along with all of us. And then they cried with us.*

*For me, the human contact of hand-holding reinforced a message I so desperately needed—that this disclosure did not make me untouchable, unlovable. And then I immediately felt the last and biggest burden of shame literally lift off my shoulders.*

*I was crying, but now I cried with relief. With release.*
*Sleep would become, once again, a place of rest and a chance for peace.*

---

*There are people who are brave because they face war and survive its horrors.*

*There are people who are brave because they save lives in spite of great danger to themselves.*

*There are people who are brave because their everyday lives are overwhelmingly difficult, and yet they put one foot in front of the other and continue on.*

*And then there are people who are brave because they overcome situations and conditions beyond one's capacity to imagine.*

*This is the bravery of those of us who survive sexual abuse.*

---

*The positive changes evolving from my group experience played out more dramatically in my individual therapy and in my social life as well. And if I have left you with the idea that all was gloom and doom in my life, it is important for you to know that nothing could be further from the truth.*

*I had friends and colleagues whose love and support sustained me through all stages of my healing. Very few truly knew the depth of my suffering but all of them own some credit for my recovery. They called to check up on me, fed me, covered for me, and kept me grounded in reality through their own lives and those of their families by way of birthdays, recitals, baseball games, and Christmas Eves spent assembling children's toys.*

*And music. Music literally did soothe my tortured soul and bring me peace. My closest friends often pulled me out of myself with tickets to a concert, a new album by a favorite singer, or just a few people sitting around talking and listening to a great guitar.*

*My resilience was due in no small part to the impact these friends, and my sisters as well, had on my daily existence. There was just enough laughter and joy to keep me wanting to stay in my life in spite of pain that often felt unendurable. And they always seem to present me with possibilities—things to look forward to, to want, to pursue.*

*Allow me to give you an example.*

*My friend's Golden had delivered a litter of gorgeous balls of fluff the color of ripened wheat fields rippling in the wind. One little girl in particular just wiggled her furry behind each time I looked her way, and she won my heart and a free trip to my home. I was thrilled.*

*Right away, I named her Willow. She was the color of new-growth weeping willow branches when they first appear in spring. She was new, and this was spring, and I was in love with her.*

*Halfway home I was ready to change her name to Whining Willow.*

*We were almost home when I thought Yowling Willow would be more fitting.*

*By the time I pulled into the garage I was sure even she thought her name was Please Stop Crying Willow.*

*Perhaps she needed to pee. I set her down in the back yard. Evidently she had never been on grass before. She picked each leg up, one at a time, and shook it before gingerly trying again. She tried to sit, but grass on her behind seemed worse than grass on her paws.*

*She made a beeline for the sidewalk and planted her butt on it, looking at me with big brown eyes, head cocked to the left.*

*I took her in. She ran through the house, sniffing each corner, scratching at the rug, nose to the floor. She headed for the living room, found the leg of the couch, squatted and peed. I picked her up, took her back outside where she sat again and gave me the look, head cocked to the right side this time.*

*"What?" I asked her.*

*I fed her. Took her out again. We played. I took her out again. She napped. We played. I took her out again. And again. And again. Nothing. I brought her in.*

*She peed.*

*When I sat down, she sat down. She stared at me, head cocked to one side or the other. I'd look at her and her furry behind would start wiggling. But still, she just looked and cocked her head.*

*"What?" I kept saying to her. "What? What? What do you want? I fed you. I played with you. I took you out. What is it that you want from me? What?"*

*One whole weekend. One long, three-day weekend, and all I said was "What?" I was not cut out for this. Dog and I were not bonding well at all.*

*On Monday she went back to her mother and siblings. I placed her back in that pen and she went prancing around, saying hello to her brothers and* sisters, wiggling that willowy behind all over the place, telling them all about me. I was sure of it. Every time she snuggled up to one of them, that puppy would turn and stare at me, cocking its own furry little head, taunting me.

"What?" I shouted, defeated.

Joking, I told people I clearly wasn't quite mature enough for a dog yet, or anything that depended on me. I suggested that I might do better dropping back and starting over with a teddy bear. And in fact, I went home and adopted a Pooh Bear from the local toy store, instantly reducing my stress factor by about ninety-nine percent.

It proved to be one of the better purchases I have ever made. I managed to tolerate family gatherings for years with the help of that bear, slipping off its red flannel vest and putting it in my pocket, holding onto it for dear life when I would eventually enter the crosshairs of my mother's AK-47 load of emotional abuse.

A few years after dog and bear, close friends gifted me with a trip to the Animal Rescue League to pick out a kitten. This proved a much better choice in terms of compatibility, and that first cat, and now her replacement, spent many years purring her way into my heart.

I found that this arrangement suited my life quite well. It worked out so well, in fact, that I established a continuum for myself: first, an inanimate object (teddy bear), then a cat, then a dog. Then, and only if and when I proved successful with all of those, I thought I might be able to move on to a decidedly more mature and intimate relationship with a human being.

I continue to strive toward this goal.

––––––––––––

WHAT THE HECK IS SHE THINKING pitching a dog story in the middle of this? No way that's going to fly. With every intention of red-lining this entire section of DJ's manuscript Cole reaches for his editing pen tucked behind his right ear. But his hand inadvertently knocks the pen backwards and it shoots through the slats of his rocker, bouncing off the side of the porch and down into the beach rose. Damn.

He slides the manuscript off his lap and onto the porch rail, lifting himself out of his chair with some effort after spending the past few hours sitting. Spotting the pen nestled securely in the bramble of rose hips Cole is reluctant to reach in for it, having previously experienced the wrath of the bush's protective thorns. He finds a piece of driftwood long enough to fish out his pen, then meticulously brushes and blows it free of the fine sand clinging to it—tiny magnets hanging on for dear life.

When Cole turns, his breath is caught by the sheer beauty of the scene in front of him. Late afternoon sun to the west is casting almost horizontal shadows across the dock. Sea gulls perch on each of the five vertical dock posts and the silhouettes of gulls and posts fall neatly along the dock and out into the water, offering the negative image of the more colorful real scene.

"Oh, wow," he whispers. "This is beautiful." He is filled with a need to share what he is seeing. But there is no one. For the briefest of seconds, he finds himself on the verge of wishing that even someone as repulsive to him as Martone were there to witness with him.

*What the hell is wrong with me?*

The sun slips low enough to dilute the images on the dock. Cole looks at his house, then back toward the empty boat slip. He sits on his bottom step and lowers his head, shaking it sadly.

*I think I'm the one who's 'neither up nor down'. Look at yourself, Alexander. You have a job, a house, and a boat. Stuff! And you don't share any of it with anybody. Hell, you even want to get rid of the damn birds, and they're the only other living things around.*

*Maybe DJ had the right idea. Start small. Maybe I should invite my kids and their families here for Christmas this year. They used to love it here, before I turned into a sour old neurotic mess with as many prickers as these bushes.*

He stands up and shouts at the birds on the roof.

"All right, you rats with wings, you get a reprieve this time. But once I work up to a cat or a dog, your days are numbered. Don't say you haven't been warned."

His shout has startled two of the post sitters off the dock, and on their brief flight to the roof top, one squawking gull drops a huge splat of guano, barely missing Cole and landing on the porch railing.

Cole struggles, wanting desperately to sit and finish the manuscript. But perhaps even more desperately he needs to clean up the sea gull mess. He manages to sit. He stares at the paperwork. He stares at the guano. He figures he's almost finished with the manuscript. He stares again at the guano. It appears to be getting bigger. He is aware that he is beginning to sweat. It's no use for him to fight this. He gets up and heads to the kitchen for bucket, brush, and soap.

By the time he's done cleaning up to his usual high level of satisfaction, darkness has descended and he has no alternative but to bring the unfinished work inside. He makes himself a sandwich, sits at the kitchen table, and returns to the manuscript.

------

*Aside from surviving the original abuse, facing it again in therapy was the hardest thing I have done in my life. To move from a place of feeling consumed by what was done to me, at times feeling responsible for it happening and of feeling unable to be free of the shame of it, to a place where it no longer defines who I am but can be understood as something that happened to me—that is not a miracle.*

*It is healing.*

*It is the nascent stage of thriving, and it is gut-wrenchingly hard work that takes courage no one on earth believes they possess. And yet we do.*

*This is certainly not everyone's experience of therapy. It is simply mine. And I do not make light of the fact that being employed and having good health insurance and income enough to handle what insurance didn't, makes me an extraordinarily privileged person. I do not know where I would be without this experience, but I truly believe it would not be a good place. Many others find healing pathways through relationships, spirituality, art, or other means. This, however, is what worked for me.*

*My history of abuse no longer controls me, no longer holds central place in my life or wakes me in the night, catapulting me into shudders of fear. While news stories of childhood sexual abuse continue to infuriate me, they do not level me, but rather energize me to work more diligently to prevent it.*

*I live as normal a life as possible these days, although the life of a writer can rarely be described as ordinary when we sequester ourselves for weeks at a time to get these words out of our heads and onto the page. That I am an author of some renown is still a wonder to me. That I am a survivor of childhood sexual abuse is the miracle of me.*

*These days I much prefer to think about and talk about the healing process than the abuse. I am desperate for people to know that there is life and joy beyond all the things that work to bring children to their knees and rob them of themselves.*

*Some people think they need to forgive the abuser in order to heal. But there are some things that are truly unforgiveable. Others think it is one's self*

*that needs to be forgiven. My concern with this is that it can contain a sug-
gestion, no matter how implicit, that the child somehow has done something
they must either be forgiven for, or for which they need to forgive themselves.
Nothing could be further from the truth.*

*Forgiveness of oneself is often mistaken for the process of letting go and
moving on. One must find a way to let go in order to heal. Letting go of
the past so that it no longer defines you, no longer holds you in its grip in a
way that weakens or disables you, is at the very core of healing. And it's as
stubborn a process as removing duct tape from just about any object you can
imagine—with all the pulling and tearing and resistance that goes with it.
Ripping it off skin, in particular, is excruciating. But it feels so good when it's
gone and your skin can actually breathe again!*

*Good therapy is like that. And the outcome... well, the outcome is life
itself, with all the joy and sadness and complexity it offers. It is at times in-
conceivable to me that I ever even considered the alternative.*

---

*There are times when mere words cannot do justice to an experience.
This is one of those times. In writing of my work in therapy, my greatest worry has been finding the right way to describe a relationship and an experience
that truly nurtured me in all the ways I needed to be nurtured, while at the
same time challenged me in the ways I most needed to be challenged. The
inner child, the one who wailed that night at the lecture in New Hampshire
so long ago and begged me to make an appointment—that was the smartest
part of me.*

*My therapist was never a silent witness to my pain. She was vital to what
I did, was in it with me in a way that rarely left me worried she would desert
me if I became too much. Nor did she ever let me off the hook if I was being
resistant or uncompromising. Her honesty with me showed me I could be
honest with myself.*

*With just the slightest lift of her eyebrow, she would let me know I was
fleeing my demons. A turned palm was her invitation to try facing them
instead. She could move me to re-think my own behaviors and motivations
with the simplest of questions: "And how has that worked for you?" This, I
might add, was long before politics changed the caring "you" to a callous
"ya", and forever etched the phrase with scorn.*

*When I began therapy, I did not care about the age, ethnicity, history* or marital status of the person I would be seeing. I cared that she would be smarter than me, have keen enough insight to know when I was trying to manipulate my way around something I needed to face head on, possess the patience and endurance required to allow me to set a pace that I could tolerate. But more than anything, whether I could have articulated it at the time or not, what I absolutely demanded was a therapist capable of the highest levels of integrity and deserving of the deepest levels of respect.

I chose wisely, it turned out.

Remarkably, I had also chosen someone who never failed to treat me with the utmost dignity, integrity, and respect in return. When I felt that I was as disgusting as the things that happened to me; when I was repulsed by re-occurring images of being covered in wet semen that I could not remove; and when my wrists ached from wanting to be cut to shreds, she believed in my power to heal and in my ability to reach for all the possibilities in life that my soul was yearning to achieve.

Therapy ended, but the words and actions of compassion and trust continue to sustain me. My therapist did not save my life, but there is not a day that I am not reminded of how, together, we were able to build a wonderful possibility out of the rubble of my life that I carried into her office so long ago.

---

When I was very little, we lived in my grandmother's house with Lena, my parents and my brother. At my grandmother's house, I held JJ's hand and danced in the sunlit back yard, played hide-and-seek beneath the rows of sheets and towels on the clothesline. I picked buttercups and held them under my chin, watched lumpy green caterpillars climb along tomato plants. Banana curls circled my smiling face, gleamed in the sunshine, and fell across the shoulders of the sweater knit by hand especially for me. I napped on the glider on the screened-in porch, robin songs filling my sleep, and I woke to the sweet scent of the evening's pasta sauce as it bubbled its way to perfection in the kitchen.

We moved when I was four. Moved away from the joys and safety of this life I was living, surrounded by love, secure in myself and confident of my place in the world—and landed directly in a full decade of hell.

What would my childhood have been like, I used to wonder, had I been fortunate enough to have danced in my grandmother's back yard for ten more years? Who would I be today?

*What would my life be like today, I often wonder, had I lacked the courage to choose healing? Who would I be today?*

*I spend my life writing romance novels, works of fiction that have very little to do with the truth of my daily life. I love my work and the pleasure it brings to those who read it. But it does not speak to all of who I am.*

*This book is the truth of my life. I offer it with hope for the future of every child. That they will be born into a world where they are free to dance in the sun, a world that has found its way to peace, and has learned to prioritize protecting our most vulnerable from all forms of abuse.*

*I ask you to imagine a world in which every child is loved and held safe.*

*A world in which home is the safest place a child can go.*

---

COLE IS FINISHED, wearied by both the task of editing and the powerful sway of DJ's words upon the page. They evoke within him feelings he has not allowed himself for many years.

He zaps a mug of warm milk and sits again, sipping slowly and staring at the closed manuscript, tapping it with his pen. His wonder and amazement at DJ have grown with each page. The man in him feels a need to cry; the editor in him feels a need to sing. Neither feeling is one he recognizes as typical for himself at all.

*Amazing,* he thinks, *truly amazing. I think I need a therapist like this one. Maybe if I'd gone when my wife wanted me to, things would have worked out. Maybe I can get DJ to tell me who she is. It might not be too late. God knows I need all the help I can get.*

Cole can't help smiling at himself.

"This has been one hell of a long weekend," he says, yawning. "I'm halfway surprised I didn't die of fright in the middle of it, and there's still tomorrow to get through before anything's resolved. Better get some sleep."

He first leaves a check for Will and instructions about closing up the house. Then he scribbles a few notes for the morning meeting, washes and dries the mug, diligently checks all doors and windows, and climbs the stairs for bed. He plans to leave for Boston at the crack of dawn.

# Tuesday

*"We gain strength, and courage, and confidence by each experience in which we really stop to look fear in the face...*
*You are able to say to yourself, 'I lived through this horror. I can take the next thing that comes along.'*
*. . . we must do that which we think we cannot."*

Eleanor Roosevelt

# FORTY TWO

BREAKFAST AT DJ'S is an informal affair this morning. Coffee, brewed dark enough to evoke memories of tall men in sombreros walking with their donkeys perfumes the air and awakens tired bodies. But the real attraction lies in the center of the table where three women armed with forks and spoons are wreaking havoc on the remaining contents of the big white box.

Tuck licks the back of her fork and smacks her lips in loud satisfaction.

"Two things," she says. "We only eat protein for lunch, or else we risk descending to the sugar point of no return. Between last night and this morning, I have personally consumed my allotment for an entire year. And I'll be riding into court this morning on a sugar high, trying to do my part to make sure the guy gets a speedy hearing." She pulls the box her way and peeks in, not wanting to leave any tidbit behind.

"You have court this morning?" DJ asks, pausing in her pursuit of the last remnants of raspberry soufflé now puddling on her plate, "that same boy from yesterday?"

"The very same," Tuck responds, her nose still inside the box. "Oh, right, we didn't get to talk last night, did we? It was the step-father who molested him. The poor kid is pretty banged up but he was very clear about who did what. We'll have to do a more thorough evaluation once he recovers, but for now, with my testimony, they'll have enough to hold his step-father. The boy will be safe. That's the important part for right now. And the mom is right on board with supporting him, too. That's always such a relief!"

"My guess is you'll be seeing the kid in therapy for a while after he's released from the hospital, too," Kate adds. "It was a great move for child protective to call you in early on. That way, he already knows you and you've both got a good head start on the trust end of things."

"Sounds like it's about time something good happened for the little guy," DJ says. "It's so hard, sometimes, when I think that kids are still being abused like this. So many years later and we still haven't figured out how to treat children with the respect they deserve."

Two heads nod in agreement.

"If my book can help, even in the smallest way, even just for a few people… If it can," DJ says, rapping her spoon for emphasis on the tabletop, "then all of this craziness about the book will have been worth it. Except for the risk it's put you two in. That will take me longer to recover from."

"Well, we're over it already, girl, so catch up!" Tuck says. "It's time to get the book out there so it can begin doing good." She stops herself and changes course. "However, that does not mean any of us can let our guard down." She points at DJ and then at Kate. "This ain't over 'til it's over. And, trust me, it ain't over yet. Old Raymond hasn't played all his cards. I can feel it in my bones."

DJ can only smile. "Well, since you're now taking messages from your bones, I guess we'd better listen."

Kate gives Tuck her most sincere look and places her hand over her heart. "I promise you I will be careful. I promise with all my heart."

Tuck throws her hands up. "I'm being serious and you're being a sarcastic bitch! Life returns to normal!"

"Two things," Kate says, taking a spoonful of mousse. She swallows and nods at Tuck. "You said there were two things you wanted to say, but you only told us one. What's the other one?"

Tuck looks puzzled for a moment and then she smiles and turns to DJ.

"Oh, yes," she says. "I remember. Deej, I know you told us last night that you weren't going to your uncle's again, right?"

"That's absolutely correct, and don't you try to talk me out of that, either. Why? What do you want?" DJ sounds suspicious.

"No, no, I wouldn't do that. It's just a question, that's all. I was wondering about the chef person, Anthony? Do you think, once Raymond's dead, you'd be inheriting him along with the house? Because, I do have to tell you, he is one hell of a fantastic baker."

Kate lets out a loud guffaw that quickly turns into a choking sound. When Tuck leans over to whack her on the back she inadvertently bumps the newspaper over the edge of the table and onto the floor. Hidden under the paper is the very last crème brûlée, now half eaten, but clearly not shared with the group.

"You sneaky son of a gun," DJ laughs. She reaches to rescue the dish before Kate can nab it for herself. "You even had one all to yourself in the car before we got here yesterday."

Tuck has a hand on each hip, glaring at her partner.

"And you had one all to yourself in the car yesterday?" she says. "You never told me that. You are such a lousy sharer, Katherine, you really are. You should be ashamed of yourself."

DJ takes two clean spoons from the kitchen drawer, hands one to Tuck, and dips into the crème brûlée with the other.

"*I'll* go halfsies with you, Tuck," she says, running the crème-loaded spoon under Kate's nose. "We, on the other hand, do know how to share." She places the rich and creamy pudding on her tongue and exaggerates a *Food Channel* chef's version of gustatory delight. Grinning widely, Tuck joins in and they taunt Kate right down to the last spoonful, which Tuck scoops up and, to her partner's surprise, places gracefully in front of Kate. She bows deeply.

"And we saved the best bite for last. For you," she says with great solemnity. "Memo to Kate, this is how to share." She tousles Kate's hair and then kisses the top of her head.

"Okay, I'm off to get dressed. Got to get to court by nine and hope they reach the case before noon. My schedule is full at the office this afternoon. When are you two heading into town?" Tuck folds the empty box and places it in their recycle bin as she speaks. She unplugs the coffee maker and dumps the grounds into the compost bucket.

"I don't know," Kate responds, looking at DJ. "What time is this meeting anyway? I've forgotten."

"I wanted to talk with you about that, Katie. I'm going solo on this one, my friend. I'm one hundred percent clear about what I want, what I'm going to say, and what I will do if they say no. Although I can't really imagine that they will. I also have to talk with Cole about whatever it was my uncle said or did to him to threaten him and why he never told me anything about all that."

DJ could see that Kate wanted to protest, but she wasn't about to give in.

"I am profoundly grateful for all the time you gave me this past weekend, to say nothing about your moral support and just plain old loving me."

She stacks the three spoons on the plate in front of her.

"But," she says, "I mean it. This is one I need to do on my own. You're both okay with that, right?"

"You know what, DJ?" Kate says. "You are more than ready. You have been for months. You were just amazing yesterday and the day before, and the day before that. You are amazing. We were glad to be asked to go with you, glad we could be there when you needed us, but you are one strong woman, more than ready to take those guys on. I'm just sorry to miss out on the fireworks, that's all."

"That goes for me, too," Tuck says. "But, at the risk of repeating myself, if you go alone you absolutely have to stay on guard. And then, of course, you have to come to our place tonight and give us the whole meeting, word for word. Deal?"

"And what makes you think, even for a minute, that I wouldn't?" DJ asks with a huge grin. "If I could call you from the bathroom floor when I started this ball rolling on Friday, the least I can do is include you both in celebrating the contract. I'd like to crash there for the afternoon, if that's still all right, maybe do a bit of shopping and then some writing. How about dinner on me at L'Espalier at, say, six-thirty? I have to get back home tonight at a reasonable hour. Got to feed the cat. Sadie will just have to stay at the kennel 'til tomorrow."

"Oh, my god," Kate fairly swoons. "L'Espalier! I've heard their pumpkin mousse is to die for. I'm in. And, yes, Tuck, protein for lunch is a must."

"So I guess there's no chance the pastry chef at L'Espalier will be chasing us down with a free box of goodies when we leave, huh?" Tuck says.

"More's the pity, I say, dearies," moans Kate.

"I hear you. So, we're all set for tonight then? I'll make reservations. Call this a thanks for the weekend. Oh, and for providing the title for the manuscript. Almost forgot. It's perfect."

"Our pleasure, Deej," Kate says. "Puts a bit of both of us in your book. It feels nice."

Tuck nods in agreement and looks up at the clock.

"Look, I'm going to be late if I don't get cracking. DJ, best of luck with the meeting. Kate, I'll see you at the office. You might have to cover for me if this hearing runs late. I'll call you on your cell if it starts to look like I might miss my one o'clock. Love you both. Oh, and you have a board meeting at four, honey. Don't forget." She blows air kisses to DJ, runs a hand under Kate's chin in a tender gesture, and leaves the kitchen.

Kate rises to clear the rest of the table.

"Why don't you take the shower first," she says to DJ. "We'll have to leave soon, too, if you want to get downtown by ten."

"Thanks, that will help a lot," DJ replies, but she remains seated with her slippered feet hugging the rungs of the chair next to her. "And thanks for the names of those two therapists in Ann Arbor. I talked with my sisters again last night and gave them to Chrissie. I actually think she was relieved to get them. It sounds like she's ready to make the next move by talking with Garret and then calling for an appointment."

"Good for her. And is she still pitching a bitch about your mother?"

"Oh, yeah, both Chris and Sarah still think she might seriously move in with one of them. Won't happen, though, my mother's all talk no action on that score anyway."

Kate asks, "Did you also bring them up to speed on what happened at Raymond's?"

DJ turns in her chair to face Kate at the sink. Her mood changes and concern shows in her hunched posture. As if to ward off a chill, she draws her bathrobe tighter around her shoulders.

"I did. First off, I couldn't have made them any happier than when I told them he's dying. It was hard to get them to listen to anything else for a few minutes."

"I don't need much of an imagination to envision that," Kate says. "They really hate him, don't they?"

"Good Lord, yes, and that's putting it mildly. I think their exact words about all of them, our father as well as uncles, was 'good riddance to bad rubbish'. Not a whole heck of a lot of emotion attached to any of it, no matter how hard I pressed them to talk about it."

"Wow," Kate says. "That's actually kind of sad, don't you think? Especially about your father."

"Well, it was a long time ago, Katie. I didn't really expect a great deal more. None of us ever actually talk about him much anyway. No reason to. Besides, I had another agenda with them last night. I wanted to know how and when they figured out what Raymond did."

"Oh, boy," says Kate, anticipating a good story. "Tell me."

"Seems they started thinking something was wrong when neither of the uncles showed up at our father's funeral. Maggie was flying then, in and out of lots of large cities along the east coast, so she started to try to find them. She came up with zilch. Nothing. Nowhere. Not even a mention of them."

"And?"

"And nothing. You know my sisters. Not much gets in their way when they decide something, let alone relying on small things like facts, or evidence. They just decided, given who Raymond is, that he killed them. And then they threw my father into the mix for good measure. That's it."

"Wow. That was a hell of a stretch. But they nailed it, didn't they? And so what happened when you told them they were right all along?"

"Kate." DJ looks at her friend as if she just fell off one of the turnip trucks she's always talking about. "Need you even ask? It totally made their day to know something I didn't. Add that to the news that he's dying and you'd have thought the Red Sox won the Series again. Really, they went nuts."

"That's it?" Kate can't quite believe that's all there is to the tale.

"Well, no, what pretty much blew them away was the news that Raymond sent our uncles packing when he found out that they were getting ready to molest them. Well, Chris and Maggie to be more precise."

"I wondered how they'd deal with that," Kate says. She pulls a chair away from the table and sits next to DJ. "How did they take it?"

"Not all that much different from me, to tell the truth. How do you hate a guy who saves you from hell, even though the things he does to save you are reprehensible? There's no real answer for that one. So they were stunned, I guess is the word."

"Makes sense they would be. I bet they never saw that one coming, huh?"

"You know, Katie, in some small way, me telling them that was kind of like them telling me that Raymond killed Ed and Joey. I think it helped them understand my initial reaction just a bit better."

"Well," Kate says, "It must have been hard for them to really believe you had no idea Raymond had killed his brothers."

DJ has to laugh at Kate's remark.

"As you well know, Katie, I am, either by nature or as a by-product of my abuse, a hyper-vigilant person. It might help make me a good writer, but it sure as hell is a pain in the butt for people close to me."

She sees that Kate is about to agree with her and puts up a hand to stop her.

"I know it. I know it. I can only apologize for it. But I have to tell you, my friend, all of that stuff that Raymond did, and what he said? I truly had not seen any of that coming, not at all. And perhaps in a convoluted sort of way, it gives me hope that my hyper-vigilant antennae are beginning to fade away from lack of use, no longer quite so necessary. That would be a good thing I think because, quite frankly, they are enormously exhausting things to carry around all the time."

Kate looks at DJ. "Good point. Now if you could only stop dreaming about ugly things hidden under rocks," she teases.

"Yeah, but I was right on target, wasn't I?" DJ laughs. "Bones and bodies and the whole nine yards. Spooky."

"I hear you. It would have been a whole lot funnier if it hadn't proven to be so true," Kate says. "And so how did you leave it with Sarah and Chris?"

"I think we're pretty much okay for now, or at least until mother starts acting up again. My guess is that they'll talk today, and that sometime during the course of their conversation, it will dawn on them that sending our uncles away was what saved the twins, but that killing them was way off the chart of reasonable. They'll figure out that killing them was to save his 'business' and his own behind, and be furious."

"Can't blame them for that," Kate says. "What do you think they'll do?"

"Frankly, I think they'll want to go to the police and charge him with murder."

"And?" Kate asks.

"And, what?"

"And what do you think of that, DJ? Surely it's crossed your mind, too?"

"Hell, yes, I can't get it *out* of my mind. But look, Kate, you and I both know that what I want, or my sister's might want in this situation doesn't amount to a hill of beans without concrete evidence. It's our word against his and just because he told us he did it, doesn't mean he's dumb enough to be caught, even now. The FBI's been on his back since the beginning and they've never been able to trap him. What chance do we have?"

DJ shakes her head, looking weary.

"And, truth be told, Katie, I'm just not sure I have the stomach for it, either. I know how I sounded when I was screaming at him yesterday, but here's the thing. Revenge works really well in the novels I write, but I'm not so sure it plays out the same in real life."

"I'm not so sure it does either, now that you mention it, DJ." She pauses. "Um… there's something else I never got the chance to tell you yesterday. It's about being at Raymond's."

"What about it?" DJ asks.

"He had a gun."

"A gun? When we were with him on the sun porch? Are you sure?"

"Oh, yeah, I'm sure. Big gun with a dark silver handle, stuck down by his side in the chair," Kate says, using her hands to elucidate. "Big gun. Scared me."

"Shit, Kate. I saw the rosary beads, but I never saw the gun." She's at a loss for words.

"Well, if he didn't use it when I blew up at him, I guess he never will," Kate says, laughing. "Maybe we're safer than we thought. And, really, you have to hand it to him—rosary beads and a gun. What every well-dressed mobster takes to a family meeting!"

DJ is still distracted by Kate's information.

"A gun. God, Katie, I am trying so hard to deal with my changing image of him, and the information just keeps piling up. I feel as if I've spent the past twenty years in la-la land. Of course he'd have a gun. Probably has a dozen of them. But why he thought he'd need one when I was there boggles my mind. And, truthfully, I don't want to think about it, don't even want it in my head. Not now. Not ever."

"I can certainly understand that, Deej. It seems like way too much, way too fast, doesn't it?"

DJ simply nods her head in agreement.

"Do you think it will change any of what you wrote about him in your autobiography? Maybe put some of this new information in it?" Kate asks.

DJ plants her feet on the floor and nervously begins to bounce one leg. She takes a full minute to answer Kate.

"I've been obsessing about that very thing since we left his place yesterday. And I honestly don't have an answer. There's just something about it that I can't quite put my finger on yet. The part of me that wants Raymond to really get what he's done is not fully satisfied. Hell, I'm not sure it ever will be. But is it really my responsibility to educate him?"

"That's a tough one, Deej."

"Yep, it is. So, I'm going to go in and see what Cole and Stan have to say. I know there'll be edits, and that will buy me some time to decide if I want this new information in the book. But my first inclination is to say no, I don't."

"And you think Sarah and Christine will be okay with that?"

"One can always hope. When they come in for Thanksgiving I should have whatever edits Cole and Stan require finished by then, and I think I need to give the girls a chance to look at it. If they decide they want to, of course."

She's quiet for some time, thinking. Kate waits.

"Once it's published, I know there'll be some fallout that we'll all have to deal with. Extended relatives and family friends will have their say about things, I'm pretty sure of that. And, my mother, of course—a bridge I'm not willing to even contemplate crossing until I have to. But with Chris and Sarah, I have no doubts they'll be supportive. Things might get sticky at times, but if there's one thing our fractured upbringing has taught us, it's that we need to stick together."

Kate utters one word.

"Survival."

"Yep," DJ says, "safety in numbers. You guys," she adds, "have always been my numbers."

"Works both ways, my friend, works both ways."

Kate stands once again and tugs at DJ's chair.

"Time to get a move on," she says. "The world awaits this new book of yours. Start those presses rolling. It will be a best seller, I'm sure of it, so don't let them tell you different. Hold your ground. Dig your heels in. Give 'em hell. Etcetera, etcetera, etcetera."

"I get it. I get it. Stop, now, please, or we'll never get going." DJ laughs, tossing a kitchen towel at Kate's head.

Kate pulls the towel down and looks at DJ.

"I mean it, Deej," she says. "Good luck with this."

"I know you do, Kate. And thanks. I'm good."

# FORTY-THREE

TUCK'S NEED TO APPEAR in court has left Kate without a car, and DJ agrees to drop her off in Sommerville before she goes into the city to meet with Cole. When they exit the house, however, they are surprised to see a black pickup truck blocking the driveway. The side door is fully open, a pair of large black shoes can be seen firmly planted on the tarmac, but their owner is hidden, slumped over behind the car door.

"Hello?" DJ calls, moving cautiously toward the vehicle. A very large head lifts up.

The women stop in their tracks. One utters "oh shit" and the other "Vincent" in unison. It is quite evident that he has been crying, and his agitation is showing in the way he is wiping his face and wringing the cloth in his hands.

DJ immediately asks, "My uncle? Vincent, is it my uncle? Is he dead?"

An agonizing "No" is heard from the driver's side.

Kate lifts herself on tiptoes and looks into the cab of the truck. There is a gun on the seat.

She leans into DJ and whispers, "He has a gun," but her mind is doing a tap dance. *Gun. Big gun. Never seen a Glock. Could be a Glock. Mobsters love Glocks, right? Must be a Glock. Guns kill. Glocks kill. Bad guys with Glocks kill good guys. We're gonna be killed by a Glock. Oh, sweet Jesus, make Tuck come back with the car right now and smash into this guy and save us. I promise I'll be good if you do. Please.*

While Kate has been pleading, DJ has quietly moved in front of Kate and inched closer to Vincent.

"You have a gun there, Vincent?" she asks. "Is that meant for me? Is that why you're here?"

Vincent reaches behind him and picks up the weapon, looking at it, turning it over, inspecting the barrel, running fingers along the grip. He looks at DJ then shakes his head from side to side, tears running down his face.

"Did Raymond send you, Vincent? Did my uncle send you to do this?" she asks, barely believing that she is even uttering these words.

Vincent looks up sharply. "No. No he did not. Since you left… all he does… he just sits in that chair and stares out the windows… he's getting sicker… you have to come back… you have to say you're sorry…" His speech is uneven, interrupted by snorts and snivels. He looks down at the gun.

Kate watches his fingers move closer to the trigger. Time slows down and merges with the strokes of his hands along the barrel, each one marking a second. *Glock. Glock. Glock. Glock…*

"All of this old stuff with you," Vincent says, glaring at DJ, "it's killing him. He was doing okay, managing okay. And then you come and it's all going to hell."

He wipes his runny nose along his sleeve leaving a long string of glistening slime. "You don't even know the half of anything, you know that, Donna?" he says, laying hard on her name. "You think everything's all about you, but it isn't. He took me in when I was a kid on the streets. He saved my life. He's been the only father I ever had."

"I do know that, Vincent," DJ says as tenderly as she can. "You've been there through just about everything. And he loves you, he really does. And you know it. And that's exactly what makes his dying so hard. You're grieving, Vincent. What you're feeling is grief. It's all mixed up in there with anger, but most of what you're feeling is sadness and that's okay. It's what you should be feeling. It means you're human."

Vincent's response is quick and it is harsh. He uses language DJ has never heard from him before.

"You know, for a girl who's supposed to be so smart, you're pretty fucking stupid." He now has the gun in his right hand and stands up. "Don't go thinking you know what the fuck I'm feeling. You don't know shit about shit."

Kate has started to tremble, and when she places her arm in DJ's, she feels her shaking as well. *This is not going well for our side,* she thinks, *not*

*well at all. We need to do something here, but I'll be damned if I know what.*
*Holy hell,* I'm *the one who's supposed to know what to do.*

DJ puts her chin up. "Just what shit don't I know shit about, Vincent?"
she says. "Enlighten me."

*Oh, crap, DJ, no, no no, that's not what to do. We have to de-escalate the*
*angry person. You're just ramping him up. We're really gonna get Glocked if*
*you talk to him like that.*

Oddly enough, however, DJ's question has reduced Vincent to tears
again, and he sits heavily back into the truck, springs bouncing in reaction
to his weight.

"You have to come... he wants... he... talk to him... he wants... oh,
God damn it," he says and grabs his head.

*Sweet mercy, this is terrible,* thinks Kate, as the situation finally begins
to make sense to her.

"Vincent," Kate says as calmly as she is able while slowly moving to
stand alongside DJ, "Raymond doesn't want you to hurt DJ, does he? He
wants you to kill *him*, though, doesn't he?"

Vincent sobs, his face in his hands, and nods his head. "Not now...
later... when he's really bad... then... it's what he wants... he says 'do it
for me Vincent, do it for me.'"

DJ is looking at Kate like she just landed from Mars. *Where in God's*
*name did that thought come from?*

"But you can't, can you Vincent?" Kate continues. "You love him and
you simply cannot do as he wishes."

"I can't," Vincent wails. "You need to help me. You need to help him,
Donna. He wants to die but I won't do it, I can't do it, not to him."

When DJ moves closer to the truck, she is somewhat relieved to see
that the gun is now tucked into the side pocket of the driver's door. "Vincent," she says, struggling to regain her composure, "put the gun under
the seat and we can talk about this, but I won't do anything with that gun
sitting there. I hate those things."

Painfully slowly he complies, grabs a handful of tissues from a pack
he finds under the same seat, and blows his nose with grand exuberance.

"He's put you in a hell of a bind, Vincent, and I can appreciate what
that's doing to you. I am no longer willing to go back to that house of his.
That's final," she says firmly as she sees him readying to argue. "However,
I will participate in whatever the doctor's plans are for him in these final
days. What I want you to do is call me to inform me of his next appoint-

ment, and I will meet you both at the doctor's office or hospital or hospice... wherever. And then we'll work together on whatever needs to be done. Can we agree on that much anyway, for starters?"

He simply nods his head, yes.

But DJ is not finished. "And no more guns, Vincent. Not near Raymond. He had one in his chair yesterday on the porch. Not in the truck either. Not anywhere near me. Got that? He will not kill himself, and you will not kill him. What we will do, you and me together, we will help him die. And that, in turn, will help us, too. Okay? I need your word on this or I will not do it at all."

Vincent spends far too much time looking at the sky before he answers, causing both DJ and Kate to worry that the message might not have been made clear enough for him. At last he lowers his eyes and faces DJ. He nods his head.

"Thank you," he says. And that is all he says. He swings his long heavy legs into the front seat, closes the door, starts the engine, and drives away without another word.

DJ and Kate stare down the country road until the truck is the size of a Tic Tac. And only then do they dare take a deep breath and will their rapidly beating hearts to believe in surviving another day on this earth. Relief washes over them and they turn to each other in an embrace of gratitude.

"Sweet Jesus, thank you," says Kate. "I didn't think we would get out of that one alive. And Tuck will be giving me holy blazes, don't you know. She kept saying it's not over 'til it's over. And she was right. Only we were almost over." She backs away a bit from DJ but still grips her arms. "Are you okay, dearie?"

DJ gives a shudder. Her legs still feel like pudding, and she sways just a bit.

"I hate guns, Katie. I mean I really hate them, and to be staring at one for what felt like half a century, thinking we might end up dead... all because of something I started... well, then I got mad when he said I didn't know shit about shit... wrong time to talk to me like that..." Her words are tumbling out like rocks down a mountainside.

"Man didn't know who he was up against, no he did not," Kate says. She leans heavily against the car.

"And you, my shero, you brilliant woman, how did you ever figure out that Raymond wanted Vincent to kill *him*?"

"For the love of mercy, DJ," Kate says, seeking the relief of humor by crowing, "I keep telling you and Tuck that I am exceptionally skilled at what I do, but you both refuse to listen. Now, tonight, you will just have to tell her this tale of my prowess. You know, pour it on, elaborate lavishly upon how I saved your life today…"

She stops when she becomes aware of DJ's hard stare.

"Oh, okay, you're being serious. Sorry," she says. "It was you, actually, and what you said to him that got me thinking."

"Me?" asks DJ. "I was just standing there quaking like the inside of a jelly donut. What was it I did?"

"When you were agreeing with him that your uncle was like a father to him I had this flash. I thought, okay, if Raymond was a father to Vincent, then maybe Vincent was a son to Raymond. Not a blood son, you know, but the closest thing Raymond would ever get to one, maybe? Like a father figure."

"Well, yeah," says DJ, "but killing your own father figure?"

Kate warms to her own ideas. "Think about it this way, DJ. Raymond fights with you and thinks he loses you, so all he has left as family is Vincent. Who else but family would you go to when you're about to die and have just about lost everything?"

"Okay," she draws out the word, "but killing isn't really a family-friendly thing to do in my book."

"Yes, but that's just it, Deej. We don't play by the same rules. God herself is probably the only one who knows what codes of honor, or whatever they're called, that those guys follow in the land of power and guns they live in. If we haven't learned anything else this long weekend, we at least know your uncle is one very messed up old dude. We mere mortals cannot begin to understand his logic… or lack thereof."

DJ takes in a huge breath of cool country air, and lets it out slowly. She leans against the car alongside Kate, surveying her house and gardens.

"I really thought we were going to die, Katie. And just when my life was feeling like it had a whole new momentum. Thank you so much for your insight. It saved our lives today."

Kate reverts back to her previously charming and mischievous self, grinning as she does so.

"DJ, darlin' friend of mine, how about in the telling of this great morning of adventure, I get to be the heroine who saved the day all by myself?"

DJ looks at Kate with disbelief.

"Really, Katie," she says, hand on her hip, "you're still wanting me to beat that drum?"

Kate has the decency to become the tiniest bit defensive.

"Okay, okay, but just with Tuck then, okay? She loves this kind of drama, and now I get to be the center of it. How about it, just this once? One time only, honest, just once?"

Her exaggerated pleading has worked its magic once again.

"Why I fall for your harebrained schemes every time is something I probably will have to go back to therapy to figure out," she says, "because it seems to have kept the monster in you alive to strike again and again. But some day, Katie dear, someday soon, I promise you, I will stop giving in to your manipulative and wily ways," DJ jokes, wagging a finger at Kate as they finally get into the car and head toward Boston.

Proud of herself, Kate keeps pushing for more.

"Ahem. And, furthermore, if I do say so myself, I also recall that I said you'll have a harder time than you think separating yourself from Raymond. Remember that, the other night when you were so pissed that you decided you were so over him, and yada, yada, yada?" She is enjoying rubbing it in.

"Remember that DJ? I was right then, too, wasn't I, especially given all you just promised Vincent? Over Raymond, my foot! You're in it up to your eyeballs. Make sure you mention that to Tuck tonight, also. She's going to be so impressed. Oh, hot damn, but I'm good." She gives DJ a poke in the rubs for emphasis.

"Ouch, cut it out. And just for a minute, Katie dear, grab your over-inflated ego and climb down from the throne you're sitting on and think about what might have happened if I hadn't said that to Vincent. And as for getting sucked back in, not only didn't I have a choice, but once again it was the right thing to do. Now please shut up for at least five minutes or I'll pull over and drop you off right here. Then see if you can fly your own way to work, Wonder Woman."

Kate got her comeuppance, but it wasn't enough to stop her from suppressing one self-satisfied smirk.

"I saw that!"

---

DJ MANEUVERS EASILY through morning traffic, much of which has thinned considerably given how late their encounter with Vincent has made them. When she drops Kate at the office DJ thanks her once again.

"You were literally a life-saver today, my friend. Thank you again. I'll see you tonight at dinner, and I promise to make Tuck proud of all you did this morning," she smiles.

"You're a peach," Kate says as she removes her seat belt and opens the door. "Good luck with Cole, too."

"Ought to be a breeze after what we just went through," says DJ.

Kate pauses before shutting the door. "Be careful there, Deej. Remember the words of the great Audre Tucker. 'It ain't over 'til it's over,' and it still might not be over."

*I am so sick and weary of all this worrying,* DJ thinks, and nods her head.

She hears Kate call "Be strong in there," as she turns toward her office.

"Precisely what I have in mind," DJ responds gripping the wheel tighter than really necessary and pulling out into traffic.

# FORTY-FOUR

COLE'S OFFICE IS ARRANGED in much the same way it was on DJ's last visit Friday morning. The manuscript again sits dead center on the massive ebony desk, although this time rainbows of sticky notes protrude from various pages throughout the tome. Cole is in his usual spot, cushioned from adversity in his huge leather chair, surveying his surroundings. Something doesn't feel quite right, however, and he drums his fingernails along the edge of the desk, deep in thought.

He knows DJ will be on time. She always is. There is no telling with Stan. He could come in early to review their position, show up just in the nick of time, or blow off the meeting altogether if something more important has developed over the long weekend. If he does come in, though, Cole will be expected to relinquish his position of power behind the desk and offer it to Stan. Problem is, Stan will accept. That would not do for Cole's sense of control. Or for his comfort level, either.

This is the very reason he has come in early, he tells himself. Problem solving before a problem actually happens is his specialty.

He glances at the clock. There's still time. He moves everything for the meeting over to the round teak conference table to the left side of the office where full length tinted windows overlook Boston's waterfront. He wheels his chair to the area and places it behind the table, against the window, knowing full well that Stan will much prefer to take a chair that allows him to watch the goings on in the harbor. Cole sets the manuscript down in the center of the table, then places pads and pens in front of each of the three seats and sits back to assess this new arrangement. He judges this to be much better for the meeting, and sits back to relax, nothing left to do at this point but to wait.

Cole allows himself just a sliver of worry that Martone has convinced DJ to pull her manuscript. He is able to acknowledge that this worry is borne more out of his fear of Martone and his grudging respect for the guy's capacity to get what he wants, than it is of thinking there is weakness in DJ. Certainly not after all he has just read. But none of this stopped him last night from making a list of arguments to use with DJ just in case her uncle has worked his charm on her.

He opens the cover of the manuscript and checks to ensure that the notes are there. They are.

There is a rapid double knock on the door and his secretary, Maya, enters the room.

"Good morning, Maya," Cole says. "How about you set us up with coffee and tea once DJ arrives, and give a call up to Stan's office to remind him of the meeting? She'll be here any minute."

"Yes, good morning, sir," she answers. "However, it seems the powers that be have changed the plan. I just received a call from upstairs. Mr. Whitman would like to hold the meeting in his office. He's expecting you and wants a word or two before Ms. Brava arrives. I'm sure his office will provide refreshments up there."

She surveys the conference table.

"Would you like me to gather your things and bring them up for you?" she asks.

"Ah, no need, Maya. Thanks, but I can manage. Would you call down to reception and have them direct DJ up to Stan's office when she comes in, please? And I expect she and I will have some work to do here once we're done upstairs. We might need more coffee then anyway."

"Certainly," she replies and leaves the office.

Cole stands, feeling quite suddenly as if the rug has been pulled out from beneath him.

*Damn you, Stan. She's my client. This meeting should be in my office. My client, my office. Shit.*

He takes a brief moment to pull himself together, tucks the manuscript under his arm, and heads upstairs to Stan's office.

COLE HATES COMING INTo Stan's large corner office with its exceptional view of the Boston skyline. Just a touch of Fenway Park's Big Green Monster is visible today in the crisp fall air as well.

Each time he enters the room, Cole is reminded that he has a serious case of desk-envy, for as much as he loves his own ebony masterpiece he is absolutely in awe of Stan's curvaceous slice of redwood. Shaped like the curl of an ocean wave, it sits regally atop six bronze pipes and gleams with so many layers of polyurethane that the entire room is reflected on its surface. Cole long ago decided it would have been better to have left the wood in its natural state, and wonders if it could, even now, be restored down to the grain. He itches to run his hands across the piece, to feel the essence of the wood, the spirit of the tree that was taken long ago and encased in ten layers of plastic. *That poor wood can't breathe.*

Stan's chair is set within the curl of the desk, wrapping him in a great sheet of reddish-brown. He is on the phone and signals for Cole to take a seat, holding up one finger to indicate he'd be free in just a minute. Cole places his copy of the manuscript on the desk, opposite Stan's copy, and allows himself the luxury of running his hand along the three-inch thickness of the desk edge.

"You know, you'd never be allowed to buy this these days," Stan says, startling Cole who is unaware that Stan is off the phone. "I got this from some old logging coot up north of San Francisco somewhere about thirty years ago. Had the bare wood shipped to Boston and made into a desk. Cost me a damn fortune, but it sure as hell looks good up here, doesn't it?"

"Sure does," Cole responds without enthusiasm, having heard the same story countless times before. He plants five fingers of one hand firmly on the desk as he sits down, intentionally leaving his mark.

*God, I'm like a dog marking his territory. This is pathetic.* Cole blushes at the thought and tries his best to be unobtrusive as he rubs a shirt cuff along the desk edge to remove the fingerprints.

"Any more contact from that son of a bitch, Zipper?" Stan asks. "And how deep do you think we're in it with this guy? Do you really think DJ's going to come in here this morning and pull the manuscript? And how the hell does he know so much about us anyway?"

Stan's questions are all over the map, usually a good predictor of how upset he is, and Cole is unsure of which question to answer first.

"No more contact, and I honestly have no idea how he knows what he knows or what he'll do next. My best guess is that DJ won't pull the manuscript, but I have no idea what he's been saying to her. I think we just have to wait and see what she says."

Stan leans across the desk.

"I want this book, Alexander. DJ's hit this one right out of the ball park. So, not only do I really want this one, I want it now. I want it ready for the holiday market. You got that?"

"I do Stan, and I want it also."

Stan levels a look at Cole.

"But here's what I want even more than I want the book. Are you listening to me, Cole?"

"Yes, sir, I am."

"I want that guy the eff out of my private life and my business. You got that?" Stan repeats. "You do whatever the hell you freaking have to do, but you get that guy the hell out of my life." Stan's face is red, his fists are balled and a fine spray of spittle is falling across the desk.

Cole, of course, can't help himself and is fixated on the desktop, all but sitting on his hands to prevent them from reaching into his pocket for a handkerchief to wipe the surface clean. But suddenly he feels something inside him go *pop,* and he grips the desk edge, glaring right back at his boss.

"Wait just one minute here, Stan," he pronounces through gritted teeth. "I didn't make this shit happen, and I can't be held responsible for fixing it either. You need to get a grip on yourself, because it sounds for all the world as if you want me to take this guy *out,* for god's sake—which, by the way, we both know I wouldn't have a fat rat's chance in hell of doing on my best day!"

Cole lowers his tone just a bit. He's aware that he may be out of line talking to his boss this way, but can't quite stem the tide of his ire.

"I still don't get what's driving him to threaten us, and that means I don't have a freaking clue what to do about it. So unless you do, which I sincerely doubt, why don't we both just calm down and wait to hear what DJ has to say."

Cole moves back in his chair, shocked by the fact that, instead of giving him hell, Stan is breaking out in a sweat—something he has never seen in all the years he has worked here. He glances with swelling satisfaction at the smudges his hands have left on the desk. And this time makes no effort whatsoever to remove them.

*Weird,* he thinks, t*his is precisely what DJ must have felt like when she was in my office Friday arguing with me about her autobiography. It does feel good. Maybe I should re-learn how to play in the mud.*

Stan swipes at his forehead with an immaculate blue handkerchief.

"You're right, Cole. You're right. It's just that I can't afford to have this… this…" he whispers, "*indiscretion* with Francine get out. It will ruin me. My marriage, my job, my relationship with my kids… I should never have gone there in the first place, and how this Zipper guy ever found out about it is beyond me. We've been very discrete." He wipes some more.

This is more information than Cole needs or wants. He blushes again, squirms a bit in his seat, and tries to avoid looking at his boss.

"We've got to find a way to publish DJ's book without any of this blowing up in our faces," Stan continues. "I want you to work this out with her. Whatever it takes in terms of a signing bonus or share of the sales, but she's got to get him off our backs. Agreed?"

"Look, Stan," Cole is cautious, "I know she wants this book published, so I'm not sure any of that kind of incentive is even necessary. But I also don't know if DJ has a clue what her uncle's been up to in terms of threatening us. This might be quite a revelation to her."

"Whatever it is, I want you to fix it." Stan raises both his hands to ward off an expected objection from Cole. "I know you didn't cause it. I'm sorry if I gave you that impression, but I'm ordering you to fix it. Period."

Cole has his mouth open to respond, when Francine knocks on the door to announce that DJ is here for the meeting.

Both men rise from their chairs and offer greetings, but not before Stan has driven home his order by stabbing his pointer finger in Cole's direction.

"Good morning, good morning. It's wonderful to see you again." Stan comes out of the curl of his desk and is now all smiles and hugs.

"Francine, how about bringing in some tea for DJ and coffee for us? Take a seat, take a seat. Cole, help her with that jacket, will you? Here, let me take your briefcase. Make yourself comfortable."

DJ gives Cole a raised eyebrow look the second Stan turns to sit behind the desk again. Cole shrugs.

When DJ sits she realizes her muscles are clenched in tight knots, especially across her shoulders and down her lower back. Taking in a deep breath and letting it out slowly she tries to discretely stretch a bit, willing her body to relax after her morning ordeal.

"You're in a great mood this morning, Stan," she says. "I hope it bodes well for this discussion about my manuscript."

"Hah!" Stan laughs and slaps the manuscript in front of him. "Getting right to the point, I like that."

He settles down and becomes serious.

"DJ," he says, "this is a phenomenal piece of work. I want you to know that we are both so sorry that this has happened to you. But you have taken these tragic events and woven a tutorial on surviving that begs to be told. Yes, we will publish it and the sooner the better. Cole and I have a few edits and he'll go over those with you later. The only question for us, then, is how quickly you can get it back to us?"

Francine enters with a beverage tray, and they take a few minutes to set themselves up with tea and coffee. Served first, DJ has a moment to reflect.

She is only slightly surprised that this is being so easy. DJ is well aware that her writing is good, the topic is relevant, and the benefit to the publisher—foremost in their minds, of course—is great. But she is not quite ready to commit until she has spoken her piece.

Stan reads her hesitation as reluctance and moves to add some guarantees to the offer.

"Because this is a different type of book from your usual work, of course, we'll set a new contract with higher figures. And you can take whatever time you need with the edits," he adds nervously, contradicting his earlier statement.

"This must have been difficult for you to write in the first place, so take whatever time you need. We'd love to have it for holiday publication, but you set the pace here, okay? You just let Cole know what you need. And, don't you worry. You still have a contract with us for the romance novels and we'll extend the timeline for the next one, you hear? Whatever you need."

"That's very kind of you, Stan. Thank you," DJ says, "but there are a few things I need to clear up first."

"Oh?" Stan questions rather innocently, and fiddles with a bronze paperclip, unbending it and twisting it into what looks like a noose from Cole's perspective across the desk. DJ ignores that and turns to Cole.

"From what my uncle has recently told me, some time ago he threatened you with harm if you published anything other than my romance novels, and I-"

Stan cannot control himself.

"In the past? Hell, he threatened both of us this weekend. Even went so far as to bring his goons up to Rockport and scare the daylights out of Cole all day Saturday. Made him take all of them for a sail in his boat! Never mind what happened years ago, that man needs to be locked up, and if he's also threatening you to not let us publish this book, then I think we need to go to the police."

Cole's anger is rising. This is his tale to tell, and he knows they need to tread more carefully around the issue of Martone's influence on DJ. Before he can organize his thoughts to break into Stan's tirade, however, DJ does it for him.

"He did what? When?"

"Saturday."

*Well, now, that's interesting,* thinks DJ. *What Raymond said the other night... about talking to a friend of mine on Saturday... some of this is starting to fit together.*

"But he told me he had threatened you in the past." She turns to Cole.

"Yes," Cole says, "he did. But he was at my house all day Saturday."

"And he went sailing with you?" she asks Cole.

He tries for humor.

"Well, it was more like he commandeered my ship."

DJ's eyes are aflame with fury. Cole becomes serious.

"He made me take him out on my boat along with his two... er... bodyguards. It took me a while to realize that none of them knew a damn thing about boats and that they'd all end up in the Bermuda Triangle if they threw me overboard." He shrugs.

DJ doesn't see any humor at all in Cole's statement.

"He's got pancreatic cancer and not much longer to live, but it doesn't stop him for a second." She shakes her head, amazed at what she is hearing. "He's consumed with preventing my book from being published. Did he hurt you? How did he know about my book?"

But Stan and Cole are no longer listening. The paperclip skids across the desktop and Cole's solar plexus begins to spasm. A huge "Thank God" escapes their lips at exactly the same moment.

Cole sees the look of surprise on DJ's face and recovers quickly.

"I'm sorry, Donna, we mean no disrespect, but this uncle of yours is one slick customer. The way you talk about him in your manuscript, you'd think he was God almighty. But the guy threatened to kill me when you first started working with us..."

"He what?" DJ is stunned. Even the information from Raymond himself yesterday hasn't prepared her for this. Her thought processes start functioning like a tilt-a-whirl. What Raymond really meant about threatening Cole in the past is finally sinking in.

"When?" She is almost stuttering.

"Wait a minute... just give me a second." She pulls at the skin on her forehead, trying to get a grip on what she is learning. She shakes her head and looks at him.

"Cole, that had to be what? Years ago. Years! And just why is it you never told me any of this? He actually threatened to kill you? Why? And you held onto this for years? You're my agent for goodness sake. We've traveled together, been in each other's lives for almost twenty years. I'm ashamed and embarrassed that Raymond has mistreated you both, but I'm also upset that you never said anything to me about what he did. And what exactly is it that he did? I want you to tell me."

DJ looks at Cole. She is not pleading or demanding, not angry or nervous. Cole recognizes a new confidence in her. It shows in her bearing, in the set of her shoulders and the lift of her head. He hears it in the measure of her voice, and the stillness of her legs now in firm contact with the floor. Whatever cloak of self-protection she previously wrapped herself in has been cast off. Writing the book has freed her.

He tells her everything—the events of sixteen years ago, and what happened Saturday. He tells her about the FBI, about how Raymond co-opted Anthony, the protection Stan arranged for him, about Raymond's frailty, and about his telling Raymond to read Chapter Twenty. He tells her that Raymond predicted she would acquiesce to his wishes and come in to the office today to remove the manuscript from publication. And, rather judiciously on his part, he omits any mention of threats regarding Stan's indiscretions.

Stan's phone rings twice during Cole's monologue, but goes unanswered. Now Francine knocks on the door and tells him he has an emergency call from one of his children. He opts to take the call elsewhere, excuses himself, and leaves the room for DJ and Cole to continue their conversation.

"Thank you," DJ says simply when Cole is done. She leans toward him, her demeanor exuding sadness, the timbre of her voice conveying resignation. "I appreciate your honesty, and I can truly understand why you haven't said anything previously. I'm amazed it never colored your treatment of me. I'm not sure I could have worked with someone whose very powerful relative was threatening to kill me."

Cole laughs nervously.

"Frankly, it was easy up until last week when I opened the mail to find *this* manuscript. I've been just a bit of a wreck since then. That uncle of yours is not to be messed with. It surprises me that you got him to listen to what you want."

"Clearly, as I am learning, it's more of an on-going battle with him than a *fait accompli,*" she says. "Something I'm only now beginning to appreciate. And there's another whole story in there for some other time. I'm just so sorry you got pulled into this. It had to be terrifying."

With Stan gone Cole risks venturing further into DJ's world. He turns his chair to face her directly and now questions her.

"What *I* don't understand, DJ, is why all this secrecy and threats in the first place? Judging by how you write about him, he was the only good thing in your early life."

DJ begins to move nervously in her seat, crossing and then re-crossing her legs.

"Yes," she responds. "He was."

"Then why is he so frightened of anything you've said about him? It's good, isn't it? At least it reads that way. And yet he's gone to great lengths to try to prevent you from saying any of this."

Cole's tone is sincere and DJ can hear that he is clearly bewildered.

"The only thing I can think of is that knowing these things about him gives information to people who might want to take over his so-called enterprise. Is that it?" Cole asks.

DJ takes a moment to collect her thoughts, purposely not willing to reveal all she now understands about Raymond and his many motivations.

"I suppose that might be some small part of it, Cole," she says. "But mostly it has to do with his own sense of guilt. He did some things he's not proud of in relation to what happened to me. I think on one level he wants the redemption that might come from telling, but at the same time fears the consequences of others knowing about it. Kind of being between the proverbial rock and a hard place, but it doesn't excuse either what he did then or how he's acting now."

Cole sits back.

"Well, that's the central theme of great novels, isn't it—the eternal dilemma of good and evil?" he says.

Any answer DJ may have given is cut off by Stan's reentry.

"Listen, folks, I have to run. My youngest grandson just broke a leg and I'm meeting them at Mass General. Where are we with this situation?"

"We're good to go," DJ says quickly. "I will deal directly with my uncle and there will be no more threats to either of you or to the publishing house. I can promise you that much at least." *I promise?* She thinks. *Like I really have any control over my uncle. Well, if I have to hound him to death to make this be the truth, then perhaps I'll do just that.*

Cole is on his feet and picks up DJ's jacket and briefcase.

"How about we go down to my office, then, and take a look at the edits? We can set up a meeting to go over contracts and timelines for some time next week if that meets with your approval, DJ."

DJ addresses Stan while he dons his overcoat and readies to leave the office.

"I apologized to Cole for all of this mess with Raymond, Stan, and I assure you both that the threats have ended." She shakes his hand and turns to join Cole at the door.

"Thank you both for believing in this new work of mine."

"And thank you for bringing it to us, DJ. This is going to be a great one. *Mazel Tov* all around!"

He hands Cole his copy of the manuscript. "My edits," he says.

DJ smiles and says, "And I hope things turn out fine for your grandson. Good bye now."

She enters the elevator with Cole while Stan gives instructions to his secretary.

# FORY-FIVE

TWO FLOORS DOWN, COLE AND DJ enter his office and sit at the teak table near the window. Maya brings in some refreshments which, due to the late hour, include some finger sandwiches and fruit.

Unexpectedly hungry, DJ is grateful for the food. She and Cole spend a good hour going over the manuscript, talking about his and Stan's editing suggestions and deciding that she can accomplish the rewrites within three weeks. Plenty of time for the holiday trade deadline.

"You know," Cole says, steering carefully into previously uncharted waters, "you'll have to do the grueling work of traveling and book signings and interviews, especially with this book, and I can't imagine it will be easy, given the personal nature of the topic. Are you ready for all that?"

DJ is pensive for a brief moment.

"Actually, Cole, this time I am. This book is about who I am, and I am not ashamed of any of who I am. With my romance novels, I always felt I was hiding behind the writing and the characters, afraid perhaps, of it being found out that I am so very different from the characters."

"I wish you had mentioned that before, DJ. It's possible I could have helped." Cole is thoughtful. "Maybe what I really mean is that I simply wish you had felt comfortable enough to have shared that with me—or that I had been brave enough to ask."

DJ looks at him. "You know, Cole, if we're being honest with each other here, I think the real truth for me is that I was always so frightened that someone at one of those events would make the connection between me and Raymond in a publically embarrassing way. You know, 'the niece of the porn king writes romance novels' kind of thing. It's still a worry. Now 'the niece of the porn king *who was molested* writes romance'. There'll be someone somewhere who'll try to make hay out of that, I'm sure."

"But surely you know there's a million miles between what he does and what you write, don't you?" Concern lines Cole's face. He remembers Martone's glib comments about this very topic so many years ago.

"Goodness, yes," DJ says. "I came to grips with that one early on. Everything I write about is adult, it's mutual, it's consensual, and it's age and gender appropriate. You know what I do, knights in shining armor, that kind of thing. No, I mean the other part. About having been molested and writing romance. I had to do a lot more thinking about that as I was writing the autobiography."

"And your conclusion?" Cole asks.

DJ shrugs. "I'm good at it. And that about sums it up. Nothing more complicated than that."

"Well, that's the truth," Cole says with relief. "But this book will certainly change your image out there. Do you have any worries about taking it on the road?"

"No, not this time. My goal with this book is to help the millions of others who have similar pasts. In fact, I want to talk to you about earmarking a small percentage of the sale of each book for a charity I have in mind."

"Hum, good idea. The PR folks will love that. And it will do some good as well. Why don't you send me the info this week by e-mail so we can have the organization vetted? What is it, by the way? Do I know it?"

"You will soon, if you don't already. It's the National Children's Advocacy Center in Huntsville, Alabama. They've developed a remarkable program where children who disclose sexual abuse can be interviewed and treated in a safe and child-focused environment. There are almost 900 centers now, mostly in the states, including many right here in Massachusetts, but also a growing number around the world. I'd love to find a way to include local or regional information for people who might want to donate or volunteer, or who may need the services of a Children's Advocacy Center. If it's possible, perhaps we can do something like that at tours and signings. What do you think?"

Cole is enthused—even more so than usual because he is being carried by DJ's exuberance.

"I think it's a wonderful idea. And speaking of PR, they tell me you did an impromptu stop at a nursing home in Atlanta. It made the society page in the local paper. Evidently, you were a hit with the older set. What was that about?"

DJ's pleasure is evident as she tells Cole the events of her long weekend—sisters, nursing home, mother, and all—leaving Raymond out of the mix for the moment.

Cole is amazed at the changes he sees in his star author. He can't quite help himself, he knows that nothing will be reciprocated, but he can't help falling under her spell. Again. *Careful, boy, this is not in the cards for you. Back off. I'm warning you.*

As they are about to wrap up the rest of their business, Maya taps on the door and comes in with a package. She seems a bit shaken.

"Uh, excuse me Mr. A," she stammers, "but some big man, really big... ah... brought this..."

She hands Cole the package.

"Never saw him before. Not one of our usual couriers." She spreads her arms. "Really big... wide...buttons barely met on his suit jacket... red face."

*Oh, boy,* thinks DJ, *this couldn't possibly be anyone but Vincent himself. What the hell has he gone and done now? I'm still a wreck about what he did this morning, and now, what's this all about?*

"Was there any message with this, Maya?" Cole asks as he weighs the package in his hands, giving it a shake. *Feels light enough to just be paper, but who knows.*

"Just that the envelope was from a Mr. Martone and that I was to give it to you immediately, while Ms. Brava was still here with you." Maya looks from Cole to DJ, clearly puzzled about what she should do next.

Cole speaks first. "It's okay, Maya," he reassures her, "thank you. You did fine. We'll take it from here."

As Maya leaves, DJ rises to her feet and comes around the table to stand next to Cole. For one brief moment he hesitates, allowing himself the fleeting fear that the envelope could explode when he opens it. Inhaling deeply, he runs a letter opener along the fold of the envelope. *Phew!* he thinks, and then swells with anger. *Stop it, dammit. I'd rather shoot myself than keep letting that asshole do this to me one more time. He sure as all hell can't die soon enough for me.*

Cole removes a two-page computer printout with a blue sticky handwritten note attached to the top page. He holds it up for DJ to see, and then reads out loud.

> "Coleman, I have written this short Appendix to my niece's autobiography. Please do me the courtesy of including this piece in her book. I accompany it with sincere apologies for my misdirected and inappropriate behavior toward you, both recently and in the past. Thank you. Raymond."

He hands the sticky note to DJ who reads it silently once again.

"Well, I'll be damned," Cole says and sits, fairly overwhelmed with relief. *The old fart must really be on his deathbed after all. Good!*

"What do you make of this?" he asks DJ.

"I find it rather odd, even for him," she responds, "but I won't know until I read what he's written, will I? My first instinct is to wonder where he gets the chutzpah to think he can add whatever he wants to my book. But, then again, this is just more of who he apparently is, I'm beginning to understand. Can I see that letter, please?"

Cole relinquishes it to her. DJ moves across to the window to gather more light as she reads aloud:

> "My niece has written eloquently of her life and her struggles to overcome the early childhood sexual abuse perpetrated upon her by my three brothers.
>
> She credits me for virtues I do not possess and for accomplishments I do not deserve. When she wrote this book and brought it to her publisher, there were things about her past that she did not know.
>
> I know these things, and I wish at this time to set the record straight. I am so much less than the person Donna Jean thinks me to be, and this is why:
>
> I knew from listening to my two older brothers that Donna was going to be sexually abused—and I did nothing.
>
> I knew from listening to them recount their exploits, that she had been abused by them—and still I did nothing.
>
> I knew that they were next going to molest her sisters—and only then did I do something. I created jobs for them in my business out of state.

*It was only when my business became threatened by their inappropriate behavior that I finally took permanent and drastic steps to have them stopped for good. They are dead, and I am to blame.*

*Donna Jean's father is dead and, while I did not kill him, I am directly responsible for the heart attack that ended his life.*

*What this boils down to is this:*

*I knew, and I did nothing.*

*And when I finally did do something, the something I did was even worse than the something I did not do.*

*What I did do by killing my brothers was to lose all my brothers whom I loved.*

*I have told myself for years that I did it to protect Donna Jean and her sisters. The truth is that I did it to ensure that my business, as publically objectionable as it is, was protected.*

*What I did when I took their lives hurt Donna very much, and it took from her the chance to both confront and, if she ever wished, to make peace with her father and uncles.*

*What I did was to lose the love and respect of my niece—the one person left who matters to me the most.*

*This is the thing I regret the most about my actions.*

*And I am to blame.*

> *Raymond Martone"*


DJ is quiet for a very long time and stands looking out at the harbor as the afternoon shadows lengthen across the docks with their container freight being unloaded and shifted onto flatbed trucks. *Well, well, well,* she thinks, *seems he was listening to at least some of what I was saying after all.*

Cole's head is about to implode. *Holy crap! This guy really is a fucking lunatic!*

"Are you all right? Cole asks, concern for her rising with her silence.

"Oh, yes," she responds in a stronger voice than he is expecting. But still, she stands by the window, deep in thought.

"What the heck is this guy thinking, DJ? He can't possibly believe you'd add this to your book, can he?" Cole is more than a bit confused, especially since DJ seems less shocked by this information than he expected her to be.

*Interesting… she's not surprised by this at all. I wonder what that's about?*

"Clearly I'm not a good reporter of what he's *ever* thought," DJ responds. "Right now, however, my guess is that he's looking for sympathy, and for forgiveness. And since he knows he can't get it from me, he's hoping my readers can give it to him. What he fails to understand is that forgiveness is neither mine nor theirs to give. And my telling him exactly that just yesterday doesn't seem to have gotten through to him."

"Let me just ask you, DJ," Cole says, unsure if he even has the right to ask. "Did you know all this? Did you know he did this to your father and uncles, because, honestly, I didn't get any sense of that from the manuscript?"

"No, I did not," she says. "I found all this out this past weekend. On Friday night my sisters told me that they suspected Raymond had killed our uncles. On Saturday evening, he didn't deny it when I confronted him, but it wasn't until yesterday that he told me why he did it."

"Saturday? That's the day he spent terrorizing me out on the boat."

"Humph," says DJ. "No wonder he and his staff all had sunburns!"

She reads her uncle's letter through one more time.

"You know, Cole," she says, "I still can't figure out how he even knew I wrote this manuscript, or that you had it. How else would he know to threaten you now? He told me he had intimidated you way back, and Stan just told me about Saturday, but something's still not right. You two never answered my question about how Raymond got involved in this again. Help me out here, Cole, because I think you know more than you're telling me."

DJ's back is to Cole as she speaks. She peers out the window, but she can also see him behind her, reflected off the glass. She watches as he runs his hands through is hair.

"That one's on me, I'm sorry to say, Donna. He threatened to kill me if I published anything you wrote about the family. But when I read how well you thought of him, it gave me the idea to call him and give him a heads up on the book. I thought he'd go easy on us. Well, on me, if I told him right up front. I'm so sorry."

Cole moves alongside DJ and stares off into the harbor, hands in his pockets to keep them still.

"I never would have called him if I had known that he killed your family, I promise you. No matter what he threatened me with, I simply would not have done so."

"There was no way for you to have known, Cole. I didn't know, and I was closer to him than anyone. Now I just have to figure out why I would never let myself really see that side of him. And, he's dying soon. It complicates things just a bit."

Both Cole and DJ share a few moments of contemplation. They turn toward each other and at the same time say, "But how did he know...?"

DJ shrugs, and continues on her own. "How does he know a lot of things... things about you way back in the beginning of our work together ... when I was coming into Boston from Atlanta the other night... getting into your house on Saturday? Clearly he's a powerful man, and the ways he uses his power are way above our capacity to even imagine. That's my guess. Anyway, we'll probably never know for sure."

Cole is thinking about Stan and Francine. "Yep," is all he contributes, grimacing. Then he changes the subject.

"Are you going to put any of this in the book?" he prods, uncertain of where this information, new to him, will now take her.

"Hum," is her only response. She seems to be half listening at best. She turns to him.

"Do you have a pen, Cole? I want to write something on this. And then, can you ask Maya to send it back to Raymond by return courier, today? It's important that it go today, please?"

"Certainly, I can see to that, if it's what you want." He hands DJ a pen and she sits to write a brief note across the top of the letter.

As she writes, Cole's thoughts are racing all over the place.

*God,* he thinks. *If she puts this in the book, it'll be a knockout runaway best seller, and we can advertise using his confession. That'll fix him, the sleazy bastard. Should I even say this to her? No, stop it, Alexander, you've already done enough damage. It's a wonder she's not talking about taking the book somewhere else. Just shut up and do as she asks.*

She finishes, places the pen carefully across the top of the letter, thinks for a brief moment, then looks up at Cole.

"That's it," she says, "done."

DJ picks up her jacket. She places Cole's copy of the manuscript, edits and all, in her briefcase and stops at the door with her hand on the knob.

"Thanks for taking care of that, Cole. I'll get the donation information to you by tomorrow and have these edits completed within a few weeks. Send me a couple of suggested times for the contract meeting, will you? Except for the edits, I should be available time-wise over the next week or so as well."

She starts to open the door, but closes it quietly and turns to him once again.

"And, Cole, thank you for all your help and support. I'm so sorry Raymond went after you the way he did, both then and now. I can imagine how terrifying that was for you, especially since you thought he'd be more reasonable. He's a strange man, my uncle. I know he's dangerous. But he has another side to him as well. Perhaps I'm the only person he's ever shown it to."

"No police, then?" Cole asks, wondering. "He gets away with what he did?"

"No evidence," she responds. "If there were, I'm still not sure what I would do. And he'll be dead soon. He can't get away from that now, can he?"

Cole picks up the pen DJ has left on the teak table and places it in his suit coat pocket, giving it a reassuring pat.

"No, he can't," he says, stalling for the time he needs to say what's really on his mind. "And, DJ..." He lets tenderness into his heart and it leaks out with his words. "Please know that I think you are as strong as you are brave. I admire you deeply."

His blushing makes her smile.

"Thank you," she says.

"And I am sorry. You have had so much loss in your life, and now all this."

"The true loss was years ago, Cole. This... this is simply disappointment spiked with grief. And anger. But in comparison... this, my dear friend, is a piece of cake!"

She opens the door again.

"Later," she says over her shoulder, and this time she closes the door quietly and walks down the hallway past the restroom she ran to just a few days before. She walks to the bank of elevators, passing every one of her framed book covers on the way.

# FORTY-SIX

COLE SITS AT THE TEAK CONFERENCE TABLE, his back to the harbor view, literally stunned by the events of the morning. He picks up the letter from Martone and reads what DJ has written across the top:

> *Uncle Raymond,*
> *I am pleased to see that you finally understand what it is you have done and are taking some responsibility for it. But this belongs in your book, not in mine.*
>
> *Fondly, DJ*

Cole reaches for the phone to call Maya, but stops himself. He has an idea, and it turns the smile on his face into a smirk of self-satisfaction.

He takes the letter with him to the Copy Room, where he photocopies each page as well as the accompanying sticky note. On the way back to his office, he gives the original letter to Maya with instructions to get it back to Martone this afternoon by courier.

Cole guides his chair across the room and back behind his desk. He sits, gloating, playing the triumphant theme from *Rocky* in his head. He fishes in his drawer for the business card Special Agent Creighton of the FBI flipped at him on Saturday. Finding it, he reads it carefully and then staples it to the upper left hand corner of Martone's letter.

He walks to the far wall of his office and stops in front of the framed picture of Tom Brady. *Conference champions! Brady, my main man!*

Cole flips the picture outward on its hinges to reveal a small wall safe.

He dials the combination and then places the letter inside with what amounts to a show of reverence—and perhaps some relief.

"Gotcha, Zipper," he says aloud to himself. He closes the safe, turns the dial, then spins it twice and flips the picture back once again.

He taps the picture frame.

"The best offense is always a good defense, isn't it, Tommy?" he says to Brady and his perfect throwing arm.

He returns to his desk and sits, surveying his kingdom, feeling rather proud of himself. The last of his lunch with DJ is on the tray table near his desk and Cole reaches for a sandwich. But when he spots Stan's copy of DJ's manuscript, he pulls his hand back as quickly as if he had just touched hot metal.

He cannot take is eyes off the tome.

*Bloody hell, Alexander,* he says to himself, *you are such a perfect ass! You really are.*

For the next thirty seconds he simply does not have any thoughts at all. But he keeps staring at the manuscript.

*Yep, you're an ass. The real question is, however, whether you want to just keep on being the ass you are, or step up and be the man you keep telling yourself you want to be. Its crunch time, pal, pick a lane.*

His eyes move from the manuscript to the Tom Brady photo and back again to the manuscript. Leaning heavily on his hands, Cole pushes himself up from the chair. He walks out from behind his desk, trailing his fingers across the title page.

Cole stands in front of the photo, noting Tom's flawless poise in the face of the charging defense.

"Time to change the game plan, Tom," Cole says, as he hears the tumblers on the wall safe click their way to opening.

Cole removes the sheaf of papers stapled together with the FBI card, and then listens with relief as they grind to confetti in the shredder.

DJ's SMILE INCREASES as she walks deliberately down the hallway, scanning each framed book cover for her picture. She catches glimpses of herself aging and maturing, changing hair color and cuts, wearing jeans and turtlenecks or business suit and pearls.

Her cell rings suddenly, echoing sharply in the vacant corridor. She checks caller ID and her smile widens.

"Marshall? Is that you?" she says, delighted that it is. "I thought you'd be in Japan another week."

"We got the contract signed and sealed, and I just delivered it to the attorneys this morning. I'm able to make the board meeting at the prevention center this afternoon, but I wanted to know if you could join me for dinner tonight. Any chance you're free?"

"I just made plans with Kate and Tuck. How about you join us at L'Espalier at 6:30?"

"Are you sure that's okay?" Marshall asks.

"Absolutely. Listen, Kate will probably be at the board meeting. Why don't the two of you drive over together and I'll grab Tuck at the office. We'll meet you there."

"That sounds good to me," he says. "And DJ...?" Marshall waits.

"Yes, Marsh?" she says.

"I'm looking forward to seeing you. I missed you." Marshall's words are carefully chosen and almost whispered—hopeful.

DJ, also, is quiet for a moment.

"Me too, Marsh, I'm really enjoying getting to know you," she says, intentionally willing her pulse to return to normal. "I'll see you tonight. There's a lot to catch you up on. We certainly haven't been idle while you've been gone."

"Looking forward to it," he says pleasantly, "see you then."

She replaces the phone in her pocket and stands just opposite the elevator, looking at the blank wall where she knows the next book jacket will be framed and hung.

"Who knew life could be so good," she smiles, and lays the briefcase holding her manuscript up against the empty wall.

"Save this space for the real me," she says, her conviction finally laced with enormous and well-deserved self-confidence.

*...And there's too much darkness in an endless night to be afraid of the way we feel.*
*Let's be kind to each other, not forever, but for real."*

# ABOUT THE AUTHOR

I am, by profession, a clinical social worker who has been working with abused and neglected children and their families for more than forty years. Wait Until I'm Dead! my first novel, is informed by the trauma, grit, and struggle to survive that I have witnessed in hundreds of remarkable children. This is their story. It is also the story of millions of adults who, as survivors themselves, will relate to its frank descriptions of the healing environment good therapy can provide.

Although I no longer practice as a therapist, I continue to present training workshops for social service professionals on topics related to child sexual abuse, interpersonal violence, compassion fatigue, and working with LGBTQ youth.

I live in Rhode Island, surrounded by an amazingly loving and diverse family, savoring a great mystery novel, getting together with friends old and new, and enjoying the excitement of adventure travel whenever my aging knees cooperate.

It is my hope that this novel will find its way to the people who may need it most.

To learn more about child sexual abuse, to comment on this book, or to Contact the Author please visit:

**www.emdawber.com, or www.waituntilimdeadnovel.com.**

# ACKNOWLEDGEMENTS

This is a work of fiction. Any resemblance to persons living or dead, or to specific events, is purely circumstantial and unintended. As is true for any author, my writing is informed by the people and events in my own life. I then take great liberties with them by contorting and distorting, dialing some quirks up and others down, until they come alive as characters and scenes within the book. They are, in truth, virtual characters. This book contains the autobiography of DJ Brava, not mine.

There are however, a great many real and wonderful human beings without whom a book of this nature would be impossible. They are not ranked here alphabetically or by importance. I am simply grateful to each of them.

My wife, Mariellen, first reader, photographer, and writing tech assistant extraordinaire is a living, breathing thesaurus, and a human treasure trove of creativity. A woman of courage, she brought me into the circle of family and each day embraces me with love. She writes young adult fiction and has an indomitable generosity of spirit. I want to be just like her when I grow up. My gratitude and love are boundless and there is no end to the ways I treasure her.

Our oldest grandson, an avid sailor, was my advisor on all things nautical. All seven grandkids remind me often that whoever I might be to the rest of the world, I am best in my role as Nana to each of them. Their joyful exuberance at simply being alive on this planet inspires me daily in our efforts to end abuse of all children.

My family of origin is now down to my two sisters and me, and it is remarkable that we are each still totally capable of behaving exactly like we did in our teens when we are together. Their support has been nothing short of phenomenal—and though even they might argue the fact—they are nothing like DJ's sisters at all. Their husbands, and my wonderful nieces and nephews, along with their children, all continue to bring light into my life.

I am eternally grateful to my early readers for their suggestions and unwavering support: my editing coach, Sandra Butler, author of Conspiracy of Silence; my pornography advisor, Cordelia Anderson; and my eagle-eyed typo pals in Dusseldorf, Germany, Carol Esposito and Liz Armstrong, who discovered that I must have been absent for the lecture on possessive plurals. Pat Stanislaski, Geri Crisci, Deborah Callins, Pnina Tobin, and Carol Plummer, who, along with Cordelia, are friends and prevention colleagues in pursuit of a world without child sexual abuse. They gave feedback with humor and style—a cheerleading section if ever there was one.

Tim Callins lent a great male and legal perspective to DJ's situation; Joan Montanari excelled as line editor and champion of just a hint of love interest for DJ. Helen Flynn, Ros Johnson, and Connie St. Pierre read the final version and were still finding things that needed my attention.

Thanks also to the exceptional support and contribution to the field from Judith Herman and Emily Schatzow, pioneers in the treatment of trauma experienced by hundreds of DJ Bravas. Deep appreciation also goes to Jim McGuire and Carol Landau, earliest of listeners, for their patience, trustworthiness, and so far beyond.

A glowing chorus of long-time friends, supportive colleagues, and my writing group, have faithfully encouraged my efforts and made my persistence at this task endurable. Jeannette Jacobs, graphic artist and transcendent quilter, brought her considerable skills to designing and formatting the cover. Visit her site at **www.jeannettejacobs.com** and be enthralled.

Pat Cook lent me her wonderful husband Pete who literally built the websites. Megan Rauscher and Shannon Lucey digitized my manuscript to e-format—skills totally out of my range but without which there would simply be no way to read my work.

There are children and children and children who have entered and left my life over the years I functioned as a social worker. I may never know what impact I had on their lives, but they have left an unforgettable mark on mine. Their pain, their suffering, as well as their profound capacity to find joy in the midst of loss and sorrow, yet be resilient enough to believe in and work for a better tomorrow, is nothing short of miraculous. This book is about them. It is because of them. It is for them. And it is for all of us in the world who work daily to stop adults from hurting children.

And then, last—but never, ever, least: this book and so much more would not have been conceivable without the patience and guidance of one very special person. (You know who you are, and you know all about It.) I honestly cannot imagine where life would have taken me otherwise. You are admired and cherished beyond mere words.

# DISCUSSION GUIDE

1. This book is uniquely structured in that it contains a story that follows the characters in real time, while it also uses memoir to evoke the past and give meaning to their current actions and emotions. As the reader, how did you react to the structure of the book? Was there enough memoir to inform the reader about DJ's past and still move the story forward?

2. The relationship DJ has with her good friends Kate and Tuck features prominently in this novel. How important do you believe they are to the story? Is the depth of friendship realistic from your perspective? Do you have, or would you want either to be such a friend, or to have friends like them?

3. In her memoir, DJ credits her survival on key figures or group of figures in her life. How important are these often overlooked "others" in helping any of us weather difficult times as children? What role do they play in DJ's ability to overcome her past?

4. Humor is used quite liberally by the author throughout the book. Was it an effective tool? Did it help relieve some of the intensity of the reality of DJ's abuse, or did it distract from its seriousness?

5. Cole held his own secret about DJ's uncle for many years, and this contributes to him being essential to the plot line involving Raymond. What role does Cole play in moving this story to its conclusion? In what ways, if any, was Cole changed by his experience and/or the memoir? Do you agree with his final act?

6. DJ and her brother, a complicated figure, shared a strong bond which impacted her greatly when it was lost. How does the rendition of his saving her from rape in the first chapter Cole reads, set the tone (or voice) of her memoir apart from the tone of the story of the novel?

7. DJ's mother was incapable of truly hearing her when she and her brother reported the attempted rape to her. How do you think DJ's fate would have evolved if her mother had taken action at that time? Would it have shaped DJ as a different adult person in the world? What message does the book convey about listening to children?

8. DJ's sisters kept vital information from her for many years. What was their rational for not telling her and, in hindsight, how might that earlier decision be viewed?

9. Some of DJ's losses also included the deaths of her brother and sister due to illness. How have she and other family members dealt with these losses when one considers them up against the loss of the father and two uncles? What effect might that have had on her response to Raymond's admissions?

10. One sister rages on with homophobic rhetoric, while the other is defensive of DJ's position. How does this exchange inform us about DJ's life?

11. DJ clearly states that even the worst of her abusers were neither all good nor all bad. As an adult, she is able to both see and understand this distinction. How difficult might that have been for her to comprehend as a child if she was told to think of her family that way?

12. Only the slightest hint of DJ being in a relationship is offered in this novel. Would you, as the reader, have wanted more information? Where would that have possibly taken the story?

13. DJ's abusers—her father and two of his brothers—are essential to the memoir and the story, but remain less well-developed than other characters. Raymond, on the other hand, is the focal point, and she is initially very defensive of him. Do you think her feelings for him are legitimate given what he does for a living? Given what she eventually learns he has done?

14. Ultimately, *Wait Until I'm Dead!* is about family secrets, and the unraveling that can occur when they are revealed. Steps people take to hide one secret, often lead to deeper and more dangerous secrets. Was one secret worse than another? Why have individual characters held onto them for so long, and why is it so difficult for one (DJ's mother) to admit that these events happened at all?

15. Which character in the book do you identify with the most and why?

16. What was the motivation for Raymond to do what he did? Protecting DJ and her sisters, or protecting his business ventures? Does choosing the former, make him a better person than if he chose the latter?

17. The book presents an interesting moral dilemma. What, if any, should be the consequences if an evil person does a good thing—or if a good person does an evil thing? Raymond tends to see what he did as clearly black and white, and is confused by DJ's anger at what he did. What did Raymond's actions take away from DJ? Should she have reported him for what he did? Why does it appear that DJ rejected that option? If you were DJ, what would you have done, and why?

18. DJ's relationship with her mother is complicated—she failed her in so many ways, but did not abuse her. DJ does not blame her, but neither does she forgive her. What would forgiveness entail and do you think it is essential for her to fully heal? Society often blames mothers for abuse that happens in their home. What path around that issue did the author take in this novel and what did you think of it?

19. DJ's accounts of her experience in therapy are formative to the later pages of the memoir. How important are they to your understanding of how she is able to function so well as a successful adult?

20. What qualities did DJ find so helpful in the therapies and therapists she utilized to help her overcome her early trauma? What were the most striking things she revealed about her experiences in treatment?

21. Vincent's appearance at DJ's home results in her going back on her decision to have little to do with Raymond. Does it seem possible for a person to resolve their inner conflict in such a way that they are capable of helping someone die who has hurt them in the way DJ has both been hurt by and holds so much anger toward Raymond?

22. DJ took us on a whirlwind long weekend of secrets, intrigue, family travails, and bonding friendships—all with the goal of accomplishing the task of telling about her memoir. Do you think she ended the task with a sense of completeness, of a job well done? Did the ending disappoint you as the reader, or did it leave you feeling more needed to be done? What would that have been?

23. What do you think Raymond had as his ultimate reason for writing the

confession for DJ's book? Were you satisfied with her response? What might you have done differently?

24. What would you imagine DJ's life to look like in the next few years as her memoir does well? How might that affect her relationships with her mother, uncle, sisters, Marsh, and with Kate and Tuck? Or Cole?

25. And finally, the author had as her goal the idea of writing an entertaining page-turner of a novel that would also educate the reader, and perhaps lead to a change in how we, as a society, work toward making children safer. As a result of completing this book, have you given any consideration to doing something different, something positive, about this serious problem? If so, what form would that take?

———————

All readers are invited to look at the following Resource Page for ideas about how to contribute to making the world a safer place for children. Support your local child welfare and social service agencies, volunteer time or services to prevention programs, lobby for laws that make adults accountable for inappropriate behavior toward children, learn how to be quiet when children are talking and really listen to what they are telling us, make yourself a tellable adult so that kids feel safe enough in your presence to disclose abuse to you, and ensure that they get the help they need when they do.

Treat children with respect. And honor the voices of adult survivors who help us daily understand their experiences when they speak out so that we will be better prepared to help the next child that discloses. And, if you are one of the many wonderful therapists with the gifts of patient listening and compassion, thank you from the bottom of this author's soul.

# RESOURCES

The following resources are available for readers who wish to have more information about child sexual abuse prevention, intervention, education, and/or treatment, and/or sexual assault. For readers who are seeking to deal with their own survivorship, please contact your local Rape Crisis Center for referral to services near you. These national services can also direct you locally:

The National Children's Advocacy Center
www.ncac.org

The National Children's Alliance
www.nationalchildrensalliance.org

National Coalition to Prevent Child Sexual Abuse Exploitation
www.preventtogether.org

The National Center for Missing and Exploited Children
www.missingkids.com

Prevent Child Abuse America
www.preventchildabuse.org

National Child Abuse Hotline
1-800-4-A-CHILD

Darkness to Light
www.d2l.org

National Sexual Violence Resource Center
www.nsvrc.org

National Alliance to End Sexual Violence
www.endsexualviolence.org

Stop It Now!
www.stopitnow.org

Childhelp USA
www.childhelpusa.org

National Council on Child Abuse and Family Violence
www.nccafv.org

American Professional Society on the Abuse of Children
www.aspsac.org

Male Survivors
www.malesurvivor.org

One in Six
www.1in6.org

———————

If you are an adult who has molested a child, or who is contemplating doing so, or if you know of someone who is doing so, please stop and contact www.stopitnow.org right away for non-judgmental assistance.

If you are being molested, or know of a child who is being physically neglected or abused, emotionally abused, or sexually abused, please call your local Child Protective Services right away.